D1363566

Contents

Contents

Preface

We have been humbly impressed with the reception that the first edition of *The Elect Methodists* has received and are grateful to the University of Wales Press for proposing the publication of this paperback edition. We have taken the opportunity to make a few minor alterations to the text of the book, but nothing that in any way alters the account and interpretations presented therein. It is our hope that this new edition will find its way into the hands of a wider readership, be they Elect Methodists, non-Elect Methodists or, indeed, anyone interested in a fascinating slice of eighteenth-century British history.

David Ceri Jones
Boyd Stanley Schlenther
Eryn Mant White
February 2016

List of Illustrations

Cover Illustration:
Engraving of George Whitefield, by J. Woolaston, after Nathaniel Hone, 1769. The National Portrait Gallery, London.

Following page 156:

1   Portrait of George Whitefield, by J. Woolaston, c.1742. The National Portrait Gallery, London.

2   Portrait of John Wesley, by N. Hone, c.1766. The National Portrait Gallery, London.

3   Engraving of John Cennick, by R. Purcell, 1754. The National Portrait Gallery, London.

4   Drawing of Howel Harris. From Gomer Roberts (ed.), *Selected Trevecka Letters (1742–1747)* (Caernarvon, 1956).

5   Miniature of Daniel Rowland, by R. Bowyer, 1790. The National Library of Wales, Aberystwyth.

6a Portrait of William Williams. From J. M. Jones and W. Morgan, *Y Tadau Methodistaidd*, vol. I (1895).

6b Painting of the first joint Association of English and Welsh Calvinistic Methodists, held at Watford, near Caerphilly, 5 and 6 January 1743, by Hugh Williams, 1912. The National Library of Wales, Aberystwyth.

7   Portrait of the Countess of Huntingdon, by J. Russell. The Cheshunt Foundation, Westminster College, Cambridge.

8   Engraving of Thomas Charles. From D. E. Jenkins, *The Life of the Rev. Thomas Charles of Bala* (2nd edition: 1910), vol. III: frontispiece.

Abbreviations

Cheshunt   Cheshunt Foundation, Westminster College, Cambridge

CMA   Calvinistic Methodist Archives (at NLW)

Drew   Drew University Library, Madison, New Jersey

Duke   Duke University Library, Durham, North Carolina

JHSPCW   *Journal of the Historical Society of the Presbyterian Church of Wales* (known also as *The Journal of the Calvinistic Methodist Historical Society*). In Welsh: *Cylchgrawn Cymdeithas Hanes y Methodistiaid Calfinaidd*

NLW   National Library of Wales, Aberystwyth

Rylands   John Rylands University Library of Manchester

SMU   Bridwell Library, Southern Methodist University, Dallas, Texas

Introduction

In common parlance, Methodism is Wesleyan Methodism, following the pattern and precepts laid down by the eighteenth-century Church of England clergyman John Wesley. Not only has his movement spread widely in the centuries since his death, but Wesleyan Methodism and its founder have received extensive, perhaps even disproportionate, academic treatment.[1] Beyond those interested in the history of religion, Methodism's association with the rising artisan classes of the nineteenth century has provided a rich field for those pursuing sociological study.[2] Theologically, Wesley's Methodism was frequently called 'Arminian', since it followed the teachings of Jacobus Arminius, an early seventeenth-century Dutch theologian who stressed man's free will in accepting or rejecting salvation. It was a theological position ideally suited to the optimistic spirit of the age, and to Wesley's overriding desire to proclaim the gospel indiscriminately to all.

However, what we today refer to as Methodism and Methodist was in reality only a portion – albeit a substantial portion – of the eighteenth-century Methodist movement. Methodism was born in the mid-eighteenth-century evangelical revivals, a swath of religious awakenings that stretched from the eastern seaboard of the American colonies to many parts of the British Isles and extended as far to the east as Bohemia, Moravia and even Siberia.[3] They were revivals that cumulatively gave birth to a new religious movement, Evangelicalism.[4] English Wesleyan Methodism was merely one constituent element of this movement. In England, a numerically smaller section, which pre-dated Wesleyanism, was Calvinistic. Rooted firmly in the English Reformed Protestant tradition, this movement maintained a markedly different theological position to Wesley's. The Calvinistic Methodists, the 'elect' Methodists, followed the teachings of John Calvin, the sixteenth-century Reformer, who in his desire to magnify

God's sovereignty laid great stress on the doctrine of divine pre-destination: that God had chosen, had 'elected', certain people for eternal salvation. As a rigid logician, Calvin went on to suppose that if God were all-supreme he also had chosen those who would experience eternal damnation. This aspect of the doctrine has been called 'double predestination' and was held by some, though not by any means all, Calvinistic Methodists during the eighteenth century.

Where Wesley's movement grew rapidly in England and later throughout the English-speaking world, Calvinistic Methodism did not. Yet this probably had very little to do with theology. While Calvinistic Methodism showed some early signs of success in England, and was certainly a viable alternative to Wesleyanism for its first decade or so, its initial growth proved to be largely fleeting. The one area of real and sustained growth was in Wales, and the religious denomination ultimately formed there in 1811 was the only branch of 'Methodism' that has ever called itself 'Calvinistic'. The English branch of the movement quickly became fragmented, the consequence of a whole host of factors, with the result that Calvinistic Methodists in England either formed their own religious networks (and there was a rich tapestry of these), morphed into evangelical Anglicans, or wound up in one or other of the various branches of more mainstream Nonconformist dissent.

Calvinistic Methodism, the smaller, almost forgotten, Methodist sibling, has received considerably less academic attention than Wesley-an Methodism. Much of the historical writing on it has been as fragmented as the movement itself, but there are a number of mile-stones that deserve attention. There has been perennial interest in the life and career of the English revivalist, George Whitefield, but much of this work has been hagiographical in nature.[5] It is only more recently that historians such as Harry Stout, Frank Lambert and Jerome Mahaffey have tried, with varying degrees of success, to understand Whitefield in his eighteenth-century context.[6] Unlike for Wesley, there has been no attempt to collate and edit Whitefield's voluminous papers, including almost 2,500 items of correspondence. To date they are an under-utilised resource. However, they have much to add to our understanding of the mid-eighteenth-century British Atlantic world, and were they more readily available they would surely add further complexity to our understanding of early Methodism, and maybe even begin to tilt the balance away from the dominant Wesleyan narrative. So also, the countess of Huntingdon and her connexion has been the subject of renewed historical attention in recent times; significant biographical studies have appeared.[7] In addition, Edwin Welch's edition of the minutes of Whitefield's London headquarters, the Tabernacle, and the countess's Spa Fields Chapel have done much to stimulate interest in the alternative Methodism of the Calvinists.[8] The later development of Calvinistic Methodism, especially following the rise to prominence of the countess of Huntingdon, has been painstakingly pieced together in Alan Harding's *The Countess of Huntingdon's Connexion: A Sect in Action in Eighteenth-Century England* (2003). However, many of the smaller fringe networks that made up the wider Calvinistic Methodist movement during the often highly chaotic development of the eighteenth-century evangelical movement have yet to receive extended analysis. We hope that one of the virtues of our book will be its drawing attention to some of these areas requiring further historical light.

In many respects historical writing on the Welsh Calvinistic Methodist movement stands in stark contrast to that on its English counterpart. Welsh Methodism has a long and at times sophisticated historiography; some of the foremost historians of Wales, particularly in the nineteenth and early twentieth centuries, have focused on it, often to the neglect of other equally important subjects. While Welsh Methodism has certainly suffered more than its fair share of hagiographers, the existence of the Calvinistic Methodist historical society and journal for very nearly a century has done much to encourage serious study of the voluminous archives bequeathed by the eighteenth-century Welsh Methodists. Much of that work has traditionally been quite narrow in focus, and too much of it has concentrated on the early phase of the revival up to the division in the movement in 1750. This trend stems partly from an understandable interest in tracing the origins of the connexion, but it also reflects the greater availability of sources for that period. It was Howel Harris who was chiefly responsible for the preservation of most of the records from the eighteenth century, so that the sources for mainstream Methodism become more scarce for the period after he withdrew from active participation in the Welsh Calvinistic Methodist Association in 1750. The legacy of extensive diaries and correspondence which he left behind means that there has been an inevitable tendency to view the Welsh revival through his eyes, since the sources are far less abundant for his colleagues in the movement, especially in the case of Daniel Rowland.

A great deal of the work on Welsh Methodism was written in the heyday of Calvinistic Methodist hegemony. The decline of Welsh Calvinistic Methodism in the twentieth century has created space for historians, sometimes having no religious or denominational affiliation themselves, to think more critically about Methodism in Wales. The teleological Methodist view of history was challenged by Geraint H. Jenkins, who argued that the idea of revival actually diverted attention away from the slow and often painstaking way in which eighteenth-century Welsh Methodism became established in Wales.[9] More recently, there have been efforts to understand the rank-and-file membership of the revival, and particularly the role of women in the Methodist movement.[10] There has been a greater appreciation of the role which improving educational and literacy levels played in creating the circum-stances necessary for the reception of the Methodist revival's message.[11] Also, in the composite volume *The Welsh Church: From Reformation to Disestablishment, 1603–1920* (2007), there is a renewed emphasis on the thoroughly Anglican nature of early Welsh Methodism.[12] Some have been keen to explore the links between early eighteenth-century Methodism and notions of Welshness.[13] Others have been keen to take a more comparative, but nonetheless complementary approach, placing events in Wales in both transatlantic and pan-Celtic con-texts.[14] This current book reflects the richness of these historiographical trends. While the authors make no apology for their close engagement with the best of recent scholarship, its claim to originality is that for the first time it attempts to tell the story of English and Welsh Calvin-istic Methodism woven into a single analytic narrative. It adopts a broadly chronological approach, switching the focus between England and Wales at appropriate points. But it also attempts to do more than that: our book tries to show how the two movements overlapped and even interpenetrated at various points during the long eighteenth century and yet reflects on some of the reasons why a full merger between them was never likely to work in the long term. The narrative concludes by reflecting on the reasons why Welsh Calvinistic Method-ism was able to go from strength to strength, particularly in the nineteenth century, while the English Calvinistic Methodists were quickly fragmented and their energies soon dissipated. Overall, by drawing Methodist history away from strict denominational- and personality-based interpretations, we hope to reflect the remarkable complexity of the eighteenth-century evangelical revival.

On stylistic matters: some Welsh spellings are even now in dispute. The thorniest problem arises with that community one mile south of Talgarth, Breconshire, which today is known as Trefecca (or Trefeca). It poses an orthographical nightmare. Historically, the name serves several functions as it is applied to: Howel Harris's home and later industrial/religious 'family'; the countess of Huntingdon's 'college' (and a later college during the nineteenth century); and a major collection of Calvinistic Methodist letters and manuscripts. To distinguish between them, we have decided to adopt 'Trefeca' when referring to Harris's home and 'family'; 'Trevecca' for the countess's college; and 'Trevecka' for the manuscript collection.[15] Indexed references will follow this pattern. Even Harris's own first (Christian) name can give rise to confusion. He clearly signed his will 'Howell', and many historians have followed this usage when referring to him. However, the more correct Welsh version 'Howel' has been followed by others, and this is the form adopted in this book, although the variant spelling will also occasionally appear when used in quotations or bibliographical references. The point to remember is that Howell Harris and Howel Harris are one and the same.

The writing of a work of this nature has not been without its challenges, not least of which have been ensuring that the voices of three separate authors meld together as seamlessly as possible. We are grateful, therefore, for the helpful and incisive comments of the anonymous reader of the original proposal and the confidence shown in our ability to produce a work that would be substantially more than an amalgam of the views and opinions of three different writers. Thanks are also due to staff at the many manuscript depositories listed in the bibliography, who have shown unflinching patience and help over the many years that the three of us have been studying and writing about the history of Methodism. Permission to quote from Howel Harris's manuscript diaries has been kindly granted once again by the Historical Society of the Presbyterian Church of Wales. We are also greatly indebted to the University of Wales Press for their forbearance over the course of the long gestation of this book.

It is the authors' wish that this book will open up Methodist studies to insights other than those of the dominant Wesleyan discourse, and at least do something to restore the perspectives of those who chose to regard themselves as the eighteenth century's elect Methodists.

David Ceri Jones
Boyd Stanley Schlenther
Eryn Mant White

Notes

[1] The extent of this academic interest can be gauged from William J. Abraham and James E. Kirby (eds), *The Oxford Handbook of Methodist Studies* (Oxford: Oxford University Press, 2009); Randy L. Maddox and Jason E. Vickers (eds), *The Cambridge Companion to John Wesley* (Cambridge: Cambridge University Press, 2010); Charles Yrigoyen Jr (ed.), *The T&T Clark Companion to Methodism* (London: T&T Clark, 2010).

[2] See David Hempton and John Walsh, 'E. P. Thompson and Methodism', in Mark A. Noll (ed.), *God and Mammon: Protestants, Money and the Market, 1790–1860* (New York: Oxford University Press, 2002), pp. 99–122.

[3] W. R. Ward, *The Protestant Evangelical Awakening* (Cambridge: Cambridge University Press, 1992).

[4] David W. Bebbington, *Evangelicalism in Modern Britain* (London: Unwin Hyman, 1989), chapter 1.

[5] John Gillies, *Memoirs of the Life of the Reverend George Whitefield* (London: Edward and Charles Dilly, 1772); Luke Tyerman, *The Life of the Rev. George Whitefield* (2 vols, London: Hodder and Stoughton, 1876–7); Arnold A. Dallimore, *George Whitefield: The Life and Times of the Great Evangelists of the 18th Century Revival* (2 vols, London and Edinburgh: The Banner of Truth Trust, 1970 and 1980).

[6] Harry S. Stout, *The Divine Dramatist: George Whitefield and the Rise of Modern Evangelicalism* (Grand Rapids, MI: Eerdmans, 1991); Frank Lambert, *'Pedlar in Divinity': George Whitefield and the Transatlantic Revivals* (Princeton, NJ: Princeton University Press, 1994); Jerome Dean Mahaffey, *Preaching Politics: The Religious Rhetoric of George Whitefield and the Founding of a New Nation* (Waco, TX: Baylor University Press, 2007).

7   Edwin Welch, *Spiritual Pilgrim: A Reassessment of the Life of the Countess of Huntingdon* (Cardiff: University of Wales Press, 1995); Boyd Stanley Schlenther, *Queen of the Methodists: The Countess of Huntingdon and the Eighteenth-Century Crisis of Faith and Society* (Durham: Durham Academic Press, 1997).

8   Edwin Welch (ed.), *Two Calvinistic Methodist Chapels, 1743–1811: The London Tabernacle and Spa Fields Chapel* (London: London Record Society, 1975).

9   Geraint H. Jenkins, *Literature, Religion and Society in Wales, 1660–1740* (Cardiff: University of Wales Press, 1978), pp. 305–9. For a partial critique of Jenkins's position, see David Ceri Jones, '"A Glorious Morn"? Methodism and the rise of evangelicalism in Wales, 1735–62', in Mark A. Smith (ed.), *British Evangelical Identities Past and Present*, vol. 1: *Aspects of the History and Sociology of Evangelicalism in Britain and Ireland* (Milton Keynes: Paternoster, 2008), pp. 97–113.

10 Eryn M. White, *Praidd Bach y Bugail Mawr: Seiadau Methodistaidd De-Orllewin Cymru* (Llandysul: Gwasg Gomer, 1995).

11 Geraint H. Jenkins (ed.), *The Welsh Language before the Industrial Revolution* (Cardiff: University of Wales Press, 1997), especially chapters 7 and 9.

12 Sir Glanmor Williams, William Jacob, Nigel Yates and Frances Knight, *The Welsh Church from Reformation to Disestablishment, 1603–1920* (Cardiff: University of Wales Press, 2007).

13 E. Wyn James, '"The New Birth of a People": Welsh Language and Identity and the Welsh Methodists, c.1740–1820', in Robert Pope (ed.), *Religion and National Identity: Wales and Scotland, c.1700–2000* (Cardiff: University of Wales Press, 2001), pp. 14–42.

14 David Ceri Jones, '*A Glorious Work in the World': Welsh Methodism and the International Evangelical Revival, 1735–50* (Cardiff: University of Wales Press, 2004); Nigel Yates, 'Wind, rain and the Holy Spirit: Welsh Evangelicalism in a Pan-Celtic Context, 1750–1850', in idem (ed.), *Bishop Burgess and his World: Culture, Religion and Society in Britain, Europe and North America in the Eighteenth and Nineteenth Centuries* (Cardiff: University of Wales Press, 2007), pp. 103–20.

15 A précis of each of the more than 3,000 letters in the Trevecka collection is included in Boyd Stanley Schlenther and Eryn Mant White, *Calendar of the Trevecka Letters* (Aberystwyth: National Library of Wales, 2003).

'A sweet prospect' for the gospel: the origins of Calvinistic Methodism, 1735–1738

Calvinistic Methodism had its roots in the sixteenth-century Protestant Reformation. Historians increasingly regard the Reformation as a long process drawn out over three centuries. The final phases of this process began with the ending of confessional conflict at the conclusion of the Thirty Years War in 1648. The signing of the Treaty of Westphalia in that year set the pattern for the future: neither Roman Catholicism nor Protestantism would prevail.[1] The easing of religious tensions, as states gave up on the policy of creating comprehensive churches within their territories, created space for alternative strains of popular spirituality to develop, pieties that tended to be more individualistic and experiential, stressing the cultivation of an inward religion of the heart.[2] These included Catholic Jansenism, Hasidic Judaism, Lutheran Pietism and Evangelicalism, one of whose offshoots was, of course, Methodism; and these groups tended to encourage what has been called religious 'enthusiasm'.[3] What united them was a desire for a more emotive and practical spirituality: one that preferred action over passivity, feeling over intellect, and informality over order, and where the clergy encouraged lay participation. Each new tradition, in its own way, endeavoured to bring about religious renewal through persuasive rather than the more coercive state-driven methods of Christianisation that had been customary.[4]

In the British Isles, strategies aimed at securing total confessional uniformity can be seen to have been gradually abandoned during the seventeenth century. The religious conflicts that had resulted in the execution of a king in 1649 and the attempt at godly reformation by the Puritans during the 1650s had been an abject failure. The restoration of the monarchy, and with it the established Church of England, largely settled religious questions; a Protestant succession was guaranteed in 1689, as was the hegemony of the Anglican Established Church.[5] But, significantly, its monopolistic hold on the religious life of the nation had certainly been loosened: a measure of toleration was granted to the Dissenters, a move which made confessional pluralism the order of the day.[6] The decades between 1660 and the beginning of the evangelical revival in the mid-1730s have often been seen by historians as a religiously quiescent period.[7] In comparison with the turmoil of the Civil War and Interregnum this may certainly be so, but these were decades of slow gestation, when important – if sometimes subtle – changes in the religious landscape of England and Wales took place; they were developments which created the context necessary for the emergence of the Calvinistic Methodist movement.

It was no accident that both George Whitefield and Howel Harris chose to define themselves deliberately as Calvinists. They were proud of the fact that they stood within a Calvinist tradition that, in Harris's words, stretched back to the 'good old orthodox Reformers and Puritans'.[8] But the spirituality and vigour of the contemporary descendants of the Puritans, the Dissenters, was a pale reflection of what had been normative in the seventeenth century. The persecution that had accompanied the re-establishment of the Church of England in the early 1660s had taken its toll, and many Dissenting congregations emerged numerically small and inward looking, preoccupied with maintaining their doctrinal purity and defending their legal status. Many of them had also become enmeshed in constricting theological debates over the nature of genuine Calvinism, a strict and increasingly popular version of which elevated predestination to such an extent that evangelism was rendered superfluous.[9] But there were also flickers of life and vitality and evidence that attitudes within the Dissenting community were becoming more fluid. Both Richard Baxter and Philip Doddridge had warned against the dangers of theological precisionism and the application of detailed doctrinal tests which tended to alienate genuine Christians from one another. Instead, they stressed the importance of what they called 'heart-work', evangelical conversion, the cultivation of the life of the soul and the necessity of affirmative spiritual nurture.[10]

These emphases were supported by a growing body of affordable and accessible devotional literature, featuring such writers as Joseph Alleine, John Bunyan and Richard Baxter himself, as well as a commitment to preaching specifically for conversions among some of the more missionary-minded members of the Dissenting community.[11]

With the hegemony of strict predestinarian Calvinism being challenged in some quarters, a more moderate version which attempted to square the sovereignty of God with human accountability was gaining in influence.[12] In provincial Baptist circles, the steady stream of ministers produced by the Bristol Baptist Academy under the leadership of Bernard Foskett were committed to an outward-looking evangelical Calvinism, which gave priority to evangelistic preaching and experiential piety.[13] It is surely no coincidence that some of Howel Harris's earliest supporters included some of the many Welsh Baptist ministers who had passed through the doors of the Bristol Academy.[14] Their priorities were reflected in what remained of the Calvinist Internationale, a network of correspondence which brought together experiential Calvinist ministers in the American colonies, Scotland, Ireland and England.[15] When news of the outbreak of a revival at Northampton, Massachusetts, in 1734 first reached the British Isles, it was this network that became the vehicle for the transmission of such apparently surprising news.[16] For Whitefield and the Calvinistic Methodists it was this embryonic tradition of evangelical Calvinism, with its twin emphases on conversion and heart nurture, which proved to be so compelling. Indeed, in many respects, Whitefield was to be the most energetic champion of evangelical Calvinism in the eighteenth century, with the result that by the end of his life it had become the dominant expression of Reformed orthodoxy favoured by Calvinist-inclined evangelicals almost everywhere.

In a sense these changes in emphasis within the Reformed tradition in England can be seen as an outworking of some of the insights of Lutheran Pietism. Recent scholarship has shown how intimately the religious life of the British Isles was connected to Continental Europe during this period.[17] W. R. Ward has shown how many of the features of what later became Methodism can actually be traced directly to central and southern Germany during the later part of the seventeenth and the early part of the eighteenth century.[18] Pietists like Philip Jakob Spener, whose *Pia Desideria* (1675) had a genuinely international

impact, stressed such things as a return to the scriptures, lay participation in small fellowship groups and the living of lives of active and
practical godliness. Among groups like the Huguenots, the Salzburghers
and later the Moravians, field preaching, camp meetings and periodic
community revivals became common. When groups such as these came
under persecution after the revocation of the Edict of Nantes in 1685,
many of them were forced to become religious refugees.[19] Their dispersal
in the early decades of the eighteenth century led to the extensive
dissemination of their ideas and practices, as many of them settled in
the southern American colonies, stopping off en route in England.

Pietistic ideas can first be detected in England during the second half
of the seventeenth century largely among Anglicans whose religious
monopoly in England, while still impressive, had nonetheless been
curtailed in the aftermath of the Glorious Revolution. Taking their
lead from August Herman Francke's pietist reformation at Halle,
organisations like the Society for Promoting Christian Knowledge,
the Society for the Reformation of Manners and the Society for the
Propagation of the Gospel, as well as a large number of private devotional societies, tried to raise the spiritual temperature through volun-
taristic means like education, the publication of devotional literature
and the inculcation of godly standards of behaviour.[20] At Oxford, the
'Holy Club', formed in 1729 by Charles Wesley, and whose members
included John Wesley and George Whitefield, was merely another
expression of this desire to recapture the spirit of primitive Christianity
through a rigorous lifestyle of ascetic piety and good works.[21]

However, it was the Moravians, who had first arrived in England
in 1728 basking in the warm glow of a revival that had taken place
on Count Nikolaus Zinzendorf's estate at Herrnhut in Saxony the
previous year, who provided the most attractive and compelling form
of heart religion.[22] The two strands of pietism, Lutheran and evangelical, were to come together in a remarkable way in 1735. The Holy
Club had run its natural course; both John and Charles Wesley, as
well as George Whitefield, had found its regimen of devotional exercises,
self-denial and sacrificial charity overly burdensome, leaving a legacy
of disillusionment and despair. The Moravians taught many of the
members of Holy Club about the nature of genuine saving faith,
which began a process by which many of them moved towards more
decided evangelical convictions.

However, by this stage there were already inklings of much more exciting times ahead. Griffith Jones, who became rector of Llanddowror, Carmarthenshire, in 1716, had for seven years engaged in extensive field preaching. He had witnessed dramatic conversions among many who flocked to these revivals as well as among parishioners in his previous parishes, perhaps especially at Laugharne. Refusing to be confined by parish boundaries, he had engaged in a widespread itinerant ministry throughout south-west Wales with considerable effect.[23] In the American colonies, according to the calculations of Michael J. Crawford, there had been at least fifteen local religious awakenings in New England between 1712 and 1732.[24] At the same time, Theodore Frelinghuysen had been stoking the fires of revival among Dutch and English settlers in New Jersey since 1720.[25] The expulsion of 25,000 Salzburgher Protestants in 1731, on account of their aggressive open-air evangelism, seemed to intimate a decisive advance for the kingdom of God.[26] The principles and techniques of revivalism were being honed and perfected well before the beginning of Methodism.

Attempts to analyse the origins of Methodism have preoccupied historians ever since Elie Halévy published his essay 'La naissance du Méthodisme en Angleterre' ('The birth of Methodism in England') in 1906.[27] Much of this work has focused predominantly on the birth of Wesleyan Methodism.[28] While Calvinistic Methodism certainly drew from the same tap-roots as what was to become its much larger Wesleyan counterpart, its own origins reflected the stronger rooting of its leaders in the Reformed tradition.[29] While the pietist stress on heart religion was certainly influential and Anglican High Church spirituality was important in jolting the revivalists out of a dependence on legalistic religion, it was the moderate Calvinist tradition, emerging in England after the Restoration, that can be said to have had the most decisive impact. When the individuals who became the leaders of Calvinistic Methodism resolved their spiritual odysseys in the experience of conversion or the new birth, it was this moderate Calvinism to which they turned: to them it gave coherence and sense to the religious upheavals they had faced.[30]

Beginnings of revival in England

The actual beginnings of Calvinistic Methodism in England are over-shadowed by the powerful narrative of Methodist origins refined by John Wesley and perpetuated by subsequent generations of Methodist historians. This narrative centres on the experience of John Wesley himself, locating the origins of English Methodism at Aldersgate Street during May 1738.[31] Until 1740 English Methodism consisted of a fairly unified network of societies in a number of locations throughout England, with its headquarters at a Moravian-dominated society which met at Fetter Lane in London.[32] From their arrival in England, the Moravians had contented themselves with working through the London religious societies, until Zinzendorf established a small society for German émigrés during his visit to London in 1737.[33] This society was the genesis of the Fetter Lane Society, which came into existence after Peter Böhler's arrival in England the following year. Böhler struck up a friendship with James Hutton, a London bookseller, who had been holding a society in his home, and the two agreed to turn Hutton's society into a formal Moravian-style band.[34] Through his connections with former Oxford Methodists, Hutton developed the society into a rallying point for many of the most religiously earnest who happened to find themselves in London during the later 1730s.

Among these was a newly ordained Anglican clergyman, George Whitefield. Whitefield had become an Oxford Methodist after joining the Holy Club in 1733; he was the first of its members to reach settled evangelical convictions. Having almost killed himself by the strict regimen of holy exercises he followed during these years, Whitefield experienced an evangelical conversion while still at Oxford in 1735. He quickly became the leader of the Holy Club in 1736, after the Wesley brothers' decision to go to the newly established Georgia colony as missionaries. Whitefield was ordained deacon at Gloucester Cathedral in June 1736 and almost immediately preached his first sermon at St Mary de Crypt in the city, reportedly driving fifteen people mad in the process.[35] The following month he deputised for his friend, and former Holy Club member, Thomas Broughton, at the chapel in the Tower of London. The predominant theme of his sermons was the new birth, but it was Whitefield's youth (he quickly acquired the sobriquet 'the boy parson'), which attracted most hearers.[36] For the next two months Whitefield relentlessly preached the new birth at the Tower, gaining both large audiences and ever greater notoriety. For much of the next eighteenth months, he deputised for a number of clergy friends, first in Hampshire and then Gloucestershire, but his decision to follow the Wesley brothers to Georgia towards the end of 1736 increased his public profile still further as pulpits were thrown open to him to preach charity sermons on behalf of the new colony.

Despite the initial goodwill of the London clergy, Whitefield did not reciprocate, and his sermons during this period were filled with denunciations of those clergy who failed to preach a full-throated evangelical message. The effect of the sermons was quite startling; allowing for his youthful exaggeration and hyperbole, Whitefield's *Journals* bristle with such observations as: 'The doctrine of the new birth . . . made its way like lightning into the hearers' consciences.'[37] Much of his time during these months was taken up with responding to invitations to preach and talking with ever increasing numbers of people 'under soul concern', a pattern that was to mark much of the remainder of his life.[38] The fame which he attracted – and he was preaching in various locations in London at least ten times a week – resulted in the publication of his first sermon, *The Nature and Necessity of our New Birth in Christ Jesus, in Order to Salvation* (1737). Recent biographers of Whitefield have attempted to understand his sensational impact during these months. Whitefield himself, of course, attributed his success solely to the superintendence of God's providence, but there were also other reasons why his preaching had the impact it did. Harry Stout has argued that Whitefield's sermons were 'dramatic scripts'; when Whitefield preached he performed, his sermons resembling theatrical events rather than theological or devotional homilies.[39]

Whitefield was also a master publicist, who used the marketing techniques at his disposal to turn himself into an overnight media sensation.[40] England was in the grip of a consumer revolution during the middle decades of the eighteenth century, which made relatively inexpensive commodities more accessible to more people than ever before.[41] These commodities included books, and Whitefield took advantage of the booming publishing industry in London to flood the market with works which carried his message, including images of himself, to a wider audience. As well as publishing his sermons, Whitefield began issuing a journal. Written with a definite eye to publication, it was issued in periodic short instalments, a clever marketing technique keeping readers abreast of the progress of his ministry and by extension the revival.

Then, at the height of his popularity, Whitefield set sail for the American colonies with the intention of establishing an orphanage in the newly founded colony of Georgia. Much of 1738 was spent in the colonies, and in his absence events back in England developed apace. First, James Hutton brought some order to the burgeoning London awakening by founding the society at Fetter Lane; it was here amidst the excitement of the London revival that John and Charles Wesley were introduced to evangelical ideas and the Methodist revival began to gather still more pace. Having returned from almost two years in Georgia in early 1738, John Wesley had found neither the salvation that he had been looking for, nor the sense of purpose and direction he might have derived from a successful mission to the Indians.[42] Wesley's spiritual discomfort had been made worse by his encounters with the Moravians, most famously in a storm en route to Georgia. When he returned to England he gravitated towards London and his old friends now meeting at Fetter Lane. Here, following intensive counselling from Peter Böhler, John Wesley was gradually brought to accept justification by faith, and then experienced its power as his heart was strangely warmed at Aldersgate Street in May 1738.[43] This experience released Wesley from years of spiritual anguish and frustration; with renewed confidence he began preaching in and around London churches, quickly meeting the same response as Whitefield had done when the clergy did not appreciate his heavy stress on the necessity of the new birth.

However, London was not the only area to experience an intensification of its religious temperature; in three other parts of England small networks of individuals were coming together intent on preaching the gospel more widely and more passionately. Benjamin Ingham, who had been a member of the Holy Club and had accompanied the Wesley brothers to Georgia in 1735, had been preaching around his home at Ossett in Yorkshire, following his early return from America in February 1737. Heavily influenced by the Moravians, by the end of 1738 Ingham had founded a number of societies in West Yorkshire and was preaching throughout the county wherever and whenever opportunities presented themselves, including in barns and even the open air.[44] Ingham also proved to be the link between the London evangelicals and a group of Methodists in Cambridgeshire and Bedford-shire. Francis Okely had been converted through Jacob Rogers of Bedford in 1736, shortly before taking up a place at Cambridge University. Almost immediately he surrounded himself with like-minded individuals in the university who met together for study, prayer and charitable acts on lines very similar to the Holy Club.[45] The society existed alongside another 'party for God in Cambridge' established by William Delamotte, who subsequently accompanied the Wesley brothers to Georgia. Delamotte was to be the link that connected the Methodists in Bedfordshire, Cambridge and Fetter Lane. His friend-ship with Benjamin Ingham led to Ingham's being invited to Cambridge in December 1738 and the outbreak of revival there.[46] Ingham was then introduced to Jacob Rogers at Bedford, where his preaching had a similar effect and led to the foundation of a Methodist society in the town. Rogers and Ingham formed a close working relationship that led to the extension of the revival to Nottingham.[47]

The final network extended west from London as far as Bristol, which was to become the second city of English Methodism. John Thorold, yet another former member of the Holy Club, had begun a society at Windsor; Charles Kinchin was the rector at Dummer in Hampshire, while John Hutchings, his curate, had been working with the religious society at nearby Basingstoke.[48] Further west, John Cennick had begun preaching at Reading, leading to the foundation of a society in the town in early 1739. However, his activities were cut short by pressing calls from Bristol, which had become the chief focus of Whitefield's ministry following his return to Britain at the end of 1738.

Bristol enjoyed its fair share of religious societies, and it was to these that Whitefield had first preached charity sermons in 1737.[49] During the year before his departure for Georgia he preached regularly in the city: on one occasion 'multitudes came on foot and many in coaches a mile without the city to meet [him]'.[50] He spent most of January and February 1737 in the city, preaching at least five times each week in churches which gladly opened their doors to him. His ministry breathed new life into many of the religious societies in the city, but he did not attempt to establish his own network of societies there at this stage. When he eventually visited Bristol again, shortly after his return to England, he found that his earlier ministry among the Bristol societies had borne lasting fruit.[51] But by this stage Whitefield's fame and notoriety had also aroused the opposition of many of the clergy in Bristol, and he found many pulpits closed to him. The lack of preaching opportunities persuaded him of the necessity of preaching in the open air, and so in February 1739, possibly inspired by the example of Howel Harris, he took the momentous step of addressing the miners at Kingswood out of doors. Whitefield was soon holding up to thirty meetings a week in Bristol, and after six weeks of this activity revival had really taken hold in the city. Unwilling to be tied down to any single locality, Whitefield established a school for the children of the Kingswood miners, and then handed over the care of the Bristol work to the newly converted John Wesley.[52] Although Wesley's preaching was not greeted with quite the same enthusiasm as that of Whitefield's, his flair for organisation really came into its own as Wesley set about arranging the new converts into societies and bands along Moravian lines.

By early 1739 the uncoordinated activities of a few individuals had become a coherent revival movement. There had been a revival underway in some parts of England for close on three years by this point, and a network of evangelical Methodists existed, stretching from Yorkshire, through parts of rural Cambridgeshire, London and as far as the West Country. At this stage all the main figures involved in the revival, the Wesleys, Whitefield and the leaders of the English Moravians, regarded Fetter Lane as the hub of the revival, each of them reporting back to it on the progress of their activities at regular intervals. The members of the society took collective responsibility for guiding the course of the whole revival, and there is much evidence to suggest that the leaders of the revival were prepared at this stage to be bound by decisions made at Fetter Lane.[53] These were the halcyon days of English Methodism, when there was a genuine combining of talents and a commitment to a national revival, but it did not take long for the cracks in this unity to appear and rival agendas to come to the surface. When this fracturing took place, English Methodism was replaced by a plethora of competing Methodisms.

Beginnings of revival in Wales

The origins of Calvinistic Methodism in both England and Wales were deeply rooted in the spirituality and structures of the Church of England.[54] Despite their tacit acceptance of the Church of England during the sixteenth century, the Welsh had never been particularly enthusiastic Protestants. The efforts of the Puritans during the middle decades of the seventeenth century had not brought about the conversion of the Welsh to a more committed form of Protestantism, and the initiatives of the Welsh Trust and the Society for Promoting Christian Knowledge following the Restoration in 1660 only confirmed the limitations of English-inspired and predominantly English-language efforts at evangelisation.[55] In many respects the seeds of the Reformation had still to flower fully in Wales.[56] Protestantism was predicated on the ability to read and understand Scripture; while the Bible had been translated into Welsh by 1588, it was not until the middle decades of the eighteenth century that the majority of Welsh people were able to read it for themselves. Fortuitously, the early years of the Methodist revival coincided with Griffith Jones's attempts to inculcate the basic skills of literacy through his highly adaptable network of peripatetic schools.[57] Once possessed of basic reading skills, many in Wales, particularly among the growing clusters of middling sorts, became fertile ground for the evangelical message of the Methodists.

Around Easter 1735 Howel Harris, a schoolmaster from Trefeca near Talgarth in Breconshire, experienced a life-changing evangelical conversion. The catalyst for the crisis occurred when his local vicar, Pryce Davies, challenged his parishioners about their fitness to receive communion on Easter Sunday, a high point in the sacramental and liturgical life of the Church. Harris passed through an intense struggle that lasted over a month until he emerged confident that he had received the 'spirit of adoption', following an intensely emotional experience of the Holy Spirit in the tower of nearby Llangasty church.[58] Within a month Harris, fired up with evangelical zeal, was visiting his neighbours and travelling to some of the surrounding villages, holding small devotional meetings, usually in people's homes, in which he urged his listeners to adopt a more earnest approach to their religious obligations. It was these activities that were to be the seedbed of the

Methodist awakening in south and mid-Wales; despite opposition from the Church, and their refusal to accept him for ordination, Harris persisted in these actions, quietly building up his followers and adding new groups to his slowly evolving itinerary. When he questioned the wisdom of his own activities, and was plagued by an inferiority complex because of his lay status, Harris was encouraged by a number of sympathetic local Dissenting ministers, and by contact with Griffith Jones, Llanddowror.

Despite Jones's wish to temper elements of Harris's over-exuberance, the friendship opened up a new world to Harris. He undoubtedly learned from the example of Jones's own evangelical preaching ministry.[59] But he also found himself exposed to the influence of European Pietism through Jones and Jones's mentor Sir John Philipps, one of the chief benefactors of the work of the Society for Promoting Christian Knowledge in Wales.[60] It is no accident that Harris first read Josiah Woodward's *An Account of the Religious Societies in the City of London* (1697) following his meeting with Jones, or that shortly afterwards he founded his first proper religious society at Y Wernos at the close of 1736. Geraint Tudur has argued that during these months Harris regarded the 'Established Church as a mission field'; he did not envisage setting up an alternative to the Church or joining the ranks of Dissent.[61] There must have been some demand for his services: within a short space of time there were over fifty societies scattered around south Wales that came under his immediate pastoral oversight.[62]

Unlike Harris, Daniel Rowland had no need to develop such innovatory forms of ministry, as his position as curate of Llangeitho and Nancwnlle in Cardiganshire since 1735 afforded him ample opportunity to hone his skills as a revivalist. Like many other Methodist leaders, Rowland had entered the ministry without evidence of an evangelical conversion. He had followed his father in the parish, but it was through the family of his wife, Elinor, that Rowland was introduced to the Puritan strain of piety. His eventual conversion, though, was secured through Griffith Jones during a sermon preached at Llanddewibrefi.[63] This revolutionised Rowland's life and infused his ministry with a new tone and sense of urgency. He was nicknamed the 'angry clergyman' (*y ffeiriad crac*).[64] But despite this, in the months immediately following his conversion and because of his obsession with the theme of God's judgement and wrath towards sinners, Rowland almost immediately began to attract significant numbers of people to Llangeitho. The tenor of his ministry was altered by his friendship with a neighbouring Dissenting minister, Philip Pugh, who counselled him to dwell much more on the grace of God in Christ in his sermons.[65] This was a change that proved decisive, and the now winsome tone of his ministry attracted increasing crowds to Llangeitho as people travelled in larger numbers and ever greater distances to sit at Rowland's feet.

Despite Harris and Rowland's common friendship with Griffith Jones, the two do not appear to have become acquainted until August 1737, when Harris first heard Rowland preach at Defynnog near Brecon.[66] The meeting was highly significant in the development of the nascent Methodist awakening. Rowland and Harris forged a strong partnership, Rowland being seemingly unconcerned about Harris's unordained status. The meeting must also have been exciting, as both men exchanged stories about their exploits and reported on what was happening in their respective communities. For his part, Harris would undoubtedly have reported on the societies he had established in Breconshire, his discovery of friendly Dissenting ministers who did their best to encourage him and the conversions he had inspired. Among the most important of these was that of Howell Davies, the schoolmaster at Talgarth, and soon to be important junior partner in the Welsh movement on account of his pioneer evangelism in Pembrokeshire.[67] The Defynnog meeting turned two embryonic religious awakenings into a more concerted movement with some semblance of centralised organisation.

The significance of the pooling of resources at Defynnog is borne out by the events which immediately followed. Harris soon travelled to Llangeitho for the first time, where he and Rowland discussed strategic matters late into the night.[68] Shortly after, Harris, whether at the instigation of Rowland or not is difficult to tell, became much more committed to preaching in the open air, grasping every opportunity to do so.[69] For the next year or more the awakening began to gather pace. Harris and Rowland maintained their tried and tested policy: Rowland continued to welcome listeners to Llangeitho, but also began itinerating on a more regular basis, while Harris travelled all over south Wales exhorting and establishing societies. By the end of 1738 Harris could boast, in a letter to George Whitefield, that there was a 'great revival' in Cardiganshire, 'a sweet prospect' in Breconshire and

Monmouthshire and some 'well-wishers to the cause of God' in Montgomeryshire and Glamorgan.[70]

These were months of experimentation and the laying of solid foundations, suffused by occasional bouts of heightened enthusiasm. In these early days, well before the revival was securely established, the tributaries that flowed into the Welsh branch of Calvinistic Methodism were already in evidence. Both Harris and Rowland were committed Anglicans, deeply moulded by the liturgical structure of the Church; both had been influenced at critical junctures in their development by sympathetic Dissenting ministers; and both passed through similar evangelical conversion experiences at roughly the same time. But it was their shared relationship with Griffith Jones, Llanddowror, that had proved to be the important catalyst to their evangelical careers. Jones exemplified the ideal of the earnest gospel minister. He was deeply influenced by pietist ideas through his associations with the Society for Promoting Christian Knowledge and the Society for the Propagation of the Gospel.[71] His dramatic preaching was something which Harris and Rowland both set out to emulate, albeit on a considerably more ambitious scale.[72]

While the English and Welsh revivals had begun independently of one another, they shared common roots. They had both begun in fairly inconspicuous, albeit intense and dramatic ways. By the turn of 1739 there were recognisable revival movements in both countries; Harris and Rowland had begun to work together in Wales, and the Fetter Lane Society was giving a measure of unity to the English revival. It was upon these foundations that the closer integration of the English and Welsh revival began following the first meeting between Harris and Whitefield in early 1739. These were the networks that were soon to evolve into English and Welsh Calvinistic Methodism.

Notes

[1] Peter G. Wallace, *The Long European Reformation* (Basingstoke: Palgrave Macmillan, 2004), pp. 165ff.

[2] Ted A. Campbell, *The Religion of the Heart: A Study of European Religious Life in the Seventeenth and Eighteenth Centuries* (Columbia, SC: University of South Carolina Press, 1991).

3 R. A. Knox, *Enthusiasm* (Oxford: Clarendon Press, 1950).
4 Eamon Duffy, 'The long Reformation: Catholicism, Protestantism and the multitude', in Nicholas Tyacke (ed.), *England's Long Reformation, 1500–1800* (London: Taylor and Francis, 1998), pp. 33–70.
5 J. C. D. Clark, *English Society, 1660–1832: Religion, Ideology and Politics during the Ancien Régime* (2nd edn, Cambridge: Cambridge University Press, 2000).
6 This process is discussed in David Hempton, 'Established churches and the growth of religious pluralism: a case study of Christianisation and secularisation in England since 1700', in Hugh McLeod and Werner Ustorf (eds), *The Decline of Christendom in Western Europe, 1750–2000* (Cambridge: Cambridge University Press, 2003), pp. 81–98.
7 As discussed in Geraint H. Jenkins, *Literature, Religion and Society in Wales, 1660–1730* (Cardiff: University of Wales Press, 1978), pp. 305–9.
8 NLW Trevecka Letter 1295; Howel Harris to James Erskine, 19 February 1745.
9 Michael Watts, *The Dissenters: From the Reformation to the French Revolution* (Oxford: Clarendon Press, 1978), p. 438.
10 Geoffrey F. Nuttall, *Richard Baxter and Philip Doddridge: A Study in a Tradition* (London: Oxford University Press, 1951), p. 19.
11 Jenkins, *Literature, Religion and Society in Wales, 1660–1730*.
12 Alan C. Clifford, *Atonement and Justification: English Evangelical Theology, 1640–1790: An Introduction* (Oxford: Clarendon Press, 1990); David P. Field, *Rigide Calvinisme in a Softer Dresse: The Moderate Presbyterianism of John Howe, 1630–1705* (Edinburgh: Rutherford House, 2004); Jonathan D. Moore, *English Hypothetical Universalism: John Preston and the Softening of Reformed Theology* (Grand Rapids, MI: Eerdmans, 2007).
13 Roger Hayden, *Continuity and Change: Evangelical Calvinism among Eighteenth-Century Baptist Ministers Trained at Bristol Academy, 1690–1791* (Milton under Wychwood: Baptist Historical Society, 2006).
14 For an indication of the sheer number of Welsh students who attended the academy, see G. F. Nuttall, 'Welsh Students at Bristol Baptist College, 1720–1797', *Transactions of the Honourable Society of Cymmrodorion* (1978), 171–99.
15 Susan O'Brien, 'A transatlantic community of saints: the Great Awakening and the first evangelical network, 1735–1755', *American Historical Review*, 91 (1986), 814.
16 D. Bruce Hindmarsh, 'The reception of Jonathan Edwards by early evangelicals in England', in David W. Kling and Douglas A. Sweeney (eds), *Jonathan Edwards at Home and Abroad: Historical Memories,*

Cultural Movements, Global Horizons (Columbia, SC: University of South Carolina Press, 2003), pp. 203–4.

[17] Tony Claydon, *Europe and the Making of England, 1660–1760* (Cambridge: Cambridge University Press, 2007).

[18] W. R. Ward, *The Protestant Evangelical Awakening* (Cambridge: Cambridge University Press, 1992); W. R. Ward, *Early Evangelicalism: A Global Intellectual History, 1670–1789* (Cambridge: Cambridge University Press, 2006).

[19] W. R. Ward, *Christianity under the Ancien Régime, 1648–1789* (Cambridge: Cambridge University Press, 1999), pp. 14, 17.

[20] Henry D. Rack, 'Religious societies and the origins of Methodism', *Journal of Ecclesiastical History*, 38, 4 (October 1987), 582–4.

[21] Eamon Duffy, 'Primitive Christianity revived: religious renewal in Augustan England', in Derek Baker (ed.), *Renaissance and Renewal in Christian History*, *Studies in Church History*, 14 (Oxford: Blackwell, 1977), pp. 290–1.

[22] W. R. Ward, 'The renewed unity of the brethren: ancient church, new sect or interconfessional movement', *Bulletin of the John Rylands University Library of Manchester*, 70, 3 (autumn 1988), 83–5.

[23] Geraint H. Jenkins, '"An old and much honoured soldier": Griffith Jones, Llanddowror', *Welsh History Review*, 11, 4 (1983), 455–7.

[24] Michael J. Crawford, *Seasons of Grace: Colonial New England's Revival Tradition in its British Context* (New York: Oxford University Press, 1991), p. 108.

[25] Carter Lindberg (ed.), *The Pietist Theologians: An Introduction to Theology in the Seventeenth and Eighteenth Centuries* (Oxford: Blackwell, 2005), pp. 78–9.

[26] Ward, *Christianity under the Ancien Régime, 1648–1789*, pp. 105–10.

[27] For an English edition, see Elie Halévy, *The Birth of Methodism in England* (trans. and ed, B. Semmel; Chicago: University of Chicago Press, 1971). See also Gerald Wayne Olsen (ed.), *Religion and Revolution in Early Industrial England: The Halévy Thesis and its Critics* (Lanham, MD: Scarecrow Press, 1990).

[28] John, 'Origins of the evangelical revival', in G. V. Bennett and J. D. Walsh (eds), *Essays in Modern Church History: In Memory of Norman Sykes* (London: Oxford University Press, 1966), pp. 141–61; John Walsh, '"Methodism" and the origins of English-speaking evangelicalism', in Mark A. Noll, David W. Bebbington and George A. Rawlyk (eds), *Evangelicalism: Comparative Studies of Popular Protestantism in North America, the British Isles, and Beyond* (New York:

Oxford University Press, 1994), pp. 19–37; Mark A. Noll, *The Rise of Evangelicalism: The Age of Edwards, Whitefield and the Wesleys* (Leicester: Inter-Varsity Press, 2004), chapter 5.

29 John Coffey, 'Puritanism, evangelicalism and the evangelical Protestant tradition', in Michael A. G. Haykin and Kenneth J. Stewart (eds), *The Emergence of Evangelicalism: Exploring Historical Continuities* (Nottingham: Apollos, 2008), pp. 252–77.

30 Walsh, 'Origins of the evangelical revival', p. 155.

31 Ibid., p. 132.

32 Colin J. Podmore, *The Moravian Church in England, 1728–1760* (Oxford: Clarendon Press, 1998), pp. 34–6.

33 Geoffrey and Margaret Stead, *The Exotic Plant: A History of the Moravian Church in Great Britain, 1742–2000* (Peterborough: Epworth Press, 2003), p. 51.

34 The circumstances surrounding the founding of the society are discussed in ibid., pp. 36–9.

35 George Whitefield to Mr H., 30 June 1736, in John Gillies (ed.), *The Works of the Reverend George Whitefield* (6 vols, London: Edward and Charles Dilly, 1771–2), I, p. 19.

36 George Whitefield, *A Further Account of God's Dealings with the Reverend Mr. George Whitefield from the time of his ordination to his embarking for Georgia* (June 1736–December 1737) (London: W. Strahan, 1747), p. 7.

37 Ibid., p. 13.

38 Ibid., p. 26.

39 Harry S. Stout, *The Divine Dramatist: George Whitefield and the Rise of Modern Evangelicalism* (Grand Rapids, MI: Eerdmans, 1991), p. 40.

40 This is a theme that has been explored by Frank Lambert in *'Pedlar in Divinity': George Whitefield and the Transatlantic Revivals, 1737–1770* (Princeton, NJ: Princeton University Press, 1994).

41 Neil McKendrick, John Brewer and J. H. Plumb, *The Birth of a Consumer Society: The Commercialization of Eighteenth-Century England* (Bloomington, IN: Indiana University Press, 1982).

42 Richard P. Heitzenrater, 'Wesley in America', *Proceedings of the Wesley Historical Society*, 54, 3 (October 2003), 87–91.

43 John H. Tyson, 'John Wesley's Conversion at Aldersgate', in Kenneth J. Collins and John H. Tyson (eds), *Conversion in the Wesleyan Tradition* (Nashville, TN: Abingdon Press, 2001), pp. 31–4.

44 Luke Tyerman, *The Oxford Methodists: Memoirs of the Rev. Messrs. Clayton, Ingham, Gambold, Hervey, and Broughton, with Biographical*

Notices of others (London: Hodder and Stoughton, 1873), pp. 90–5; Richard P. Heitzenrater (ed.), *Diary of an Oxford Methodist: Benjamin Ingham, 1733–1734* (Durham, NC: Duke University Press, 1985), pp. 43–7.

45 John Walsh, 'The Cambridge Methodists', in Peter Brooks (ed.), *Christian Spirituality: Essays in Honour of Gordon Rupp* (London: SCM Press, 1973), pp. 249–83.

46 Ibid., p. 258.

47 Podmore, *The Moravian Church in England*, p. 50.

48 George Whitefield, *A Continuation of the Reverend Mr Whitefield's journal from his arrival at London to his departure from thence on his way to Georgia (December 1738–June 1739)* (London: James Hutton, 1739), pp. 20–1; Tyerman, *The Oxford Methodists*, pp. 368–9.

49 Jonathan Barry, 'Introduction', in Jonathan Barry and Kenneth Morgan (eds), *Reformation and Revival in Eighteenth-Century Bristol* (Bristol: Bristol Record Society, 1994), p. ix.

50 Whitefield, *Further Account*, p. 16.

51 Whitefield, *A Continuation of the Reverend Mr Whitefield's Journal from his arrival at London to his departure from thence on his way to Georgia*, p. 27.

52 Ibid., p. 66.

53 Podmore, *The Moravian Church in England*, p. 48.

54 William Jacob, 'Methodism in Wales', in Sir Glanmor Williams, William Jacob, Nigel Yates and Frances Knight, *The Welsh Church from Reformation to Disestablishment, 1603–1920* (Cardiff: University of Wales Press, 2007), pp. 165ff.

55 See Eryn M. White, 'Popular schooling and the Welsh language 1650–1800', in Geraint H. Jenkins (ed.), *The Welsh Language before the Industrial Revolution* (Cardiff: University of Wales Press, 1997), pp. 319–25.

56 Glanmor Williams, 'Wales and the Reformation', in idem., *Welsh Reformation Essays* (Cardiff: University of Wales Press, 1967), p. 30.

57 White, 'Popular schooling and the Welsh language 1650–1800', pp. 325–37.

58 For an account of his conversion experience, largely in his own words, see Richard Bennett, *The Early Life of Howell Harris* (London: The Banner of Truth Trust, 1962).

59 See Eifion Evans, 'Spirituality before the Great Awakening: the personal devotion of Griffith Jones, Llanddowror', in idem., *Fire in the Thatch: the True Nature of Religious Revival* (Bridgend: Evangelical Press of Wales, 1996), pp. 61–2.

[60] Mary Clement, *The S.P.C.K. and Wales, 1699–1740* (London: SPCK, 1954), pp. 63–6.

[61] Geraint Tudur, *Howell Harris: From Conversion to Separation, 1735–1750* (Cardiff: University of Wales Press, 2000), p. 20.

[62] Eifion Evans, *Howel Harris, Evangelist 1714–1773* (Cardiff: University of Wales Press, 1972), p. 22.

[63] Eryn M. White, 'Daniel Rowland (1711?–1790)', in *Oxford Dictionary of National Biography* (Oxford: Oxford University Press, 2004).

[64] John Owen, *Coffhad am y Parch. Daniel Rowlands, gynt o Langeitho, Ceredigion* (Caerlleon: Edward Parry, 1839), p. 17.

[65] Eifion Evans, *Daniel Rowland and the Great Evangelical Awakening in Wales* (Edinburgh: The Banner of Truth Trust, 1985), pp. 37–9.

[66] See Howel Harris's Diary, 3 August 1763, in Tom Beynon (ed.), *Howell Harris, Reformer and Soldier (1714–1773)* (Caernarvon: The Calvinistic Methodist Bookroom, 1958), pp. 187–8.

[67] Derec Llwyd Morgan, 'Howell Davies (?1717–1770)', in *Oxford Dictionary of National Biography* (Oxford: Oxford University Press, 2004).

[68] Evans, *Daniel Rowland*, p. 54.

[69] Howell Harris, *A Brief Account of the Life of Howell Harris, Esq.* (Trevecka, 1791), p. 25.

[70] NLW Trevecka Letter 136, Howel Harris to George Whitefield, 8 January 1739.

[71] Ward, *The Protestant Evangelical Awakening*, pp. 317–19.

[72] For Griffith Jones's preaching, see Jenkins, '"An old and much honoured soldier"', 455–9.

2

'A great pouring out of the Spirit': the forging of a movement, 1739–1740

Prior to 1739 there had been little tangible contact between the English and Welsh revivals. This was to change when George Whitefield wrote to Howel Harris as Whitefield crossed the Atlantic on his way back from Georgia at the end of 1738. The three months following Harris's receipt of this letter were critical months for both the English and Welsh revival movements: they set in motion a process by means of which their fortunes became ever more closely intertwined.

The Harris–Whitefield relationship

The arrival of Whitefield's first letter came at a particularly opportune moment for Howel Harris, the freelance revivalist. Having been exhorting informally for almost three years, Harris had begun to harbour serious reservations about the validity of his activities and had been counselled by both Griffith Jones and his local parish priest to quit preaching if he wished to be considered a serious candidate for ordination in the Church of England.[1] In his letter, Whitefield immediately recognised the validity of Harris's ministry; being 'united to [him] in spirit', he 'rejoiced to hear how the good pleasure of the Lord prospered in your hand' and hoped that he would 'be the spiritual father of thousands, and shine, as the sun in the firmament, in the kingdom of your heavenly Father'.[2] Whitefield then sketched in some details about the 'great pouring out of the Spirit in

London', before rounding off his letter by requesting a reply.[3] In an almost immediate response, Harris expressed his solidarity with Whitefield and then penned a sweeping account of the beginnings and progress of the Welsh revival up to that point. He ended his letter by inviting Whitefield to visit Wales. It is no surprise that following this exchange of correspondence, and with an evangelical network whose sinews already connected London and Bristol to Wales and the American colonies, Whitefield began to refer to the 'whole world' as his parish.[4]

Before arriving in Wales for the first time in early March 1739, Whitefield had taken the decisive step of beginning to preach in the open air.[5] Having met Griffith Jones in Bath on two separate occasions, it is highly likely that Whitefield would have heard much more about Harris's ministry, as well as Jones's perspective on his own experience of field preaching.[6] He was accompanied by his business manager, William Seward, and Whitefield's first visit to Wales consisted of a whistle-stop tour of the societies which Harris had established in south-east Wales since 1736. Seward kept the London Methodists up to date with Whitefield's itinerary and introduced many of them to the Welsh revival for the first time.[7] The personal bond between the two revivalists was confirmed and cemented, and Whitefield was deeply impressed by the interdenominationalism of the Welsh revival: at this stage, Dissenters and Churchmen were cooperating harmoniously and with a measure of success.[8] However, it was the practical discussions between Harris and Whitefield, during which they decided 'on such measures as seemed most conducive to promote the common interest of our Lord', that proved to be of most long-term significance.[9] Neither Whitefield nor Harris recorded the details of these discussions in their journals, but we know from related correspondence that they made plans to translate some of Whitefield's sermons into Welsh and made arrangements for a new edition of the Welsh-language Bible, although the latter never came to anything.[10] Within three weeks Whitefield was back in Wales again; on this occasion he stayed longer and accompanied Harris on a more extensive preaching tour, which saw the two revivalists going 'from place to place as Joshua did when he took Caanan, from conquering to conquer'.[11] Whitefield reflected that Wales was a 'noble soil for Christianity' and its inhabitants 'much readier to receive the Gospel than [the people] in England'.[12]

The Harris–Whitefield axis was firmly drawn following Whitefield's two visits to Wales. For Harris, meeting with Whitefield had been decidedly affirming. While many considered Harris's unordained status to be an impediment, Whitefield's desire to 'catch some of his fire' indicated that he thought Harris possessed the sanction of a higher authority than the Church of England.[13] Although Whitefield did not meet Daniel Rowland during these visits, he was quickly integrated into the leadership and decision-making processes of the Welsh revival. To Harris personally, Whitefield became his 'dearest and Elder Brother', to whose judgement Harris invariably deferred whenever major decisions needed to be taken.[14] At the end of Whitefield's second visit to Wales, Harris accompanied him to London where he spent the following six weeks immersed in the swirling currents of the London revival. By the end of this visit, a new pattern had, therefore, emerged. Whitefield became a regular visitor to Wales, and Harris began to spend increasing amounts of his time in London and Bristol. A Calvinistic Methodist leadership structure for England and Wales was beginning to take shape.

Harris and the London Methodists

Geraint Tudur has written that the six weeks which Harris spent in England during April and May 1739 was a traumatic period in his personal and spiritual development.[15] Although most of his time was spent in London itself, he visited each of the four centres of English Methodism: London, Bristol, Oxford and Gloucester. During his first days in London he attended the Fetter Lane Society, and quickly made the acquaintance of John and Charles Wesley, John Cennick and the Moravians James Gambold and Count Zinzendorf. Meeting these 'ripe saints' for the first time dragged Harris down into the depths of depression, as all of his old insecurities emerged once again.[16] The Fetter Lane Society was bursting at the seams by this point as different groups jostled with one another for the ascendancy. On his first night, Harris was party to a bitter disagreement in the society following John Shaw's assertion that an ordained priesthood was entirely unnecessary. As a layman himself, Harris might have been expected to speak up for Shaw, but his loyalty to the Church and sensitivity over the reputation of the Methodists ensured that he became one of the loudest voices calling for Shaw's immediate expulsion.[17] What the Shaw debacle demonstrates is that from his first night in London, Harris was fully incorporated into the embryonic leadership structures of English Methodism.

However, it was problems associated with the Moravian influences at Fetter Lane that caused the most damaging divisions and became the cause of Harris's greatest difficulty. Many at Fetter Lane had become infected with 'stillness', a teaching which stated that since faith was a gift from God there was little, if anything, anyone could do to achieve it. Practically, this meant that prayer, Bible reading, attendance at the means of grace and the performance of good works were actively discouraged, seekers being told that they had to wait passively until God gave them the gift of faith.[18] Impressed by the spirituality of the Moravians at Fetter Lane, Harris was initially drawn to their stillness teaching, and it was not long before he started to think that since his own conversion experience had been an agonising process it must have been inferior, or possibly even false. His diary entries during his stay in London betray the depth of this spiritual crisis:

> I did not know what to do. I was afraid to write these convictions down lest it was 'working'. I was afraid to pray, though I had desires put in me, lest it was 'doing' . . . I went along (much humbled inwardly) fearing every step . . . dreading the name of 'doing' or anything like it.[19]

The corollary of this was that if his conversion was suspect then maybe his whole ministry in Wales might be invalid also. Only very gradually did Harris's despair lift, largely through the patient counsels of George Whitefield and Harris's close observations of the Wesley brothers' growing unease at the direction in which the Fetter Lane Society was going.[20]

Whitefield also helped Harris to come to settled convictions about the doctrine of justification by faith alone.[21] And for much of his time in London Harris devoted himself to serious theological study, immersing himself in works of a Calvinist flavour.[22] This process, of course, had already begun in Wales; Harris had benefited from the ministry of Thomas Lewis, the curate at Merthyr Cynog.[23] He had also picked up some elements of Reformed theology from Daniel Rowland, who was himself coming to more settled Calvinist convictions during 1737 and 1738.[24] At one point he worriedly confessed that he was spending more time reading Puritan works than the Bible itself.[25] However, the whole experience proved deeply formative, and Harris emerged from his depression 'enlightened . . . more and more . . . since I came here to London'.[26] Whitefield himself had also recently passed through a period which had seen his theological opinions become more refined and finely tuned. At the beginning of his ministry he had been content to define himself via the basic formularies of the Church of England but, as the revival in London became increasingly complex, Whitefield was forced to adopt a more clearly articulated theological position. Through a re-examination of the Thirty-Nine Articles of the Church, immersion in a wide range of Puritan literature and possibly through contact with the Scottish Calvinist evangelicals, Ebenezer and Ralph Erskine, Whitefield came to more settled Reformed theological convictions.[27] In a sense Whitefield and Harris were following a similar theological trajectory and, by the time Whitefield left England for the American colonies in June 1739, both had become thoroughgoing Calvinists.

However, this outline of their theological development needs qualification, particularly in the light of the disagreements over predestination that were to engulf the English Methodist movement in 1740. Whitefield and Harris were not supralapsarian double predestinarians. In other words, they both rejected the most extreme version of Calvinistic predestination which claimed that God's choosing some people for eternal life and others to eternal death had taken place before the Creation of the world and the Fall of Adam. By the early eighteenth century the popularity of Calvinism had declined markedly in England and Wales; those who retained Reformed convictions, particularly among certain Baptist groups, tended towards such hyper-Calvinistic positions as double predestination, positions that were insular and which severely blunted evangelistic initiative.[28] Whitefield and Harris adopted a more moderate Calvinism, akin to that of Isaac Watts.[29] This was being popularised at the time by the Bristol Baptist Academy.[30] Harris confessed to having been delivered from a belief in Reprobation in 1737, and consistently referred only to God's positive election of grace.[31] Free from the fatalism of double predestination, the Calvinism adopted by Harris and Whitefield was wedded to their passionate commitment to the indiscriminate preaching of the gospel. It was this evangelical Calvinism that was to be characteristic of Calvinistic Methodism, at least as Whitefield and Harris envisaged it.[32]

These weeks in London, therefore, tied Harris and Whitefield, and consequently the revivals they superintended, still closer to one another. Yet it would be a mistake to assume that Harris's firm relationship with Whitefield precluded close engagement with other kinds of evangelicals in London. His relationship with the Moravians is indicative. Encountering the Moravians had led Harris into serious difficulties but, unlike both Whitefield and the Wesleys, who gradually distanced themselves from them, Harris never formally disowned them; indeed, he always harboured a secret admiration for them. During the earliest days of his spiritual pilgrimage he had avidly read pietist works including those of Jakob Böhme and August Herman Francke.[33] Later in his career he was to be widely suspected of being a Moravian on account of his patripassian views.[34] He never publicly criticised them; while others wrote disparagingly of the Moravians, Harris 'was made inwardly to rejoice in their success . . . & to pray for their preservation – & found the highest esteem in my soul for them'.[35] A similar pattern emerged in his dealings with the Wesley brothers. While the bond with them was not as strong as that which he enjoyed with Whitefield, their mutual admiration remained undimmed, even in the midst of their acrimonious theological disputes. On meeting John Wesley in Bristol in June 1739, Harris wrote:

> I had not been long there, before my spirit was knit to you, as it was to dear Mr Whitefield, and before you had done, I was so overpowered with joy and love that I could scarce stand still, and with much difficulty got home.[36]

While a formal separation between them did take place in the early 1740s, Harris's personal admiration for the Wesley brothers meant that he attempted to act as a bridge between them and the other factions of the revival for much of the rest of his life.

The strength of the relationships which Harris established during his first visit to London shaped the rest of his career. He had begun to contribute to the decision-making process within the higher echelons of the London revival following his timely intervention in the dispute over John Shaw. He had made strong friendships with many within Whitefield's immediate circle of friends, had formed strong links with leading London Moravians and had begun to get to know the Wesley brothers. While he was closely allied with Whitefield, even at this early stage his sympathetic attitude to the Moravians and the close bond he had formed with John and Charles Wesley were to bear fruit as he became an important agent of peace and reconciliation between the various factions of the English revival, his efforts at bridge building often preventing their divisions from descending into bitterness and recrimination.

The international dimensions of the revival

The Harris who returned to Wales in June 1739 was in some important respects very different from the Harris who had gone to London six weeks earlier. With a new self-confidence, a renewed sense of mission and perhaps a more coherent theological understanding, Harris re-engaged with his societies with increased vigour. But he also returned to Wales with exciting news that 'in many nations the Gospel is spreading its healing wings'.[37] Having unified the Welsh revival at Defynnog during 1737 and joined forces with Whitefield and English Methodism in early 1739, Harris was then able to introduce his fellow Welsh Methodists to the wider international revival community, which Whitefield, in the main, had been patiently piecing together.

Harris had read Jonathan Edwards's account of the revival at Northampton, Massachusetts, *A Faithful Narrative of the Surprising Work of God* (1736), shortly after the publication of its first British edition in 1737. He had discussed the book in some detail with Daniel Rowland during November 1738, and this led Harris to make positive comparisons between what was happening in New England and what was underway in Wales.[38] Whitefield had returned from his first missionary expedition to Georgia at the end of 1738 and, although he did not have much opportunity to travel beyond the colony on this occasion, the visit whetted his appetite for future transatlantic travel. When he returned to the colonies in late 1739 he did so as a revivalist and for fifteenth months preached up and down the eastern seaboard of the colonies to spectacular effect.[39] He commented in his diary that 'there was never such a general awakening, and concern for the things of God known in *America* before'.[40] From this point forward Whitefield began splitting his time between England and the American colonies, a commitment which was strengthened following his establishment of an orphan house near Savannah, the foundation stone of which he laid in March 1740.[41] For the rest of his life, the orphan house became a burden necessitating the constant raising of funds. None were more supportive of the venture than the Welsh Methodists, their sacrificial financial contributions giving them a tangible stake in the progress of the gospel overseas.[42] But Whitefield's commitment to Georgia also had implications for the leadership of the Welsh revival, as Harris was increasingly called upon to take charge of the English Calvinistic revival during Whitefield's frequent and prolonged absences in the colonies.

With both Whitefield and Wesley claiming the world as their parish, Whitefield carried his ministry to Scotland.[43] His first visit, which lasted over three months from July to October 1741, was not a resounding success, and Whitefield had to extricate himself from being monopolised by the leaders of the separatist Associate Presbytery, Ebenezer and Ralph Erskine.[44] When he returned the following spring for the second of his fourteen excursions to Scotland, Whitefield spent five months working in partnership with William McCulloch and James Robe, fanning the flames of the revivals in their parishes at Cambuslang and Kilsyth.[45] He confessed that the revivals 'far out-did all that I ever saw in America'.[46] Harris was tempted to join him on a number of occasions, but never had the opportunity; instead, he maintained a warm and regular correspondence with McCulloch, by means of which news of events in Scotland became common currency among the Welsh Methodists, and Harris became 'much beloved' among the Scottish evangelicals.[47] In a similar way, Harris maintained an interest in revival events in Ireland, largely through his correspondence with John Cennick who had established a number of Moravian settlements in the north of Ireland by the mid-1740s.[48] At a later point William Williams had 'strong thoughts of going to Ireland'.[49] However, the dominance of the Irish Methodist societies by John Wesley's brand of Methodism must have acted as a powerful deterrent. Wesley had proven significantly more successful in Ireland than Whitefield, whose several attempts to establish a foothold there had ended in failure.[50]

The areas that interested Whitefield and Harris were very much focused along the British North Atlantic world axis.[51] Revivals in the various parts of continental Europe did not engage their attention to the same extent. Unlike John Wesley, neither Harris nor Whitefield had any pressing desire to visit either Herrnhut or Halle. Pietist influence, therefore, continued indirectly, or surfaced when Harris flirted with their ideas and tried to bring about some sort of recon-ciliation between the Wesleyans, the Calvinists and the Moravians during the mid-1740s. The Moravians remained a minor irritant throughout the 1740s as a result of the gradual defection of members from Whitefield's Tabernacle Society, and by 1753 Whitefield was forced into print, formally setting out his differences with them for the first time.[52] There was an unusual European dimension for some Methodists in the late 1740s when a number, including some Welsh Methodists, serving in British armies in northern France and the Low Countries during the War of the Austrian Succession (1740–8) wrote letters back to friends in the British Isles telling them about their evangelistic endeavours among fellow soldiers.[53]

The international dimensions of the evangelical revival led Whitefield to attempt to link the various national and local awakenings into a more organic movement. Initially, Whitefield himself, and his inter-revival itinerancy, became the glue that bound the various awakenings together; but once the revival began to expand, both numerically and in terms of its geographical spread, Whitefield was forced to come up with more sturdy means of binding them. Despite surface cultural differences, converts from each of the revival communities were united by a shared experience of the new birth, and they used similar language when they spoke about it. This common language was fostered by the early publication of some of Whitefield's sermons and journals, especially those which dealt with the subject of conversion.[54] These became a model whereby others could give expression to their experi-ences and also evaluate their authenticity.

The dissemination of Whitefieldian literature necessitated an efficient distribution network. Whitefield came to rely on a few hand-picked secretaries who facilitated the creation of what Susan Durden has called a vibrant early evangelical 'print culture'.[55] At first he worked in partnership with the wealthy former stockbroker, William Seward, but after Seward's death at the hands of a mob in 1740 he made use of a number of printers and booksellers who had links with his Tabernacle Society, including John Lewis, John Syms and Thomas Boddington. However, the circulation of printed literature was only a small part of their activity. In the early phase of the revival, Seward acted as Whitefield's 'chief reporter and press agent', advertising his itineraries in the local presses, circulating up-beat reports of White-field's preaching as advance publicity and managing the international letter-writing network.[56]

The communications network depended heavily on correspondence between the pioneer revivalists themselves, between the revivalists and their followers and sometimes among rank-and-file members of the movement as well. Letter writing was, of course, the means by which the pioneer revivalists had first made contact with one another; but, once contact had been made, the letter-writing network, which took shape as letters rapidly changed hands throughout the evangelical community, was put to more sophisticated uses. Letters became the primary means for spreading news, especially news about the latest progress of the revival. As the revival matured, a wider range of subject matter appeared in the letters. Accounts of individual conversions were commonplace.[57] However, the letters also came to be used for pastoral purposes as converts raised problems, both personal and spiritual, which were then answered in further letters. At times of tension within the wider evangelical movement the letter network became a means by which issues were aired and some form of con-sensus sought. The letter-writing network had a number of focal points. Whitefield's Tabernacle in London was the main distribution centre, but Howel Harris's Trefeca and Thomas Prince's base in Boston, Massachusetts, also became places where letters were collected and then distributed more widely. Also key were the regular Letter Days. Following the practice initiated by the Moravians, which had also been adopted by the Wesleyans, the latest letters were read out to expectant monthly gatherings at Whitefield's Tabernacle, and it quickly became common practice for individuals to send letters in to the Tabernacle in advance.[58]

Whilst the coverage of the letter-writing network was much wider, access to it could still often be limited. In response to this, John Lewis established a weekly magazine, *The Christian's Amusement*, the first issue of which appeared in September 1740.[59] Produced inexpensively, each issue was four pages long and contained the choicest letters to have been sent in to the Tabernacle in any given week. It was not an instant success, and for the first six months Lewis laboured in vain to make it financially viable. The change in its fortunes did not occur until Whitefield suggested taking over editorial control in March 1741, following his acrimonious split with John Wesley. Whitefield suggested that it be renamed *The Weekly History*, and he guaranteed a regular supply of quality material for it.[60] Under his direction the magazine was transformed, and it quickly became the official mouthpiece of the newly separate Calvinistic wing of the Methodist movement. There was no distinct Welsh edition of the magazine; Howel Harris did consider translating some of its contents into Welsh but eventually decided against it, preferring to circulate copies of the London-based edition.[61] In practical terms this meant that the magazine was only really likely to appeal to those in Wales who could read in the English language. To circumvent this problem, Harris arranged for public readings where bilingual exhorters would read ad hoc précised translations from the latest letters. Although it is uncertain to what extent this was put into practice, the very intention to do so suggests on the part of the movement's leaders a clear desire for the magazine to become an important expression of the joint identity of English and Welsh Calvinistic Methodism, especially after 1741. It was supplemented by two other magazines, the short-lived Scottish *Glasgow Weekly History*, and the American *The Christian History* first published by Thomas Prince in Boston during March 1743.[62] Material was shared between them, ensuring that readers in each constituency were looking at broadly similar information and receiving a steady supply of the most up-to-date accounts of the fortunes of the revival.

The splintering of the Methodist consensus and the emergence of Calvinistic Methodism

The communications network gave a sense of identity to widely scattered evangelical converts throughout the British Atlantic world. Individuals who would not normally have come into contact with one another were brought into the community, becoming beneficiaries of the revolution that was taking place in methods of communication and in the demand for consumer goods.[63] From Whitefield's and Harris's perspective the communications network really came into its own following the splintering of the evangelical revival into three distinct factions: Moravian, Wesleyan and Calvinist, in 1740 and 1741. Its contents and participants were rigorously managed as it came to be used to support and reinforce a distinct identity for the Calvinistic Methodists.

The initial energy unleashed by the revival had given a veneer of unity to the mixed bag of German Pietists, Moravians, Huguenots, Anglicans and Dissenters, Arminians and Calvinists who gravitated to it. The corollary of this inclusiveness were the tensions that arose as different groups vied for influence, indeed, ascendancy. These tensions were exacerbated by the emergence of the leadership of John Wesley. Re-energised by his conversion experience at Aldersgate Street in May 1738, Wesley, with his combination of evangelical enthusiasm and Anglican propriety, was determined to bring order to the revival and establish himself as its outright leader. The months between his emergence as the leader of the Bristol Methodists and his final split with Whitefield in 1741 witnessed Wesley's carving out his own revival movement, sidelining those who might be regarded as more appealing alternative leaders and separating from those with whom he had deep-seated theological disagreements.

The splintering of the Fetter Lane Society was probably inevitable. The dispute over John Shaw's views in April 1739 was indicative of this, but it was the influence of Philip Henry Molther and August Gottlieb Spangenberg, with their theology of 'stillness', that first broke the unity of the English revival. Charles Wesley was the first to speak out publicly against stillness, for which he was expelled from Fetter Lane during Easter 1740.[64] John Wesley then led the fight against stillness, although the dispute quickly revealed the extent of Wesley's ambitions to head the revival on his own terms. A faction which looked to Wesley for leadership had already begun to form within the society, and he had started preaching to a newly established group in London in December 1739. At some point early in 1740 he had purchased the old Foundery in Moorfields in anticipation of the almost inevitable separation.[65]

The actual separation did not finally take place until July 1740, and only after protracted discussion of the issues at stake.[66] There were also efforts at pacification by Howel Harris, who had been called to London in the aftermath of the dismissal of Charles Wesley from Fetter Lane.[67] Harris convened a meeting between the Wesley brothers and Molther to air their differences; they each appear to have attended with an open mind, and Molther initially distanced himself from some of the excesses at Fetter Lane. However, when Harris pressed him on who were fit to attend communion, he found that Molther was unwilling to retract his previous quietist position.[68] Consequently, the meeting ended in stalemate and, following an acrimonious gathering in Fetter Lane at which John Wesley provocatively read a paper outlining his disagreements, he withdrew from the society taking with him eighteen or nineteen other members.[69] The society Wesley had quietly established at the Foundery was then set in order and became the base of his operations. However, neither Harris nor Whitefield followed Wesley by separating formally from Fetter Lane at this point. While they undoubtedly shared Wesley's strong disagreement with stillness teaching, Whitefield's absence in America for much of 1740 meant that he was away at precisely the time when his own converts in London and Bristol were vulnerable and crying out for strong leadership.

At the same time as he was distancing himself from Fetter Lane and setting up his own headquarters, Wesley was also waging war on his other *bête noire*, predestination and Calvinism. Following his return to England in December 1738, Whitefield had spent a year preaching extensively along the well-trodden London–Bristol axis. The crowds that gathered to listen to him at Moorfields and Kennington in London continued to grow, but it was in Bristol that some of the greatest advances had been made. Whitefield had arrived in the city in February 1739 to find that his reputation had preceded him. The religious societies in the city had already received a new lease of life, and Whitefield initially concentrated his activities around them; but his desire to preach the gospel more widely led Whitefield into the open air at Kingswood, a notoriously rough mining area outside the city well known for its thousands of poor and dispossessed colliers. The image of the Kingswood colliers listening to Whitefield's sermons with tears running down their cheeks creating white gutters in their coal-stained faces has passed into Methodist folklore.[70] By early April, Whitefield had solicited enough funds to set the foundation stone for the school for Kingswood miners.[71] But then, after laying the foundation of Bristol Methodism, he left the city, not coming back again until he returned from his extended trip to America in 1741.

It was only after much persuasion, and not wishing to be outdone by his younger colleague, that Wesley was persuaded to preach out of doors and take on the leadership of the Bristol work.[72] Within a month he had followed his practice in London and bought a piece of land in the Horsefair in Bristol, where he built a room large enough to contain at least two societies, a move which gave him an independent foothold in the city. Wesley had been warned by Whitefield not to preach against election and predestination at Bristol.[73] However, Wesley seems to have been surprised at the tenacity with which the Bristol Methodists held to Calvinist opinions, the result both of Whitefield's own preaching and that of John Cennick, who had been appointed schoolmaster at Kingswood.[74]

The vacuum left by Whitefield's departure for America in August 1739 gave Wesley the freedom to deal with the Calvinist issue; he preached regularly against predestination and attempted to expel members of the Bristol societies who persisted in holding Calvinist opinions. In Wales, Howel Harris began receiving letters from disgruntled evangelicals.[75] However, he refused to get involved until the simmering tensions finally erupted in April 1740 when Wesley dismissed the Calvinist, John Acourt, from his Foundery society.[76] Harris solemnly warned Wesley that if he persisted with the expulsion of Calvinists from his societies 'you must exclude Bro Whit__d, Bro Seward and myself and if you go as to take such methods as to let those who are without rejoice in our divisions will you not grieve the Spirit of God in all the Brethren'.[77] Harris's intervention seemed to smooth over the tensions in the short term, until William Seward arrived in Wales with the news that he had just broken all links with Charles Wesley.[78]

Charles Wesley appears to have been even more belligerent in his anti-Calvinist stance than his elder brother.[79] It was often his precipitate actions, rather than those of his brother, that led to the most serious breakdown in relations. By the end of 1740 Harris confessed that he was 'stagger'd about th[e]m w[ha]t to do'.[80] His solution was to invite Charles Wesley to Wales for discussions; although Wesley was initially prickly, he appeared to assure Harris that he did, after all, believe in predestination.[81] The main point of contention was the Calvinist insistence on a limited, rather than general, doctrine of the atonement.[82] Harris took this to be a major concession on Charles Wesley's part and in the pages of *The Christian's Amusement* warned his fellow Calvinists to be careful with the words they used since 'there are some sincere of every particular party'.[83] There is no doubt that Harris was misled into thinking that the differences between the Calvinists and the Wesleyans were not so great after all. Quite why Charles Wesley acted in this way is difficult to ascertain. It may have been out of personal regard for Harris, but seems more likely to have been a stalling mechanism, aimed at buying the Wesleys enough time to act more decisively against the Calvinists. What is clear is that with Whitefield's absence in America, John Wesley was free at Bristol to act with a new determination against the 'hellish infection' of predestination.[84] This was underscored by Charles Wesley's hymn on 'Universal Redemption', which was published together with his brother's sermon on 'Free Grace'.[85] When he read this publication, while still in America, Whitefield wrote to the Wesleys: 'Why did you throw out the bone of contention? Why did you print that sermon against predestination? Why did you, in particular, my dear brother Charles, affix your hymn . . .?'[86] Not helped by reports that John Cennick's preaching was more popular than his own, John Wesley engineered a showdown, where insults were traded in a heated confrontation.[87] The upshot was that Cennick, together with fifty-two of the Bristol Calvinists, were forced to withdraw from the society, leaving the remaining ninety members in the care of John Wesley.[88]

Having gained the upper hand at Bristol, there was now only one further obstacle in the way of Wesley's total dominance of English Methodism: George Whitefield. Whitefield had been absent in America as relations between his followers and those of Wesley were rapidly deteriorating in England. There is no doubt that John Wesley took full advantage of Whitefield's extended absence to grasp control of the English revival, using tactics that were unprincipled and possibly even dishonourable.[89] Whitefield was restricted to relying on Howel Harris's shuttle diplomacy to smooth over the worst of the difficulties.[90] He also wrote impassioned letters from America pleading with Wesley to refrain from 'driv[ing] John Calvin out of Bristol'.[91] But Whitefield did not return to England until after Wesley had successfully purged the Bristol Society of its Calvinist elements. He returned shocked to discover just how wide a chasm had opened up between the two sides. Wesley was reluctant to meet Whitefield face to face, and when they did meet Whitefield told Wesley not only that he thought they now preached different gospels, but that he was no longer prepared to stand by and let him take over the entire revival.[92] Reluctantly, and at last giving his followers the kind of leadership that they had lacked over the course of the previous eighteen months, Whitefield went into print against Wesley with *A Letter to the Rev Mr John Wesley: In Answer to his Sermon Entituled Free Grace* (1741). Whitefield's letter was a reasonable and well-argued rebuttal of the main points that Wesley had raised. In his original sermon, Wesley had caricatured all Calvinists as fatalistic double predestinarians who did not believe in the free offer of the gospel, and it was this accusation that Whitefield dealt with in most detail. While he admitted that he certainly did believe in the doctrine of reprobation, Whitefield clarified by explaining that what he meant by it was very different from what Wesley had imagined. Whitefield reiterated the moderate Calvinist position that only those 'left of God to continue in sin', those who would receive their just deserts, would be reprobated, not because of any decree of God, but as a consequence of their unbelief.[93] Whitefield stressed throughout that the gospel had to be preached indiscriminately, since 'none living, especially none who are desirous of salvation, can know that they are not of the number of God's elect'.[94] Whitefield's response was unlikely to change any minds by this stage: positions had become too entrenched; but it did at least bring some clarity to discussions and an end to the worst of the rancorous public disputation. Howel Harris, whilst fully supportive of Whitefield's position, remained in conversation with Charles Wesley; but when Harris learned that Wesley had been warning his followers against going to listen to Harris preach he was reluctantly led to conclude that 'their scheme is all of the Devil & Man'.[95]

Tensions between the two movements did not abate in the months following the publication of Whitefield's reply to Wesley; indeed, the unity of the revival had effectively been shattered. Where there had once been a unified renewal movement, there were now three separate groups: the Moravians, the Wesleyans and the Calvinists. They were each equally committed to evangelical renewal, but each now competed for the same space in a religious marketplace that was becoming decidedly overcrowded.

Notes

[1] NLW Trevecka Letter 78, Howel Harris to Griffith Jones, 27 June 1736; Trevecka Letter 80, Howel Harris to Griffith Jones, 31 July 1736; Trevecka Letter 54, Howel Harris to Pryce Davies, 16 August 1735; Trevecka Letter 65, Pryce Davies to Howel Harris, 27 February 1736.

[2] NLW Trevecka Letter 133, George Whitefield to Howel Harris, 20 December 1738.

[3] Ibid.

[4] George Whitefield to Daniel Abbot, 3 March 1739, in Graham C. G. Thomas (ed.), 'George Whitefield and friends: the correspondence of some early Methodists', *National Library of Wales Journal*, 27, 1 (summer 1991), 91.

[5] George Whitefield, *A Continuation of the Reverend Mr Whitefield's Journal from his arrival at London to his departure from thence on his way to Georgia* (London: James Hutton, 1739), p. 36.

[6] Ibid., pp. 37, 44.

[7] William Seward to Samuel Mason, 7 July 1739, in Thomas (ed.), 'George Whitefield and friends', *National Library of Wales Journal*, 27, 1 (summer 1991), 312–13.

[8] NLW Trevecka Letter 136, Howel Harris to George Whitefield, 8 January 1739.

[9] Ibid.

[10] George Whitefield to Daniel Abbot, 10 March 1739, in Thomas (ed.), 'George Whitefield and friends', *National Library of Wales Journal*, 27, 2 (winter 1991), 175–6.

[11] William Seward to Joseph Stennett, 5 April 1739, in ibid., 196.

[12] George Whitefield to Samuel Mason, 7 April 1739, in Thomas (ed.), 'George Whitefield and friends', *National Library of Wales Journal*, 27, 2 (winter 1991), 197.

[13] Whitefield, *A Continuation of the Revd Mr Whitefield's Journal*, p. 49.

[14] NLW Trevecka Letter 788, Howel Harris to George Whitefield, 21 August 1743.

[15] Geraint Tudur, *Howell Harris: From Conversion to Separation, 1735–1750* (Cardiff: University of Wales Press, 2000), pp. 51, 55.

[16] John Thickens, *Howel Harris yn Llundain* (Caernarfon: Argraffdy'r Methodistaid Calfinaidd, 1938), p. 179.

[17] Colin J. Podmore, *The Moravian Church in England, 1728–1760* (Oxford: Oxford University Press, 1998), pp. 52–3.

[18] Kenneth J. Collins, *John Wesley: A Theological Journey* (Nashville, TN: Abingdon Press, 2003), p. 110.

[19] NLW Howel Harris's Diary, 30 April 1739.

[20] Henry D. Rack, *Reasonable Enthusiast: John Wesley and the Rise of Methodism* (London: Epworth Press, 1989), p. 203.

[21] Tudur, *Howell Harris*, p. 55.

[22] Eifion Evans, 'Howel Harris and the printed page', *JHSPCW*, 23 (1999), 40–1.

[23] Richard Bennett, *The Early Life of Howell Harris* (London: The Banner of Truth Trust, 1962), p. 134.

[24] Eifion Evans, *Daniel Rowland and the Great Evangelical Awakening in Wales* (Edinburgh: The Banner of Truth Trust, 1985), pp. 60–1.

[25] Tom Beynon, *Howell Harris's Visits to Pembrokeshire (1739–1752)* (Aberystwyth: The Cambrian News Press, 1966), p. 3.

[26] NLW Howel Harris's Diary, 16 May 1739.

[27] Whitefield's theological development is discussed in some depth in Arnold A. Dallimore, *George Whitefield: The Life and Times of the Great Evangelist of the 18th Century Revival* (2 vols, London: The Banner of Truth Trust, 1970), I, pp. 403–10; David Ceri Jones, '"We are of Calvinistical principles": how Calvinist was early Calvinistic Methodism?', *The Welsh Journal of Religious History*, 4 (2009), 45–8.

[28] Peter Toon, *The Emergence of Hyper-Calvinism in English Nonconformity, 1689–1765* (London: Olive Tree, 1967).

[29] Herbert Boyd McGonigle, *Sufficient Saving Grace: John Wesley's Evangelical Arminianism* (Carlisle: Paternoster, 2001), pp. 121–3.

[30] Roger Hayden, *Continuity and Change: Evangelical Calvinism among Eighteenth-Century Baptist Ministers Trained at Bristol Academy, 1690–1791* (Milton under Wychwood: Baptist Historical Society, 2006).

[31] Bennett, *The Early Life of Howell Harris*, p. 135.

[32] Jones, 'We are of Calvinistical principles', 37–54.

[33] Geoffrey F. Nuttall, *Howel Harris, 1714–1773: The Last Enthusiast* (Cardiff: University of Wales Press, 1965), pp. 63–4.

[34] See p. 94 n.79 of the present work.

[35] NLW Howel Harris's Diary, 27 May 1739.

[36] Quoted in A. H. Williams, 'The leaders of Welsh and English Methodism, 1738–1791', *Bathafarn: Historical Society of the Methodist Church in Wales*, 16 (1961), 37.

[37] 'Extract of a letter from a minister in the country to his friend in London, 3 February 1742', in John Lewis (ed.), *The Weekly History*, 46, 20 February 1742.

[38] NLW Howel Harris's Diary, 27 November 1735; Evans, *Daniel Rowland*, p. 69; David Ceri Jones, '"Sure the time here now is like New England": what happened when the Welsh Calvinistic Methodists read Jonathan Edwards', in Kelly Van Andel, Kenneth Minkema and Adriaan Neele (eds), *Jonathan Edwards and Scotland* (Edinburgh: Dunedin Press, 2011), pp. 50–2.

[39] See Thomas S. Kidd, *The Great Awakening: The Roots of Evangelical Christianity in Colonial America* (New Haven, CT: Yale University Press, 2007), chapter 4.

[40] George Whitefield to G__ L___, 22 May 1740, in John Gillies (ed.), *The Works of the Reverend George Whitefield* (6 vols, London: Edward and Charles Dilly, 1771–2), I, p. 179.

[41] Neil J. O'Connell, 'George Whitefield and Bethesda Orphan-House', *The Georgia Historical Quarterly*, 54 (1970), 50–2.

[42] David Ceri Jones, *'A Glorious Work in the World': Welsh Methodism and the International Evangelical Revival, 1735–1750* (Cardiff: University of Wales Press, 2004), pp. 301–2.

[43] John Wesley to [John Clayton], [28 March 1739], in Frank Baker (ed.), *The Works of John Wesley*, vol. 25, *Letters I, 1721–1739* (Oxford: Oxford University Press, 1980), pp. 614–17.

[44] Dallimore, *George Whitefield*, I, pp. 83–92; Andrew L. Drummond and James Bulloch, *The Scottish Church, 1688–1843: The Age of the Moderates* (Edinburgh: St Andrew Press, 1973), pp. 51–3.

[45] Stewart J. Brown, 'Religion in Scotland', in H. T. Dickinson (ed.), *A Companion to Eighteenth-Century Britain* (Oxford: Blackwell Publishing, 2002), pp. 261–7; Arthur Fawcett, *The Cambuslang Revival: The Scottish Evangelical Revival of the Eighteenth Century* (Edinburgh: The Banner of Truth Trust, 1971).

[46] George Whitefield to Elizabeth Whitefield, 7 July 1742, in Gillies (ed.), *The Works of the Reverend George Whitefield*, I, p. 405.

[47] Jones, *'A Glorious Work in the World'*, pp. 140–2; 'The copy of a letter from the Rev. Mr Whitefield in Scotland to Mr Howel Harris in Hoxton, near London, 16 September 1741, in Lewis (ed.), *The Weekly History*, 81, 23 October 1742.

[48] David Hempton and Myrtle Hill, *Evangelical Protestantism in Ulster Society, 1740–1890* (London: Routledge, 1992), pp. 7–8.

[49] NLW Trevecka Letter 1471, William Williams to Howel Harris, 5 June 1746.

50 Dallimore, *George Whitefield*, I, p. 211; Dallimore, *George Whitefield*, II, pp. 339–42, 396–9.
51 Boyd Stanley Schlenther, 'Religious Faith and Commercial Empire', in P. J. Marshall (ed.), *The Oxford History of the British Empire*, vol. 3, *The Eighteenth Century* (Oxford: Oxford University Press, 1998), pp. 128–50.
52 George Whitefield, *An Expostulatory Letter, addressed to Nicholas Lewis, Count Zinzendorf, and Lord Advocate of the Unitas Fratrum* (London: G. Keith and J. Oswald, 1753).
53 Jones, 'A Glorious Work in the World', pp. 325–6.
54 Whitefield's sermon on *The Nature and Necessity of our New Birth in Christ Jesus, in Order to Salvation* was published as early as 1737, and was translated into Welsh in 1739. See George Whitefield, *Angenrheidrwydd a Natur o'n Genedigaeth Newydd yng Nghrist Iesu* (Bristol: Felix Farley, 1739). George Whitefield's, *A Journal of a voyage from London to Savannah in Georgia. In two parts. Part 1. From London to Gibraltar. Part II. From Gibraltar to Savannah* (London: James Hutton, 1738), went through five editions in little more than a year of its first publication. It was followed by, idem., *A Continuation of the Reverend Mr. Whitefield's Journal, from his arrival at Savannah, to his return to London* (London: James Hutton, 1739).
55 Diane Susan Durden, 'Transatlantic communications and literature in the religious revivals, 1735–1745' (unpublished Ph.D. thesis; University of Hull, 1978), 51.
56 Frank Lambert, *'Pedlar in Divinity': George Whitefield and the Transatlantic Revivals, 1737–1770* (Princeton, NJ: Princeton University Press, 1994), p. 57.
57 David Ceri Jones, 'Narratives of Conversion in English Calvinistic Methodism', in Kate Cooper and Jeremy Gregory (eds), *Revival and Renewal in Christian History*, Studies in Church History, 44 (Woodbridge: Boydell, 2008), pp. 128–41.
58 Susan O'Brien, 'A transatlantic community of saints: the Great Awakening and the First Evangelical Network, 1735–1755', *American Historical Review*, 91 (1986), 826–7.
59 David Ceri Jones, 'John Lewis and the promotion of the international evangelical revival, 1735–1756', in Dyfed Wyn Roberts (ed.), *Revival, Renewal and the Holy Spirit* (Milton Keynes: Paternoster, 2008), p. 17.
60 Susan Durden, 'A study of the first evangelical magazines, 1740–1748', *Journal of Ecclesiastical History*, 27, 3 (1976), 260–1.

[61] NLW Trevecka Letter 319, Howel Harris to John Lewis, 19 March 1741.

[62] Durden, 'A study of the first evangelical magazines', 266–70; J. E. Van Wetering, 'The Christian history of the Great Awakening', *Journal of Presbyterian History*, 44 (1966), 122–9.

[63] See Neil McKendrick, 'The consumer revolution in eighteenth-century England', in Neil McKendrick, John Brewer and J. H. Plumb (eds), *The Birth of a Consumer Society: The Commercialization of Eighteenth-Century England* (Bloomington ID: Indiana University Press, 1982), pp. 9–33. This theme has been developed in reference to early evangelicalism in Lambert, *'Pedlar in Divinity'*, chapters 1 and 2.

[64] Podmore, *The Moravian Church in England*, pp. 67–8.

[65] Rack, *Reasonable Enthusiast*, p. 204.

[66] A full discussion of John Wesley's differences with the Fetter Lane Moravians can be found in Richard P. Heitzenrater, *Mirror and Memory: Reflections on Early Methodism* (Nashville, TN: Abingdon Press, 1989), chapter 6.

[67] NLW Trevecka Letter 232, anon. to Howel Harris, 27 March 1740.

[68] NLW Howel Harris's Diary, 6 June 1740.

[69] W. Reginald Ward and Richard P. Heitzenrater (eds), *The Works of John Wesley*, vol. 19, *Journal and Diaries II (1738–43)* (Nashville, TN: Abingdon Press, 1990), p. 162.

[70] John Gillies, *Memoirs of the Life of the Reverend George Whitefield* (London: Edward and Charles Dilly, 1772), pp. 37–8.

[71] Whitefield, *A Continuation of the Reverend Mr Whitefield's journal, from his arrival at London, to his departure from thence to Georgia*, pp. 66–7.

[72] Ward and Heitzenrater (eds), *The Works of John Wesley*, vol. 19, pp. 46–7.

[73] John Wesley to James Hutton and the Fetter Lane Society, 30 April 1739, in Baker (ed.), *The Works of John Wesley*, vol. 25, p. 639.

[74] J. H. Cooper (ed.), *Extracts from the Journals of John Cennick: Moravian Evangelist* (Glengormley: The Moravian History Magazine, 1996), pp. 6–7.

[75] NLW Trevecka Letter 196, Joseph Stennett to Howel Harris, 8 November 1739; Trevecka Letter 232, anon. to Howel Harris, 27 March 1740.

[76] A. Brown-Lawson, *John Wesley and the Anglican Evangelicals of the Eighteenth Century* (Edinburgh: The Pentland Press, 1994), pp. 162–3.

[77] NLW Trevecka Letter 260, Howel Harris to John Wesley, 6 July 1740.

[78] NLW Trevecka Letter 286, John Stock to Howel Harris, 12 November 1740.

[79] Gareth Lloyd, *Charles Wesley and the Struggle for Methodist Identity* (Oxford: Oxford University Press, 2007), p. 57.

[80] NLW Trevecka Letter 282, Howel Harris to John Cennick, 27 October 1740.

[81] Tom Beynon (ed.), 'Extracts from the diaries of Howell Harris', *Bathafarn: The Journal of the Historical Society of the Methodist Church in Wales*, 4 (1949), 57.

[82] Peter J. Thuesen, *Predestination: The American Career of a Contentious Doctrine* (New York: Oxford University Press, 2009), p. 92.

[83] John Lewis (ed.), *The Christian's Amusement: containing letters concerning the progress of the Gospel both at home and abroad*, 12.

[84] George Whitefield to John and Charles Wesley, 1 February 1741, in Luke Tyerman, *The Life of the Rev. George Whitefield* (2 vols, London: Hodder and Stoughton, 1876), I, p. 465.

[85] John Wesley, *Free Grace: A Sermon Preach'd at Bristol* (Bristol: S. and F. Farley, 1739).

[86] Frank Baker (ed.), *The Works of John Wesley*, vol. 26, *Letters II, 1740–1755*, p. 48.

[87] Ward and Heitzenrater (eds), *The Works of John Wesley*, vol. 19, p. 175.

[88] Ibid., Sunday 8 March 1741, p. 186; Dallimore, *George Whitefield*, II, pp. 38–40.

[89] Lloyd, *Charles Wesley and the struggle for Methodist Identity*, pp. 57–8.

[90] Harris's role is discussed in more detail in David Ceri Jones, '"The Lord did give me a particular honour to make [me] a peacemaker": Howel Harris, John Wesley and Methodist infighting, 1739–1750', *Bulletin of the John Rylands University Library of Manchester*, 82, 2 and 3 (summer and autumn 2003), 73–88.

[91] George Whitefield to John Wesley, 25 August 1740, in Gillies (ed.), *The Works of George Whitefield*, I, p. 205.

[92] Ward and Heitzenrater (eds), *The Works of John Wesley*, vol. 19, pp. 188–9.

[93] George Whitefield, *A letter to the Reverend Mr John Wesley: in answer to his sermon, entituled, Free-Grace* (London: W. Strahan, 1741), p. 10.

[94] Ibid., p. 15.

[95] NLW Howel Harris's Diary, 26 June 1740.

3

An 'outward settled agreement': shaping a structure and a spirituality, 1741–1743

George Whitefield had begun the task of reinvigorating Calvinistic Methodism following his return to England in March 1741, but the split with the Wesley brothers shortly afterwards made that a still more pressing necessity. Whitefield's converts had been picked off as a result of the incursions of the Wesleys during his absence, and the remaining rump were thoroughly demoralised because of the lack of leadership they had experienced. It is probably fair to say that Whitefield, unlike John Wesley or Howel Harris, did not have much flair for the day-to-day work of organisation and administration, and that he had never envisaged heading his own religious movement. Nonetheless, he was now forced into precisely this role. Whitefield, therefore, committed himself to staying in Britain for almost two years and, with the necessary assistance of Howel Harris, revived the societies that he had already established and developed an organisational structure that tied together Calvinistic Methodism in England and Wales.

Calvinistic Methodism in 1741

Following the split with the Wesleys, and once sides had finally been taken, Calvinistic Methodism had emerged with four main centres of strength: London, Bristol, Gloucestershire and Wales. The primary flashpoint of the controversy between the Wesleyans and the Calvinists had been in Bristol. John Cennick had been forced out of the Bristol society, but those he had taken with him formed the core of a new and exclusively Calvinist society in the city. Cennick, a layman, had officially been made one of Whitefield's assistants following Whitefield's return from America, and the new Bristol society was placed under his leadership. It experienced significant growth and was soon attracting a regular attendance of about 120 people.[1] They had acquired new premises, Smith's Hall, the refectory of a former monastery, and another school was opened at Kingswood.[2] Cennick had also tentatively begun preaching in some villages in his native Wiltshire towards the end of 1740.[3] This was slow and painstaking work, as he divided his energies between Bristol and Wiltshire, but by 1742 Cennick had attracted enough of a following to enable him to establish some societies, and in October he opened a Calvinistic Methodist meeting house at Tytherton, just east of the market town of Chippenham.[4]

Gloucester was an important stopping-off point between London and Wales, and Gloucestershire quickly became an important area of Calvinistic Methodist activity. Whitefield's familial ties ensured that he visited the city regularly and preached in a number of congregations, both within the Church and also among some sympathetic Dissenters.[5] However, it was in the rural areas surrounding the city that the Calvinistic Methodists were strongest. Thomas Adams had been converted while listening to Whitefield preach on Minchinhampton Common in April 1739.[6] He had erected 'a fine new house' in the town, at which a sizeable society regularly met.[7] Adams became one of Whitefield's most trusted lieutenants and was to stand in for him regularly at the Tabernacle Society in London during the later 1740s; but his labours in Gloucestershire bore significant fruit, eventually leading to the building of the Rodborough Tabernacle, near Stroud.[8] By early 1742 the Calvinistic Methodists, therefore, had a patchwork of societies and preaching places in the south-west of England, conveniently located between London and Wales.

These societies all looked to London, and more specifically to George Whitefield, for leadership and direction. At this stage the network of societies that depended on him did not possess an administrative structure, and so relied on Whitefield's physical presence and interest to maintain their momentum. But the Whitefield who returned from America in March 1741 was very different from the man who had left England eighteen months earlier. He had departed as the un-questioned leader of a successful and growing religious renewal move-ment. He returned to be confronted with problems on every side; the crowds that came to listen to him preach had dwindled, his old converts were scattered and his reputation was in tatters. This had been badly damaged in a raft of hostile publications which followed the printing of his letter *To a Friend in London Concerning Archbishop Tillotson* (1740), in which he accused this seventeenth-century archbishop of Canterbury, whose moralistic version of Christianity was remarkably popular in mid-eighteenth-century England, of knowing no more about 'Christianity than Mahomet'.[9] At the same time, John Wesley was publicly tearing up copies of some of Whitefield's published sermons.[10] Whitefield's publisher, James Hutton, was reluctant to print anything more bearing Whitefield's name, and many of his 'spiritual children' were sending him 'threatening letters, that God will speed-ily destroy me'.[11] The prospects for recovery were far from auspicious.

Whitefield had also returned to England encumbered by weighty financial problems. William Seward's untimely death at the hands of a mob in south Wales had left him saddled with a substantial debt, for which he faced the real possibility of imprisonment if it could not be settled.[12] But it was his responsibility for the orphan house in Georgia which he had opened a year earlier that now weighed most heavily on Whitefield's mind. He had been preaching charity sermons for Georgia since 1737, but had returned from America with sub-stantial debts accrued since its opening in March 1740.[13] The task of raising a steady supply of funds for the project fell squarely on White-field's shoulders, and he assumed that he would be able with ease to commend the scheme to the thousands of listeners to whom he was accustomed to preach on a regular basis in London and Bristol. The future of the orphan house, therefore, depended on Whitefield's ability to reinvigorate the revival he had abandoned eighteen months earlier, to sell his vision for it as widely as possible.

Despite these unpromising circumstances, Whitefield plunged into a gruelling programme of open-air preaching in London in order to regain the initiative from John Wesley. Within a week he reported to John Cennick in Bristol the good news that 'some that have been led astray, begin to recover'.[14] The one positive development that occurred when Whitefield had been absent in America was that the small band of supporters who remained loyal to him had built a temporary structure at Moorfields, in reality little more than a shed, hastily erected to enable his hearers to shelter from the worst of the weather during his open-air sermons. Whitefield was initially worried that the building would be regarded as a Dissenting meeting house in all but name, and that its close proximity to Wesley's Foundery would exacerbate the frictions between them; but the low morale of what remained of his revival persuaded him to keep the structure and to use it regularly. He suggested that it be called the Tabernacle, to reinforce its temporary nature, but it was not long before it became the base of all his operations. Within a month of his return to London the numbers attending the Tabernacle had begun to grow, to such an extent that Whitefield was forced to add to the structure by building a society room adjacent to it.[15] The new headquarters began to look more permanent, an impression reinforced by the takeover of *The Christian's Amusement* magazine. As *The Weekly History*, under Whitefield's active direction, this became the public mouthpiece of the Calvinistic revival. Its pages were filled with letters reporting on Whitefield's activities and the success of Calvinistically-minded evangelicals everywhere. The relaunched publication had an important symbolic use: it galvanised the scattered Calvinists, drew them together and gave them a sense of permanency and identity.[16]

The Tabernacle Society, as it became known, was part of a network of other Calvinist societies in London, the most influential being that led by Joseph Humphreys at Deptford. While a student at the Dissenters' Academy at Deptford, Humphreys had established a society for Whitefield's followers; but he had initially become more closely associated with John Wesley, being appointed one of his earliest assistants and deputising regularly for him at the Foundery.[17] However, when the Calvinist controversy broke out Humphreys sided with Whitefield, bringing his people under the oversight of the Tabernacle Society. In this way the structure of Calvinistic Methodism began to take shape. It took five weeks of continual preaching and pastoral work before Whitefield felt confident to leave London and catch up with what had been taking place in the other Methodist communities who had allied themselves with him and his Calvinism. At Bristol he found that 'sad tares have been sown'.[18] Even within Cennick's new Calvinist society perfectionist teachings had gained a foothold.[19]

Whitefield spent over three weeks in Bristol, at the end of which he wrote, with evident relief, that 'error is, in a great measure, put a stop to'.[20] By this stage he felt that his ministry had begun to bear fruit once more; he reported to Howel Harris that his congregations were now 'very large and solemn' and that he 'had never had greater freedom in preaching'.[21] It was at this stage that invitations started to come in, both from other parts of England and from a new network of evangelicals in Scotland; in the following weeks Whitefield ventured beyond London and Bristol, conducting 'a circuit into Hertfordshire, Essex, Bedfordshire, Cambridgeshire and Suffolk' and another covering Wiltshire and Gloucestershire, before returning once more to Bristol.[22]

Whitefield had seemingly learned the lesson regarding the neglect of his converts while in America and so turned to Howel Harris, inviting him to take over the interim leadership of the Tabernacle Society during his extended leave of absence.[23] Harris agreed and eagerly picked up the reins of Whitefield's work, arriving in London at an opportune moment; the worst of the infighting between the Moravians, Calvinists and Wesleyans had died down, and Harris now began to use his contacts and warm personal relationships with members of each group to work towards some sort of reconciliation, or at least pacification. Up to this point Harris had been busy organising the Welsh revival, drafting in Whitefield to advise at certain points, but it was only during Harris's extended stay in London that the possibility of uniting the English and Welsh Calvinistic revivals under a single organisational structure began slowly to germinate. The special relationship between English and Welsh Calvinistic Methodism was further cemented in November 1741, when Whitefield married Elizabeth James, a widow from Abergavenny, who had already been betrothed to Harris.[24] In a bizarre incident, Harris sacrificially handed her over to Whitefield, who was confident that his new wife would not detract too much of his attention, nor 'attempt to hinder me in [God's] work for the world'.[25]

Whitefield's three-month-long visit to Scotland in the late summer and autumn of 1741 had a major effect on his attitude to the movement which circumstances had led him to establish in England. He had been invited to Scotland by the Erskine brothers, Ralph and Ebenezer. The Erskines assumed that Whitefield would be a natural ally, but their hopes were soon dashed. While Whitefield certainly sympathised with their Calvinism, he did not agree with their separatist ecclesiology. Consequently, the Erskine brothers quickly turned against him, dismissing his preaching as 'only delusion, and by the agency of the devil'.[26] Those who thought that Whitefield, by forming a Calvinistic grouping in England, was giving tacit approval to others who wished to separate from Established Churches and set up their own doctrinally pure organisations, misunderstood what both Whitefield and the English Calvinistic Methodists were all about. While much of Whitefield's actions and attitudes can be seen as undermining Anglicanism, he utilised his ordination to facilitate his work and made no active move towards leaving the Church of England. Calvinistic Methodism was intended to be a network of societies in connection with one another, whilst working towards the renewal of the Church. Despite having the seeds of secession within it from the beginning, Calvinistic Methodism was never designed to be an *ecclesiola in ecclesia*, or an alternative to the Church altogether. Whitefield resisted all 'tempt[ations] . . . to come over to some particular party'.[27] His experience in Scotland reinforced his determination not to get sucked into the quagmire of denominationalism, but to remain above the fray as the roving freelance evangelist. This goes some considerable way to explain Whitefield's often ambivalent attitude to the Calvinistic Methodist movement which he had created, almost by default. At times he devoted considerable time and energy to it, while at others he abandoned it all too easily for seemingly greener pastures elsewhere. As James L. Schwenk has recently argued, Whitefield was committed to an 'evangelical ecumenicity' which sought to 'bring evangelicals together under the banner of conversion'.[28] His vision tended to a capaciousness wider than Calvinistic Methodism.

Having said this, Whitefield's renewed commitment to his work in England following his return from America in March 1741 had paid handsome dividends. His congregations had recovered to the size which he had become accustomed to seeing in the later 1730s; and, despite damaging divisions first with the Moravians and then with the Wesleyans, Whitefield now controlled a network of Calvinistic Methodist societies in the south and south-west of England, and his influence in Scotland, Wales and the American colonies was growing all the time. Little wonder that he wrote to a close friend in 1741 that 'the work is beginning afresh in England'.[29]

Calvinistic Methodist spirituality

From the disagreements over the nature and definition of Methodism during the early 1740s, there emerged a variety of competing Methodisms. But what did it mean to be a Calvinistic, rather than Wesleyan Methodist, or for that matter a Moravian? Was the experience of the humble rank-and-file Calvinistic Methodist appreciably different or distinct? In recent years considerable attention has been given to the lived experience of Methodism, to the various expressions of Methodist piety and spirituality.[30] The richness of the primary sources has meant that much of this material has focused on Wesleyan Methodism; there has been comparatively little investigation into the nature of Calvinistic Methodist spirituality. However, there is no shortage of sources for such an investigation; Whitefield's largely unpublished correspondence is particularly rich as is the even more expansive correspondence of Howel Harris. These sources can be supplemented by the published material which the Calvinistic Methodists produced, including not only journals, books and theological treatises, but the evangelical periodical, *The Weekly History*, which, together with its sister publications in America and Scotland, provides compelling evidence of the existence of a fairly sophisticated Calvinistic Methodist public sphere.[31]

The kinds of people who were attracted to Calvinistic Methodism were not markedly different from those drawn to other forms of Methodism, or evangelical religion more generally. They tended to be predominantly, though not exclusively, from the middling orders. There was always a sprinkling from the upper echelons of society, and some drawn from the lower orders, but the majority were merchants, shopkeepers, booksellers or craftsmen, while in rural areas small farmers and industrious labourers tended to predominate.[32] Women made up at least, and sometimes considerably more than, half of the total membership.[33] In general, members were literate, tending to be eager to learn, and they were industrious and frugal, all qualities which predisposed them to the self-improving undercurrent of the Methodist message. There was an obvious similarity in that message, and in its cultural expression, across all kinds of Methodism. The Bible was the foundational text, and the widespread use of biblical imagery and terminology ensured that a common biblical language developed throughout the Methodist movement.[34] The other common factor was the experience of conversion or, as they preferred to call it, the new birth. Most Methodists experienced conversion in a similar way, perhaps while reading an evangelical sermon or book, or more commonly while listening to one of the Methodist revivalists preaching. Conversion involved the realisation of one's innate sinfulness and a move towards trusting in Christ, which could happen instantaneously or over a more protracted period of time. It was a process that was often accompanied by extremes of emotion, from initial conviction and despair to subsequent relief, joy and peace. It was this transitional process as one travelled from darkness to light that actually felt like being born a second time.[35]

The newly awakened were quickly organised into small cell groups, known by the Methodists as societies. These could vary in size from the large society that met at Whitefield's Tabernacle, consisting of many hundreds of members subdivided into smaller bands, to the smaller societies, usually made up of about fifteen to twenty members, scattered around the Welsh countryside. Whitefield urged his converts to

> meet once a week, to tell each other what is in your hearts, that you may then also pray for and comfort each other, as need shall require. None but those who have experienc'd it can tell the unspeakable advantage of such an union and communion of souls: By this means brotherly love will be excited and encreased amongst you, and you will learn to watch over one another for good.[36]

Each society was placed under the oversight of a steward, and a structure of local and national leadership was soon to develop to administer their growing number. The conditions of membership in a society were rigorous, with candidates being expected to pass a probing interrogation regarding their spiritual condition, and in Wales to agree with the Calvinist theology of the movement.[37] Once admitted, the societies kept up a demanding regimen of Bible reading, catechising, prayer, singing and self-examination. Every aspect of life was open to the scrutiny of the society, and there were often strict consequences for those who transgressed its norms. Having said this, the societies were a highly successful and efficient means of spreading, in

John Wesley's famous words, 'scriptural holiness throughout the land'.[38] They were the bedrock of the Methodist movement and the context in which most rank-and-file Methodists lived out their lives. But to many outsiders they appeared secretive, even subversive, and from their earliest days they had within them the genesis of an alternative religious structure.

Despite obvious generic similarities across the Methodist movement, each expression of Methodism also had its own distinctive features. The most obvious distinguishing feature of those attracted to White-field's brand of Methodism was their commitment to Calvinism, something that only became more pronounced after the split with the Wesley brothers. Those Calvinistic Methodists who penned accounts of their conversion did so within the framework of the Calvinist *ordo salutis* – this 'order of salvation' of ruin, redemption and restoration.[39] Taking their lead from Whitefield's published journal, they reflected his moderate Calvinism, bringing to the foreground the themes of unconditional election, the distinguishing love of God and the imputed righteousness of Christ. Whilst there tended to be little discussion of the shades of opinion within Reformed theology in these narratives, they were often overlaid with Calvinist rhetoric; interjections such as 'O Free Grace and rich mercy' or 'O what wonder's [*sic*] has God's Free Grace wrought in me!' were commonplace.[40] This is an indication of the extent to which these themes had become contested in the wake of the divisions with the Wesley brothers. The disagreements were about far more than a mere difference of emphasis, as James L. Schwenk has suggested.[41] Much of the language of these narratives indicates that many Calvinistic Methodists were engaging in a process of conscious self-definition as much as in theological reflection.

Calvinist soteriology was supplemented by the Calvinistic Method-ists' stress on the progressive nature of sanctification in the life of the believer. Unlike the Wesleyans, Calvinistic Methodists did not expect to achieve a state of perfection or entire sanctification. When White-field encountered perfectionistic ideas among some of his followers in Bristol during 1741, he reacted strongly.[42] And, while he frequently urged his converts to 'study to be holy, even as he [Christ] is holy, and walk even as he also walked', he stopped well short of suggesting that it was ever likely that a Christian would attain a state of sinless perfection.[43] Calvinistic Methodism did not experience the kind of periodic outbreaks of hysteria that often accompanied fresh claims of Perfection among the Wesleyans.[44] Rather, Calvinists were taught, in a rather more understated way, to expect the Christian life to be characterised by a gradual process of conquest over indwelling sin and training in the habits of practical godliness. The dark 'clouds and heaviness and temptation' that one of Howel Harris's correspondents complained about, were the very stuff of the normal experience of Calvinistic Methodists.[45] They were to be expected, borne with patience and dependence on Christ and alleviated through the regular liturgical use of the means of grace.[46] Doubt, temptation, lethargy and discouragement were as much a part of the life of the typical Calvinistic Methodist as were peace, joy, certainty and triumph.

Wesley's ministry in Bristol during 1739 had been accompanied by the whole gamut of emotional behaviour, and the Wesleyan movement experienced periodic outbursts of highly emotional, often bizarre behaviour, especially following a spate of fresh claims to entire sanctification. Wesley seems to have actively encouraged such outbursts, taking them to be an indication of God's blessing on his ministry.[47] Whitefield sometimes took a more cautious approach. While his own preaching was often dramatic and highly emotional in both its style and effects,[48] Whitefield tended to be more wary of claiming that groanings, convulsions, trances, dreams, or glossolalia were reliable indicators of the presence of the Holy Spirit. At least, in 1739 he cautioned Wesley against 'those convulsions which people have been thrown into under your ministry' since they 'take people from the written word, and make them depend on visions, convulsions, &c, more than on the promises and precepts of the gospel'.[49] In adopting this way of reasoning, he was both reacting to the excesses he had witnessed under Wesley's ministry and betraying his indebtedness to Jonathan Edwards who, in the aftermath of the Northampton awakening and some of the excesses of the early stages of the colonial revivals, cautioned against assuming that physical manifestations were of necessity the work of the Holy Spirit.[50] English Calvinistic Methodists, therefore, tended to be wary of charismatic manifestations; the atmosphere of their meetings was certainly characterised by intense emotion, but only rarely descended into enthusiastic excess.[51]

In Wales, by contrast, the early stages of the revival were characterised by profound emotion; converts could frequently be heard weeping, groaning and shouting out in both agony and ecstasy, but it was not until the second wave of the revival, following the awakening at Llangeitho in 1762, that critics started branding the Methodists the 'Welsh Jumpers', on account of their proclivity for dancing, jumping and exuberant singing.[52] Howel Harris himself was more open to immediate impressions of the Spirit; his diaries record dreams, impressions on his mind and a tendency at times to value the prophetic over the written word of God.[53] He repeatedly used these charismatic insights as a way to bolster his position and authority, and it was his increasing dependence on the prophetic gifts of Mrs Sidney Griffith, which he used against his ordained contemporaries within the Methodist movement, that would become one of the contributory factors to his expulsion from the movement in 1750. For much of the early decades of the revival Daniel Rowland and William Williams were much more cautious about the physical manifestations that accompanied their preaching. This may have been the consequence of their dealings with Harris, but following the fresh outbreak of revival in 1762 they were forced to defend the authenticity of the sometimes bizarre behaviour of their converts from the virulent attacks of those who wished to discredit the revival. They argued that the physical manifestations were an indicator, albeit an imperfect one, of spiritual life, the implication being that it was better to grapple with some of the excesses of genuine piety than the somnolence of spiritual decline.[54] In their readiness to reason in this way they proved themselves to be dedicated disciples of Jonathan Edwards.[55]

Despite sharing the same organisational structure, similar spiritual experiences and common theological language, the English and Welsh Calvinistic Methodists were temperamentally quite different. The English Calvinistic Methodists were a much more restless and fissiparous bunch than their Welsh counterparts. Their development is littered with disagreements, personality clashes, switches of allegiance and secessions which had effectively reduced the movement to little more than a rump of Whitefield's most loyal supporters by the 1750s. They had become accustomed to defending their Calvinist viewpoint during the conflict with the Wesley brothers, but it seems that their contentiousness never really left them. In the absence of the strong leadership of Whitefield, whose commitment to his converts blew hot and cold, a vacuum was created, one of the consequences of which was that many different theological ideas were able to circulate freely within the movement. Some in Bristol were attracted to the perfectionist teachings of Wesley, antinomianism reared its ugly head on more than one occasion, and John Cennick took 400 members of the Tabernacle Society over to the Moravians by the end of 1745.[56] Many others merely ran after the latest fad to appear within the Methodist communities. Some found themselves drawn into the various Dissenting communities, particularly Congregationalism; others wound up in all sorts of weirdly wonderful fringe sects, while not a few even abandoned their faith altogether.

The Welsh Methodists were a much more homogenous group. Their organisational structure was tighter, and a greater degree of central control was maintained. This ensured that the lay leaders of the movement were held accountable and that the rank-and-file members were strictly disciplined. In its first decades Welsh Methodism did not succumb to the debilitating switching of allegiances that bedevilled English Calvinistic Methodism, largely because there was usually no alternative Methodist community in Wales to which individuals could defect, neither the Wesleyans nor the Moravians being viable alternatives at this stage. There was a greater degree of accountability among the leaders of the Welsh movement: Howel Harris, Daniel Rowland, Howell Davies and William Williams were each based in different parts of Wales and, despite Harris's claims to primacy as 'the first to sound the trumpet around the country', there was not really a single outright leader of the movement.[57] Welsh Methodism enjoyed a more collegiate style of leadership, something which enabled the revivalists to keep focus and maintain strong discipline. When there were divisions and disagreements in Wales, as there inevitably were, it was possible for them to be dealt with without jeopardising the whole of the movement. The problems surrounding Howel Harris in the later 1740s are an obvious illustration of this. While the loss of Harris and his most loyal followers would be deeply damaging to the revival and resulted in a period of stagnation, it did not bring the revival to a grinding halt.[58]

Developing a joint organisational structure

While Whitefield was busy trying to re-energise his converts in England throughout much of 1741, the leaders of the Welsh Methodist revival were deciding on and then refining an organisational structure that made the best use of the revivalists themselves, and that ensured that the rank-and-file members had the best pastoral support possible. Whitefield had been the key to this process ever since he and Harris had discussed the state of the Welsh societies during his first visit to Wales in March 1739.[59] After this visit he began to be included in the discussions over the organisation of the Welsh revival on a regular basis and soon came to be regarded as a type of father figure or elder brother by the Welsh revivalists.[60]

Whitefield's vision for the societies was laid out fully in his *Letter ... to the Religious Societies Lately Set on Foot in Several Parts of England and Wales* (1740), and was almost immediately translated into Welsh.[61] Whitefield's *Letter* had two aims. It was bitingly critical of the perform-ance of the Church of England; Whitefield argued that its bishops were more interested in indulging in 'the diversions of the age' than with supporting initiatives to 'promote the power of Godliness'.[62] It was no surprise, therefore, that alternative forms of spiritual nurture had sprung up to the plug the gaps. Having given an apology for the existence of the societies, Whitefield, in what is one of the best de-scriptions of their function, went on to more practical matters. He urged his readers to ensure that the highest possible standards of entry into the societies were maintained, and that evidence of a conversion experience was essential; but this had also to be supplemented by the possession of full assurance of faith, a somewhat rarer commodity. There was also a more specific doctrinal test, firmly rooted in the doctrine of justification by faith which Whitefield identified as being the key point of difference between the Methodists and others within the Church of England.[63] Yet this doctrinal exactness was to be tempered by an irenic spirit, as members were encouraged to unite with other evangelicals 'in one common interest against spiritual wickedness in high places'.[64]

On a still more basic level, Whitefield offered practical advice on what were to be the core activities of each society. That the societies were to be characterised by reading, singing and praying together was taken for granted; instead, Whitefield focused on three more demanding spiritual disciplines: the confession of one's faults to both God and fellow members, paying testimony to God's work in one's life and the building of communal interdependency. These he held to be essential if the societies were not to follow the same trajectory as many of the old religious societies in London which, according to Whitefield, had degenerated into a 'dull formality'.[65] Although Whitefield had written this pamphlet with his Bristol societies mainly in mind, its swift translation into Welsh shows the extent to which there was substantial agreement over the nature and function of the societies between the leaders of the English and Welsh Calvinistic Methodists. By 1740 there was already unanimity over the strict rules of entry, over their core theological commitments and over the basic activities in which society members were to engage across both countries, a foundation which became the basis on which a more all-encompassing administrative structure could be built.

Up until 1740 the Welsh societies remained under the informal control of Howel Harris and Daniel Rowland, each man taking responsibility for the societies he himself had set up. However, the growth in the number and geographical dispersal of these societies and Harris's desire to spend increasing amounts of time in London meant that a more efficient system of administration was required. In some prefatory remarks to the official minute book of the Welsh Methodist Association, Harris claimed that the Welsh Methodists had begun organising their converts in 1739 when Harris left his societies in the care of three men, two of whom were Dissenting ministers, as he accompanied Whitefield back to London during March.[66] On his return, he met formally with his three newly appointed assistants, a practice which he then maintained throughout the rest of that year.[67] These gatherings gradually evolved to become the Monthly Society. The first official meeting of the Monthly Society took place at Mynydd Meio in Glamorgan during January 1740; its importance to the administration of the movement is seen by the fact that it was in this forum that Harris issued the Welsh societies with their first set of codified rules and regulations.[68] For much of 1740 the monthly meeting embedded itself, slowly evolving to become the main decision-making body within Welsh Methodism. By the end of the year both Harris and Rowland were agreed on the need for a more coordinated approach and, therefore, called upon all the leaders of the revival to meet at Defynnog in order to bring the societies to an 'outward settled agreement'.[69]

To their credit, Harris and Rowland welcomed an impressive group of Welsh evangelicals to Defynnog on 1 October, including members of the Church and some prominent sympathetic Dissenting ministers, including John Oulton from Leominster and Edmund Jones of Pontypool. At the meeting they discussed Harris's rules in more detail, before he took the important step of placing the care of his own societies under the new body, thereby vesting it with autonomy and control over the whole revival.[70] However, the meeting was not entirely successful, and tensions between Harris and some of the Dissenting ministers quickly surfaced, bringing to an abrupt end the possibility of meaningful further collaboration.[71] The Defynnog meeting was, therefore, something of a watershed for the Welsh Methodists. While important to the developing organisation of the revival, it brought an end to any hopes they may have had of leading a broad movement of renewal encompassing Welsh evangelicals of many different denominational affiliations. In its aftermath, Harris, disappointed at the lack of vision of some of his associates in Wales, redoubled his efforts at seeking still closer links with Whitefield and his English Methodists. Therefore, the failure to broaden the base of Welsh evangelicalism contributed directly to the consolidation of the Welsh and English branches of Calvinistic Methodism.

For two years between early 1741 and early 1743 the Welsh Methodists, aided by the periodic secondment of Whitefield, held a series of further meetings at which a joint administrative structure for Welsh and English Calvinistic Methodism was hammered out. The first of these meetings took place at Llandovery during February 1741. Although Whitefield did not attend on this occasion, the meeting marked an important point in the developing relationship between his revival and the Welsh Methodists. It formally adopted the tiered connexional structure that had been gradually taking shape under Harris's close tutelage. The seventy societies that existed in south Wales by this stage were split into small groups of five or six; each group was then instructed to meet once a month. There was also a meeting every other month at which the society leaders of neighbouring counties were to meet; a gathering of the leaders of the Welsh revival was to take place quarterly; and an annual meeting at which all of the leaders of English and Welsh Calvinistic Methodism met in conference.[72] Under the direction of Daniel Rowland, the meeting then proceeded by examining and assigning various laymen to take charge of individual societies and discussing and refining the society rules that Harris had drawn up earlier.[73] From this point on, all of the leaders of the Welsh revival were committed to strategic meetings every two months. The new body, now known as the Public Society, effectively became the executive arm of the Welsh revival.[74]

The wider context of the Llandovery gathering was equally important, meeting as it did against the backdrop of the damaging splits over predestination that were occurring among the London Methodists. Harris put discussion of these theological problems at the top of the agenda at Llandovery and began the meeting by reading two letters. One had been written by him to Charles Wesley outlining Harris's difficulties with Arminian and Perfectionist views.[75] The other, from Whitefield to John Wesley, outlined a similar array of objections.[76] After a discussion of the merits and demerits of each position the assembled Welsh Methodists enthusiastically came down on the side of Harris and Whitefield, a decision that formally aligned the Welsh revival with Whitefield's Calvinistic Methodists.[77] After the meeting Harris spent three months working tirelessly to implement what had been agreed at Llandovery: he travelled around south Wales, visiting the societies, ensuring that each of them had adequate leadership, that the authority of the Public Society was widely accepted and that the new structures were working with the necessary efficiency.

Once he was happy that matters were in order, Harris responded to Whitefield's invitation to return to London to help him reorganise his revival after the split with the Wesley brothers, and to share in its leadership with John Cennick during Whitefield's planned absence in Scotland. Harris now immersed himself in the fractured English revival, with the disapproval of some of his Welsh colleagues ringing in his ears.[78] When in London, his activities were centred on Whitefield's recently established Tabernacle Society; he preached there twice daily to its 300 regular attendees and examined the various smaller bands.[79] However, he frequently ventured further afield as well, preaching in Bristol, Gloucestershire and Wiltshire, the three other places in England where there was the strongest concentration of Calvinistic

Methodists. But the Tabernacle Society itself was still very much in its infancy and so Harris's considerable pastoral and organisational skills were drawn upon extensively during these months in London.

The Tabernacle Society was always smaller than the totality of those who gathered regularly at Moorfields to listen to Whitefield preach, individuals only being admitted to the private society after a strict examination of their suitability. Harris helped Whitefield introduce a system of bands divided according to sex and marital status, coming together for a whole group meeting once a week. Each band was placed under the care of a leader who in turn reported on progress to whoever happened to be occupying the ministerial role at the Tabernacle at the time.[80] The system was extended to the other English Calvinistic Methodist societies as well and seems to have facilitated considerable further growth. Within eighteen months the Tabernacle Society was thriving, and its 1,200 members necessitated the building of a substantial extension to the structure.[81] By this time the Tabernacle also hosted a sizeable school which catered for the needs of over a hundred children.[82] The members of the society also collected considerable sums of money to distribute to the poor and destitute in the immediate vicinity of the Tabernacle.[83] Other activities at the Tabernacle had also mushroomed, and the instituting of a monthly letter day at which the latest accounts of the progress of the revival around the Anglo-American world were read aloud reflected the newly acquired self-confidence of Whitefield's followers.[84] But the growth of the English Calvinistic Methodist societies, particularly during 1742, flagged up the need for an administrative structure that covered the whole of the country. Consequently, the English movement was divided into four associations: London, Bristol, Gloucestershire and Wiltshire.[85] Each association was placed under the oversight of a superintendent, who in turn had responsibility for the exhorters and stewards who laboured in the local societies under their supervision. The superintendents were required to send comprehensive monthly reports to John Syms at the Tabernacle, who presented them to Whitefield, Harris or John Cennick for careful examination.[86] In this way a close watch could be kept on the progress of the revival in each of its localities, problems could be identified early and the attention of the revivalists deployed accordingly.

At its best this proved to be a highly efficient way of managing the English revival, but it depended too heavily on the active involvement of Whitefield, and he was too often distracted by other demands on his time and energies. Neither John Cennick nor Howel Harris, who had to split his time between England and Wales, of course, proved quite able to fill his shoes. Nonetheless, by the end of 1742 there were in England a substantial number of 'Whitefieldian Methodist Societies', and fifteen full-time preachers.[87] The fullest figures relating to the extent of the connexion date from 1747 when English Calvinistic Methodism could boast thirty societies and twenty-four preaching places, with over twenty full and part-time preachers and exhorters in active service.[88] While English Calvinistic Methodism was never as widespread as the movement led by John Wesley, by 1742 it consisted of an extensive network of societies and preachers, mostly in the south and south-west of England. Where there were pockets of strength and committed local leaders, the organisational structure put in place by Whitefield and Harris actually worked extremely effectively.

Nowhere was this truer than in Wales, where by early 1742 a structure parallel to that in England was firmly in place. At the end of 1741 Whitefield was invited to a gathering of the leaders of the Welsh Methodist revival at Dugoedydd in Carmarthenshire. Although, in the end, he was unable to attend the meeting held during the first few days of 1742, he wrote a lengthy and detailed letter analysing the state of the Calvinist societies, pinpointing the areas where there were still weaknesses that needed to be addressed. Whitefield first made two general points: he reiterated the importance of the distinction between those who were engaged in public work among the societies and those who were concerned with more private matters, and he addressed the still thorny issue of the status of the societies in relation to the Church of England and the Dissenters, advising that they should remain loyal to the Church until 'cast out' and that they should seek out sympathetic clergy prepared to administer the sacraments to them.[89] But these points were only the prelude to the substantive practical matters Whitefield wanted to be raised at the meeting. By this stage the English and Welsh Calvinistic awakenings had become intertwined, and Whitefield attempted to capitalise on this by requesting the more regular assistance of some of the Welsh preachers in the personnel-strapped English work. He was particularly concerned about the lack of regular pastoral oversight for the Calvinists at Kingswood and in Wiltshire and suggested that Thomas Lewis be released from his responsibilities in Breconshire to assist in England on a more regular basis.[90]

Whitefield was also concerned about the channels of communication between the two revivals and suggested that they follow his example of incorporating a monthly letter day into their communal life. He reminded them of their obligation to send a monthly report of the revival to the Tabernacle in preparation for the English letter day and promised that he would ensure that the Welsh received a similar report from England. The unity that Whitefield envisaged for the English and Welsh revival, therefore, operated on two levels: there was to be a coordinated organisational structure within which manpower could be freely shared, and there was to be a 'spiritual' connection by means of which the rank and file of the revival were to be drawn closer together through regular communication.

The Dugoedydd meeting followed Whitefield's agenda to the letter, and Harris reported to him that 'every one agreed with your thoughts, we had much union sweetness concord and brotherly love together'.[91] In the following months the Welsh Methodists met regularly, fine tuning the structure which had been agreed; and at a meeting at Llwynyberllan in Carmarthenshire during February they produced a final version of the society rules and arranged to have them printed.[92] These were then circulated throughout Wales.[93] By mid-1742 the Welsh and English Calvinistic Methodist revivals had been brought to some sense of order and had developed structures that were broadly parallel. By October 1742 Whitefield was of the opinion that 'the awakening seems in some measure to be over . . . there are so many living stones it may be time to think of putting them together'.[94]

Consequently, during the first week of 1743 the leaders of Calvinistic Methodism in both England and Wales assembled for the first Joint Association of English and Welsh Calvinistic Methodism, at Watford near Caerphilly. Whitefield was accompanied by John Cennick, Joseph Humphreys and Herbert Jenkins. Harris and Rowland were joined by William Williams and John Powell.[95] Despite its prominence in most discussions of the early history of Calvinistic Methodism, the Watford meeting did not actually make any major new recommendations. It authorised a number of the decisions which had already been made, and it officially adopted many of the policies and procedures that already had been agreed. The most significant decision made was the appointment of Whitefield to the position of moderator of the association. Despite its obvious Presbyterian connotations, the role actually had more symbolic than practical significance.[96] However, his appointment was indicative of the respect and affection with which Whitefield was held, particularly in Wales.[97]

The practical discussions at the association were largely concerned with the appointment of the leaders of the Welsh revival to various offices within the movement. Public and private exhorters were assigned to various spheres of work; twenty-four private exhorters were given responsibility for larger groups of societies which they were instructed to bring together for fellowship on a monthly basis. The country was divided into different areas, each under the control of a superintendent, to whom the exhorters were to report at quarterly meetings. The superintendents then met together once a year in the annual gathering of the Association of English and Welsh Calvinistic Methodism, under the direction of Whitefield or, in his absence, Harris or Rowland.[98] The association also attempted to draw a line under the persistently thorny issue of the relationship between the Methodist societies, the Church of England and the Dissenters. The oft-repeated policy of cooperation with those evangelical Dissenters who were sympathetic to them and loyalty to the Church until 'the Lord should open a plain door for leaving her Communion' was now written into the formal minutes of the association.[99]

A few months later Whitefield was again at Watford to discuss some of the matters that had not been resolved at the January meeting. On this occasion reports were received from the exhorters, and some of the gaps in coverage were plugged. This association also made a number of other far-reaching decisions which included the setting apart of William Williams as Daniel Rowland's personal assistant in south-west Wales, a move that enabled them to turn the area into the powerhouse of Methodist growth; this was a development that was to have important ramifications for the future of Welsh Methodism after the expulsion of Harris in 1750. In some respects one of the most important tasks which the association faced was finding an appropriate role for the unordained Harris. Much of this pioneering organisational work had been carried out by him, of course, and in recognition of this and his significance in the wider evangelical movement the association conferred on him the title of general superintendent. Nebulous in and of itself, the title in effect gave him joint oversight with Whitefield of the English and Welsh Calvinistic societies.[100] It was a decision that bore all the hallmarks of Whitefield, who coveted Harris's organisational gifts for his own societies in England, and it opened the way for Harris to devote an even greater proportion of his time to the English societies.

In many regards the two Watford meetings were actually little more than a rubber-stamping exercise, but they had a significant psychological impact. The annual associations were to become important days in the Methodist calendar: feast days lasting two, sometimes three, days as large crowds gathered to listen to sermons and renew old friendships. Whitefield's presence at Watford put the final seal on the organisational structure that had been gradually evolving over the previous two years, and it shored up the beleaguered English societies which benefited from the extra resources available from Wales. The months immediately following the Watford meetings saw a fresh spurt of growth and further consolidation. For most of 1743 Whitefield kept a closer eye on events in Wales than he might normally have done, but by the end of the year the draw of the American colonies had once again become too strong for him to resist. The interdependence of the two revivals continued, but the balance of their relationship began to alter, largely because of their contrasting fortunes. For the moment, the revival in Wales went from strength to strength, but as Whitefield sailed for America in 1744 he could not have imagined that by the time of his return four years later his English societies would have been brought to the verge of collapse.

Much of the historiography on Methodism has attributed the very differing long-term fortunes of the Wesleyan and Whitefieldian movements to Whitefield's overriding priority of preaching, and his apparent lack of ability or interest in the day-to-day pastoring and organising of his converts.[101] The evidence presented here perhaps suggests otherwise. Whitefield, with the example and assistance of Howel Harris, put in place a highly effective organisational structure in England which mirrored that established by the Welsh Methodists. When his attentions were fully concentrated on making this system work effectively it served Whitefield's needs perfectly. Problems arose when those attentions were diverted elsewhere, particularly when he spent protracted periods of time in the American colonies. Those he left in charge were not able to make the system work as effectively, either through their own lack of ability or, as in the case of Howel Harris, being overburdened by the responsibility of leading the Welsh revival as well. Had Whitefield been able to concentrate on the English revival, he might well have proved able to establish a Calvinistic Methodist body that would have become a serious rival to that version of Methodism set up by John Wesley. In the final reckoning, the Calvinistic Methodist structure largely fashioned by George Whitefield suffered severely owing to his frequent absence from it. Its organisation was unable to thrive without the presence of its chief architect.

Notes

[1] John Cennick, *The Life of Mr J. Cennick* (Bristol: John Lewis and James Hutton, 1745), p. 38.

[2] John Cennick, 'An account of the most remarkable occurrences in the awakenings at Bristol and Kingswood till the Brethren's labours began there in 1746', ed. H. J. Foster, *Proceedings of the Wesley Historical Society*, 4, 8 (December 1908), 140; Arnold A. Dallimore, *George Whitefield: The Life and Times of the Great Evangelist of the 18th Century Revival* (2 vols, London and Edinburgh: The Banner of Truth Trust, 1970 and 1980) II, p. 152.

[3] Cennick, *The Life of Mr J. Cennick*, pp. 38–9.

[4] Colin J. Podmore, *The Moravian Church in England, 1728–1760* (Oxford: Oxford University Press, 1998), p. 88.

[5] See Geoffrey F. Nuttall, 'George Whitefield's "curate": Gloucestershire dissent and the revival', *Journal of Ecclesiastical History*, 27, 4 (October 1976), 375–6.

[6] George Whitefield, *A Continuation of the Reverend Mr Whitefield's Journal, during the time he was detained in England by the Embargo* (London: W. Strahan, 1739), p. 13.

[7] Dallimore, *George Whitefield*, II, p. 152.

[8] C. E. Watson, 'Rodborough Tabernacle: an account by John Knight, written in 1844', *Congregational Historical Society Transactions*, 10, 6 (September 1929), 278; George Hasking Wicks, *Whitefield's Legacy to Bristol and the Cotswolds* (Bristol: Taylor Bros, 1914), pp. 104–11.

[9] George Whitefield, *Three letters from the Reverend Mr G. Whitefield: viz to a friend in London, concerning Archbishop Tillotson* (Philadelphia: B. Franklin, 1740), p. 2.

[10] Luke Tyerman, *The Life of the Rev. George Whitefield* (2 vols, London: Hodder and Stoughton, 1876), I, p. 473.

[11] George Whitefield to Joseph Humphreys, 25 March 1741, in John Gillies (ed.), *The Works of the Reverend George Whitefield* (London: Edward and Charles Dilly, 1771), I, p. 256; ibid., p. 257.

[12] Geoffrey L. Fairs, 'Notes on the death of William Seward at Hay, 1740', *JHSPCW*, 58, 1 (March 1973), 12–18. George Whitefield to Joseph Humphreys, 25 March 1741, in Gillies (ed.), *The Works of the Reverend George Whitefield*, I, p. 256.

[13] Neil J. O'Connell, 'George Whitefield and Bethesda Orphan-House', *The Georgia Historical Quarterly*, 54 (1970), 48, 52.

[14] George Whitefield to John Cennick, 25 March 1741, in Gillies (ed.), *The Works of the Reverend George Whitefield*, I, p. 258.

[15] George Whitefield to Samuel Mason, 27 April 1741, in Gillies (ed.), *The Works of the Reverend George Whitefield*, I, p. 259.

[16] David Ceri Jones, *'A Glorious Work in the World': Welsh Methodism and the International Evangelical Revival, 1735-1750* (Cardiff: University of Wales Press, 2004), pp. 64–5.

[17] Richard P. Heitzenrater, *Wesley and the People called Methodists* (Nashville, TN: Abingdon Press, 1995), pp. 114–15.

[18] George Whitefield to William W__, 16 May 1741, in Gillies (ed.), *The Works of the Reverend George Whitefield*, I, p. 261.

[19] John Cennick, 'An account of the most remarkable occurrences in the awakenings at Bristol and Kingswood till the Brethren's labours began there in 1746', ed. H. J. Foster, in *Proceedings of the Wesley Historical Society*, 6, 6 (June 1908), 108–10; Kenneth Morgan, *John Wesley in Bristol* (Bristol: Historical Association, 1990), p. 9.

[20] George Whitefield to Mr S__, 5 May 1741, in Gillies (ed.), *The Works of the Reverend George Whitefield*, I, p. 261.

[21] George Whitefield to Howel Harris, 6 June 1741, in Gillies (ed.), *The Works of the Reverend George Whitefield*, I, p. 268.

[22] George Whitefield to James Habersham, 12 July 1741, in Gillies (ed.), *The Works of the Reverend George Whitefield*, I, p. 276. George Whitefield to Howel Harris, 6 June 1741, in Gillies (ed.), *The Works of the Reverend George Whitefield*, I, p. 269.

[23] George Whitefield to Howel Harris, 6 June 1741, in Gillies (ed.), *The Works of the Reverend George Whitefield*, I, p. 269.

[24] See Roger Lee Brown, 'The marriage of George Whitefield at Caerphilly', *JHSPCW*, 7 (1983), 24–30.

[25] George Whitefield to Rev. Mr G[ilbert] T[ennent], 2 February 1742, in Gillies (ed.), *The Works of the Reverend George Whitefield*, I, p. 363.

26 George Whitefield to Howel Harris, 26 August 1742, in Gillies (ed.), *The Works of the Reverend George Whitefield*, I, p 426.

27 George Whitefield to Howel Harris, 13 August 1741, in Gillies (ed.), *The Works of the Reverend George Whitefield*, I, p. 313.

28 James L. Schwenk, *Catholic Spirit: Wesley, Whitefield, and the Quest for Evangelical Unity in Eighteenth-Century British Methodism* (Lanham, MD: Scarecrow Press, 2008), p. 2.

29 George Whitefield to Mr B__, 24 July 1741, in Gillies (ed.), *The Works of the Reverend George Whitefield*, I, p. 280.

30 Good starting points are D. Bruce Hindmarsh, *The Evangelical Conversion Narrative: Spiritual Autobiography in Early Modern England* (Oxford: Oxford University Press, 2005); Phyllis Mack, *Heart Religion in the British Enlightenment: Gender and Emotion in Early Methodism* (Cambridge: Cambridge University Press, 2008).

31 The extent of the Methodist and evangelical public sphere is only beginning to be appreciated. See Isabel Rivers, 'The First Evangelical Tract Society', *The Historical Journal*, 50, 1 (March 2007), 1–22; Jennifer Snead, 'Print, predestination, and the public sphere: transatlantic evangelical periodicals, 1740-1745', *Early American Literature*, 45, 1 (2010), 93–118.

32 C. D. Field, 'The social composition of English Methodism to 1830: a membership analysis', *Bulletin of John Rylands University of Manchester Library*, 76 (spring 1994), 153–69; Eryn Mant White, '"The world, the flesh and the devil" and the early Methodist societies of south west Wales', *Transactions of the Honourable Society of Cymmrodorion*, 3 (1997), 45–61.

33 David Hempton, *Methodism: Empire of the Spirit* (New Haven, CT: Yale University Press, 2005), p. 5.

34 Bebbington, *Evangelicalism in Modern Britain* (London: Unwin Hyman, 1989), pp. 12–14; Eryn M. White, *The Welsh Bible* (Stroud: Tempus, 2007), p. 92.

35 For more on the process of evangelical conversion, see Bebbington, *Evangelicalism in Modern Britain*, pp. 5–10; idem., 'Evangelical conversion, c.1740–1850', *Scottish Bulletin of Evangelical Theology*, 18, 2 (autumn 2000), 102–27.

36 George Whitefield, *A letter from the Rev. Mr George Whitefield to the religious societies, lately set on foot in several parts of England and Wales* (London: W. Strahan, 1740), pp. 23–4.

37 David Ceri Jones, '"Like the time of the Apostles": the fundamentalist mentality in eighteenth-century Welsh evangelicalism', *Welsh History Review*, vol. 25, no. 3 (June 2011), 380.

[38] Quoted in Heitzenrater, *Wesley and the People Called Methodists*, p. 214.

[39] D. Bruce Hindmarsh, "'My chains fell off, my heart was free": early Methodist conversion narrative in England', *Church History*, 68, 4 (1999), 925.

[40] From M__y L__y (a young girl in Merchant's Hospital, Edinburgh) to the Rev. Mr Whitefield', in John Lewis (ed.), *The Weekly History*, 62 (12 June 1742), 3. 'The copy of a letter to a friend in the country to Brother Howell Harris', in John Lewis (ed.), *An Account of the Most Remarkable Particulars relating to the Present Progress of the Gospel*, 2, 1 (1743), 62.

[41] Schwenk, *Catholic Spirit*, p. 123.

[42] Dallimore, *George Whitefield*, II, pp. 66–7.

[43] George Whitefield to James Habersham, 18 February 1741, Gillies (ed.), *The Works of the Reverend George Whitefield*, I, p. 247.

[44] Henry D. Rack, *Reasonable Enthusiast: John Wesley and the Rise of Methodism* (London: Epworth Press, 1989), pp. 395–410; Herbert Boyd McGonigle, *Sufficient Saving Grace: John Wesley's Evangelical Arminianism* (Carlisle: Paternoster, 2001), chapters 6 and 10.

[45] NLW Trevecka Letter 727, Anne Davies to Howel Harris, 6 November 1742.

[46] See, for example, 'From the Reverend Mr Daniel Rowland (a Church of England minister) in Wales to two Welsh sisters of his flock in London', in Lewis (ed.), *An Account of the Most Remarkable Particulars Relating to the Present Progress of the Gospel*, 4, 2, 13–16.

[47] Rack, *Reasonable Enthusiast*, p. 195.

[48] Harry S. Stout, *The Divine Dramatist: George Whitefield and the Rise of Modern Evangelicalism* (Grand Rapids, MI: Eerdmans, 1991), pp. 40–4.

[49] George Whitefield to John Wesley, 25 June 1739, in Frank Baker (ed.), *The Works of John Wesley*, vol. 2, *Letters I, 1721–1739* (Oxford: Oxford University Press, 1980) pp. 661–2.

[50] See George Marsden, *Jonathan Edwards: A Life* (New Haven, CT: Yale University Press, 2003), pp. 233–8.

[51] However, for examples of such excess, see NLW Trevecka Letter 1903, Mary Biggs to James Ingram, 27 November 1749; Trevecka Letter 1904, Mary Biggs to Howel Harris, 18 December 1749; Trevecka Letter 1936, Mary Biggs to Howel Harris, 14 May 1750.

[52] Geraint H. Jenkins, *The Foundations of Modern Wales, 1642–1789* (Oxford: Oxford University Press, 1987) p. 366.

[53] Geoffrey F. Nuttall, *Howel Harris, 1714–1773: The Last Enthusiast* (Cardiff: University of Wales Press, 1965), pp. 46ff.

---

54 See Eryn M. White, "'I will once more shake the heavens": the 1762 Revival in Wales', in Kate Cooper and Jeremy Gregory (eds), *Revival and Resurgence in Christian History*, Studies in Church History, 44 (Woodbridge: Boydell, 2008), pp. 160–1.

55 David Ceri Jones, "'Sure the time here now is like New England": what happened when the Welsh Calvinistic Methodists read Jonathan Edwards', in Kelly Van Andel, Kenneth Minkema and Adriaan Neele (eds), *Jonathan Edwards and Scotland* (Edinburgh: Dunedin Press, 2011), pp. 55–6.

56 Podmore, *The Moravian Church in England*, pp. 90–5.

57 Tom Beynon, 'Howell Harris's visits to Kidwelly and District', *JHSPCW*, 24, 1 (March 1939), 56.

58 See Tudur, *Howell Harris*, chapters 7 and 8; Eryn White, "'A breach in God's house": the division in Welsh Calvinistic Methodism, 1750–63', in Nigel Yates (ed.), *Bishop Burgess and his World: Culture, Religion and Society in Britain, Europe and North America in the Eighteenth and Nineteenth Centuries* (Cardiff: University of Wales Press, 2007), pp. 85–102. See also chapter 5 of this present work.

59 NLW Trevecka Letter 148, William Seward to Daniel Abbot, 10 March 1739; George Whitefield, *A Continuation of the Reverend Mr Whitefield's Journal from his arrival at London to his departure from thence on his way to Georgia (December 1738–June 1739)* (London: James Hutton, 1739), p. 49.

60 See, for example, NLW Trevecka Letter 650, George Whitefield to Howel Harris, 16 September 1742; Trevecka Letter 1152, Howel Harris to George Whitefield, 19 March 1744.

61 George Whitefield, *Llythyr Oddiwrth y Parchedig Mr George Whitefield at Societies neu Gymdeithasau Crefyddol a Osodwyd yn Ddiweddar ar Droed Mewn Amriw Leodd yng Nghymru a Lloeger* (Pontypool: Samuel and Felix Farley, 1740).

62 Whitefield, *A Letter from the Rev. Mr George Whitefield to the Religious Societies*, p. 4.

63 Ibid., pp. 12–13.

64 Ibid., p. 21.

65 Ibid., p. 23; Henry D. Rack, 'Religious societies and the origins of Methodism', *Journal of Ecclesiastical History*, 38, 4 (October, 1987), 586, 589ff.

66 W. G. Hughes-Edwards, 'The development and organisation of the Methodist Society in Wales, 1735–50' (unpublished MA thesis; University of Wales, 1966), 247–8.

67 NLW Howel Harris's Diary, 5 June 1739; Howel Harris's Diary, 5 August 1739; Howel Harris's Diary, 2 September 1739; Howel Harris's Diary, 30 November 1739.
68 Hughes-Edwards, 'The development and organisation of the Methodist Society in Wales', 249.
69 NLW CMA Trevecka 2945 Records of Associations, I, p. 2.
70 Tudur, *Howell Harris*, pp. 74–5; Evans, *Daniel Rowland*, pp. 109–15.
71 NLW Howel Harris's Diary, 1 October 1740; M. H. Jones, *The Trevecka Letters* (Caernarvon: Calvinistic Methodist Bookroom, 1932), pp. 262–4.
72 See NLW Howel Harris's Diary, 29 December 1740.
73 Hughes-Edwards, 'The development and organisation of the Methodist Society in Wales', 253–5. For an English translation of these rules, see Evans, *Daniel Rowland*, pp. 123–4.
74 NLW Howel Harris's Diary, 13 February 1741.
75 NLW Trevecka Letter 312, Howel Harris to Charles Wesley, February 1741.
76 It is not entirely clear which letter this was, although it seems likely to have been the one Whitefield wrote to John Wesley from Philadelphia on 9 November 1741. See Gillies (ed.), *The Works of George Whitefield*, I, p. 219.
77 NLW Howel Harris's Diary, 13 February 1741.
78 See, for example, NLW Trevecka Letter 363, Thomas Price to Howel Harris, 8 August 1741.
79 NLW Trevecka Letter 361, Howel Harris to George Whitefield, 4 August 1741; NLW Trevecka Letter 644, Howel Harris to Daniel Rowland, 14 September 1742.
80 NLW Trevecka Letter 618, Howel Harris to Howell Griffith, 2 September 1742.
81 NLW Trevecka Letter 628, Howel Harris to Marmaduke Gwynne, 7 September 1742; NLW Trevecka Letter 685, Howel Harris to George Whitefield, 12 October 1742.
82 NLW Trevecka Letter 618, Howel Harris to Howell Griffith, 2 September 1742.
83 Edwin Welch (ed.), *Two Calvinistic Methodist Chapels, 1743–1811*, pp. 21, 29, 32, 39, 41–2, 113–14.
84 NLW Trevecka 2946 Records of Associations, II, flyleaf; Welch (ed.), *Two Calvinistic Methodist Chapels*, p. 19; Susan O'Brien, 'A transatlantic community of saints: the Great Awakening and the First Evangelical Network, 1735–1755', *American Historical Review*, 91 (1986), 826–7.

[85] NLW CMA Trevecka 2946 Records of Associations, II, p. 1; Welch (ed.), *Two Calvinistic Methodist Chapels*, p. 19.

[86] See, for example, NLW Trevecka Letter 994, Howel Harris to John Syms, 6 October 1743; Trevecka Letter 1220, Howel Harris to John Syms, 29 August 1744; Trevecka Letter 1278, Howel Harris to John Syms, 11 January 1745.

[87] Dallimore, *George Whitefield*, II, p. 154.

[88] See appendices A and B of this present work.

[89] George Whitefield to the Brethren in Wales, 28 December 1741, in *Evangelical Magazine* (1826), 469.

[90] Ibid; J. T. Lloyd and R. T. Jenkins (eds), *The Dictionary of Welsh Biography down to 1940* (London: Transactions of the Honourable Society of Cymmrodorion, 1959), s.v. Lewis, Thomas.

[91] NLW Trevecka Letter 460, Howel Harris to George Whitefield, 14 January 1742.

[92] They were published under the title *Sail Dibenion, a Rheolau'r Societies neu'r Cyfarfodydd Neilltuol a Ddechreusant Ymgynull yn Ddiweddar yng Nghymru* (Bristol: Felix Farley, 1742).

[93] NLW Howel Harris's Diary, 11 February 1742; Hughes-Edwards, 'The development and organisation of the Methodist Society in Wales', 260–1.

[94] 'The conclusion of the letter begun in our last', Lewis (ed.), *The Weekly History*, 80 (Saturday 16 October 1742).

[95] Lloyd and Jenkins (eds), *The Dictionary of Welsh Biography*, s.v. Powell, John.

[96] Jones, *The Trevecka Letters*, p. 280.

[97] See, for example, NLW Trevecka Letter 811, Howel Harris to George Whitefield, 1 March 1743.

[98] NLW CMA Trevecka 2945 Records of Associations, I, pp. 5–6.

[99] Ibid.

[100] NLW CMA Trevecka 2945 Records of Associations, I, pp. 13–15.

[101] See, for example, Robert Philip, *The Life and Times of George Whitefield* (London: George Virtue, 1837); Tyerman, *The Life of the Rev. George Whitefield*, I, p. iii–iv; John Charles Ryle, *The Christian Leaders of England in the Eighteenth Century* (London: Chas J. Thynne, 1902), pp. 30ff.

4

From high hopes to 'miserable divisions': the consolidation and splintering of Calvinistic Methodism, 1744–1750

When George Whitefield arrived in New England in October 1744, at the beginning of what was to be his longest continuous period in the American colonies, he walked straight into the storm that was raging over the legitimacy of the revivals of the previous few years.[1] In his absence the colonial revival had become enmeshed in controversy, and Whitefield's ministry was being held responsible for unleashing a spirit of discord, even unbridled fanaticism. New England ministers were nervous at reports that Whitefield had 'a design to turn out the generality of ministers in the country, by persuading people to discard or separate from them as being unconverted, and to get a supply of converted ones, many of which were to be foreigners'.[2] So he was quickly forced into print to distance himself from what he called the 'wild-fire' of some of the more extreme elements of the colonial awakening.[3] He then embarked on a nine-month preaching tour of New England, described by one historian as a 'tour of pacification', dampening down much of the turmoil that his earlier ministry had stirred up.[4]

Finding New England less fertile ground than in the early 1740s, Whitefield travelled south, spending most of the next three years in the southern plantation colonies, especially Georgia where his Bethesda orphanage took up ever increasing amounts of his time and energy. Mired in debt, Bethesda had lost the services of both its manager, James Habersham, and its chaplain, Jonathan Barber.[5] Following the lukewarm reception of his plan to raise subscriptions in support of the orphanage, in spite of the use of Benjamin Franklin's formidable public relations expertise, Whitefield acquired a plantation in the neighbouring colony of South Carolina.[6] 'As for the lawfulness of keeping slaves' he wrote, 'I have no doubt'.[7] So he embarked on an ambitious campaign of recruiting subscriptions from leading planters, eventually raising £300 for the purchase of still greater numbers of slaves.[8] While John Wesley was a bitter opponent of slavery, Whitefield was to emerge during this period in America as one of the most prominent slave holders and a persuasive voice in calls for the legalisation of slavery in the Georgia colony.[9] He was also one of the most committed evangelical defenders of the institution of slavery more generally.[10]

Harris's leadership of English Calvinistic Methodism

In his absence, Whitefield had left the temperamentally unsuitable John Cennick in charge of the London Tabernacle Society and, therefore, of the English Calvinist revival. Cennick's success in leading the Bristol society and establishing Calvinistic Methodist societies in Wiltshire was probably sufficient qualification in Whitefield's eyes for his appointment, but doubts about his suitability seem to have lain behind Whitefield's policy of tying Howel Harris into a more regular pattern of dividing his time roughly equally between England and Wales.[11] Initially this arrangement worked well: Harris, using his powers of diplomacy, managed to persuade the members of the Tabernacle Society to stop bickering.[12] And the Calvinistic Methodists began to make further inroads into the south-west of England with the establishment of a new society at Plymouth in July 1744.[13] This followed Whitefield's unexpected six-week ministry in the city while he was awaiting the arrival of a naval convoy to grant his ship safe passage through the English Channel en route to the American colonies.[14]

However, it did not take long for all the old tensions to bubble to the surface once more, initially surrounding a young preacher and teacher at the Tabernacle school, William Cudworth. Cudworth at one point audaciously claimed he had introduced the real gospel to the Tabernacle Society, a gospel which he thought had not been preached faithfully in London for over a century.[15] He was accused of propagating antinomian views in the Tabernacle, a somewhat vague catch-all charge bandied about with some enthusiasm by the early Methodists.[16] Harris was forced to lead the opposition to Cudworth within the Tabernacle Society, Cennick seemingly reluctant to differ publicly with him.[17] Characteristically, in June 1745 Harris issued Cennick with an ultimatum: 'if Bro Cudworth would stay, I must go out, and if Brother Cennick choses him before me, I believe he will find himself mistaken'.[18] Manoeuvred into a corner, Cennick was forced to take decisive action: Cudworth was expelled from the Tabernacle, but not before taking with him a substantial number of its members to the new Independent chapel which he had established in nearby Spitalfields.[19]

The Cudworth fracas revealed the weaknesses at the heart of English Calvinistic Methodism and the lack of confidence which many had in John Cennick's ability to lead the movement effectively. Cennick's prominence within Calvinistic Methodism was probably based more upon his proven evangelistic gifts and reputation for personal sanctity than upon his flair for organisation or diplomacy.[20] There was also the issue of Cennick's relationship with the Moravians, something that intensified during his leadership of the Tabernacle. Despite their having divided formally from the Moravians in 1740, many Calvinistic Methodists remained fascinated by them. Whether it was their more overtly emotional spirituality, or their preference for living in tightly knit religious communities, the Moravians proved to be the final destination of choice for many who, at one time or another, had been part of either the Wesleyan or Calvinistic Methodist communities. By September 1745, Cennick had repudiated his Calvinist beliefs and adopted universal redemption, much to the concern of some of the more doughty champions of Reformed theology within the Tabernacle Society.[21]

Furthermore, Colin Podmore suggests that Cennick had also begun to resent Whitefield, confiding to James Hutton at one point that he suspected Whitefield had recently left England because he thought that the whole revival was on the verge of imploding.[22] This, together with his suspicion that he had not been Whitefield's first choice as leader of English Calvinistic Methodism, seems to suggest that Cennick had become paranoid and that the pressure of leading the English Calvinists had brought him to the verge of a nervous breakdown.[23] Cennick's decision to leave the Whitefieldians was finally made public on the eve of the English Calvinistic Methodist Association that met at the Tabernacle in early December 1745.[24] His decision seems to have been made easier by his knowledge that Howel Harris was now ready to take his place, but Harris feared that Cennick's decision to quit would see the Tabernacle finally 'torn to pieces'.[25] Cennick left, taking 400 members of the Tabernacle Society with him as well as all of the societies that he had established in Wiltshire; this was a loss which left English Calvinistic Methodism severely depleted, both in terms of numbers and morale. The impact of this secession seemed to cement in place the hostile relations between the Calvinists and the Moravians. Calvinist preachers were prevented from preaching in the Wiltshire societies, the Moravians dismissing them as 'vainly puffed up bitter enemies of Christ'.[26]

Harris was left with little choice but to take on the leadership of the English movement, but he agreed to do so only until Whitefield returned from America or an alternative leader could be found.[27] However, this did not mean that Harris was prepared to relinquish his position in Wales, since to do so would have meant that he would have had to hand over complete control of the Welsh revival to his friend and rival Daniel Rowland. A small band of younger preachers, including James Beaumont, Thomas Adams, James Relly, Andrew Kinsman and Herbert Jenkins, were therefore drafted in and took their turns deputising as leader of the English revival during the short intervals when Harris was back in Wales.[28] This arrangement was far from ideal, and it did not prevent further high profile secessions from the Tabernacle. Both John Syms, who had served as Whitefield's secretary for much of the 1740s, and John Lewis, the printer and bookseller, soon followed Cennick into the welcoming arms of the Moravians.[29]

Despite this, Howel Harris's leadership of the English Calvinistic revival was not a complete failure. Between early 1746 and Whitefield's return to England in July 1748, Harris worked tirelessly to reposition the Calvinist revival and, if not to enthuse it with new life, at least to give it a measure of coherence and stability. For almost eighteen months there was very little contact between Whitefield and his London Calvinistic Methodist friends. Harris wrote to him at regular intervals, but waited in vain for a reply to his lengthy letters outlining many of the problems at the Tabernacle.[30] When Whitefield did eventually respond, he wearily bemoaned the 'miserable divisions . . . amongst my English friends', something that contrasted markedly with his recent successful attempts at smoothing over some of the divisions that his colonial evangelism had caused in the early 1740s.[31] Without being overtly critical of Harris's leadership, he complained: 'I suppose when I come to England, I shall have all to begin again.'[32] Whitefield was, therefore, strongly supportive of Harris's strategy of ameliorating some of the tensions within English Calvinistic Methodism, and also of his attempts to re-engage in constructive dialogue with the Wesley brothers and the Moravians.[33]

Almost immediately following the split between Wesley and Whitefield in 1741, Harris had applied himself to the task of keeping open the lines of communication between the two sides. As early as August 1741 Harris, following a meeting with John Wesley, confessed that he felt 'vast love' to him and seemed genuinely hopeful that the 'L[or]d [would] remove all mountains [between us]'.[34] A couple of weeks later, after another meeting with John Wesley, Harris recorded their resolution to 'forget all that is past to this [September] 10',[35] He naively concluded that the reason for the tensions between them had more to do with simple misunderstanding than with tangible theological issues.[36] Harris worked hard at persuading Whitefield to re-consider his attitude to the Wesley brothers.[37] He had an extended meeting with John Wesley in south Wales in March 1742.[38] After this Harris drew up a discussion paper which outlined the key areas where there was unanimity between the Whitefieldians and the Wesleyans, before highlighting those areas where further discussion was needed to ease outstanding tensions.[39] More substantial results came from a meeting convened by Whitefield in February 1743 and attended by John Wesley and Harris, James Hutton having turned down the invitation on behalf of the Moravians.[40] The occasion was cordial, and the two groups agreed on a number of points concerning their relations with the Church of England and their legal position in the light of increasing levels of persecution.[41]

Following the meeting, Wesley prepared another discussion document in which he outlined the theological areas in which he still differed from the Calvinists. These he reduced to just three: unconditional election, irresistible grace and the final perseverance of the saints. Despite these being fairly substantial points of difference over some key distinctive Calvinist doctrines, Herbert McGonigle has suggested that the concessions Wesley made in this document, particularly his readiness to accept any form of predestination that did not necessitate a belief in an active decree of reprobation, was the nearest he ever got to coming to terms with Calvinistic opinions.[42] In the end relatively little concrete, beyond the restoration of cordial relations between Whitefield, Harris and Wesley, came of these discussions. While the revivalists managed to put their differences to one side to some extent, their followers usually did not have the same capacity for tolerance.

By the time Harris was in charge of the English Calvinist movement the doctrinal differences of the early 1740s had been thoroughly institutionalised, and Harris's mediatorial role became ever more necessary as the different groups tried to navigate around one another. In January 1747 Harris and Wesley met for another summit-style discussion at Bristol, at which they tried to 'remove any hindrances of brotherly love which have been'.[43] Harris brought twelve of the most prominent and trusted leaders of the Calvinist revival with him, and Wesley was accompanied by four of his most faithful preachers.[44] The background of the meeting was the controversy at Neath in south Wales where Wesley had established a society following one of his preaching visits in August 1746.[45] This society was in direct competition with the Welsh Calvinist society that had been organised in the town some years earlier.[46] The two societies had found it almost impossible to coexist peaceably, and there was considerable two-way traffic between them. Harris was determined to extract from Wesley a promise that he would not establish societies in 'any town in Wales where [there] is a society already'.[47] Once this potentially damaging issue was settled, discussions between the two groups broadened out further, and Harris drew up yet another document, this time listing ten points of agreement between them. Both sides resolved that they would no longer compete directly for the same souls, and that whenever they preached for each other they would endeavour to 'stren[gth[en], not . . . weaken, each others hands', in other words that they would steer well clear of contentious topics like free will, predestination and perfection.[48]

The harmony that resulted from this conference did not last long. The problems at Neath that necessitated the meeting in the first place were being played out on an even bigger stage in the south-west of England. Wesley had sent one of his preachers, John Godwin, to

Plymouth; Godwin had vigorously opposed the leader of the recently established Calvinist society there, Herbert Jenkins, with the result that it had become polarised into Calvinist and Wesleyan factions.[49] By early 1747 the society had actually split: the Calvinists continued to meet in Plymouth while the Arminians had established an alternative society at nearby Devonport; both sides barred one another from attending each other's meetings.[50] The tensions in Devon were discussed at a meeting of the revival's leaders at Bristol, and Wesley and Harris were instructed to visit Plymouth to restore order by 'endeavouring to heal the breach there, and to insist on a spirit of love and its fruits among the people'.[51] Harris's diplomatic skills were once more pressed into use. On meeting the Plymouth Calvinists he chided them for their 'evil spirit' and criticised them severely for their attitude towards Wesley, since 'stabbing him is stabbing me'.[52] Harris came under intense pressure from members of the Calvinist society for apparently selling out to Wesley and not defending their interests with sufficient conviction; this obviously unexpected response forced Harris into taking a more aggressive stance against Wesley, whom he accused of sending his brother Charles to Plymouth to exploit the differences in the society.[53] John Wesley tried his best to exonerate his brother of any intentionally provocative behaviour (although his protestations had a hollow ring given that he was not averse to using the same kind of divide and conquer behaviour himself).[54] He then reaffirmed his commitment to abide by the recommendations passed at the Bristol meeting a few months earlier. The two societies were re-established, one at Devonport, with the other in Plymouth now placed under the leadership of a local man, Andrew Kinsman; and both groups agreed not to interfere with one another's affairs or poach members from each other.[55]

For Harris the work of smoothing relations between the Methodist factions was never ending. Even after these important developments, and after Whitefield's return to England in 1748, Harris kept working at maintaining the lines of communication between the various English Methodists. There is no doubt that he and Whitefield were well-intentioned in their desire to repair the damage that had been done by their theological contretemps in the early 1740s. If left to them, then perhaps the truce that they had reached with Wesley in early 1748 might actually have worked; but in practice it proved impossible to implement, since many of their followers never quite shared their leaders' respect for each other. In the end, far from re-establishing good relations, these meetings became almost an admission of failure by the English revivalists; since they had been unable to work closely and harmoniously together, arrangements had to be made to keep them apart. In a sense, despite Harris's wish to see unity among the English revivals restored, it was under his period of interim leadership that the inevitability of multiple Methodisms became fully apparent. Harris had taken over the leadership of the English Calvinistic Methodist movement in the midst of a crisis following the secession of John Cennick. To his credit he had steered the movement through some challenging times and had brought a measure of stability to the fractious Tabernacle Society. The irony of his leadership was that at the very time that Harris's diplomatic skills were beginning to bear tangible fruit in London, the more combative and angular sides of his personality were placing an unbearable strain on the revival in Wales.

The deterioration of relations in Wales

The division of Harris's time between England and Wales during the second half of the 1740s, and the heavy demands which the Tabernacle Society made upon his energies, meant that his involvement in the Welsh revival suffered to some extent. In a sense this did not have an enormous day-to-day impact since the organisational structure that had been set in place by early 1743 made ample provision for Harris's absences, and there were many other gifted leaders to step into his shoes. What his absences did ensure was that the balance of power within Welsh Methodism began to shift very definitely away from Harris and towards Daniel Rowland. The south-west of Wales had the greatest number of societies, the strongest leadership structure and was served by some of the best qualified of the Welsh revivalists. Howell Davies had superintended the revival in Pembrokeshire since its beginning.[56] And from 1743 Daniel Rowland had been assisted by William Williams, who despite owing his conversion to Harris, became ever more closely associated with Rowland and the revival at Llangeitho.[57] In many respects, much that has been written on the development of Methodism in Wales during the mid- and later 1740s has been overshadowed by the division between Harris and Rowland which finally became public in 1750.[58] While the causes for the expulsion of Harris had roots that probably stretched back to the birth of the revival itself, the mid-1740s were actually years characterised by further steady growth, healthy debate and a number of important new initiatives.

By 1750 there were over 420 Calvinistic Methodist societies in Wales, the overwhelming majority in the south and west.[59] On the reckoning that each society had between twenty and twenty-five souls, the Methodist movement could have numbered between ten and twelve thousand fully committed members, a not insignificant number given the difficulties which earlier Protestant groups had encountered in Wales.[60] This was a growth facilitated by the efficiency of the organisational structure that had been finally agreed upon at Watford in January 1743. The system of monthly and quarterly associations organised on a county basis gave ample opportunity for new leaders to be identified and to find a niche to exercise their gifts, as new waves of converts regularly brought new faces into the movement. This made it easy for the expansion of the movement into virgin areas through the appointment of exhorters to individual societies, and superintendents to manage smaller groups of them. The painstaking work of setting up this structure was bearing considerable fruit by 1743, and there was evidence of further renewal. In March of that year, for example, Harris informed Whitefield that 'every where there is a reviving' in Wales, 'the Holy Spirit is uncommonly powerful' in some of the private societies and fresh 'doors are opening daily' for the gospel.[61] Measuring the extent of the revival is a difficult and imprecise science. It is likely that the number of society members represents merely the tip of a Methodistic iceberg since there were inevitably a much greater number of people influenced by the preaching of the revivalists, but who, rather than joining a society, committed themselves afresh to worshipping in their local parish church or Dissenting meeting house. It was in this way that the evangelical impulse tended to spill over from Methodism into many of the other Protestant groups in Wales and elsewhere, giving some grounds for concluding that the mid-eighteenth-century revivals amounted to a Great Awakening.[62]

The link between England and Wales was also flourishing during these years. Always a reliable barometer of the ebbing and flowing of the revival, the Calvinistic Methodist magazine, by this point re-branded with the rather cumbersome title *An Account of the Most Remarkable Particulars Relating to the Present Progress of the Gospel*, was packed with letters from Wales throughout 1743, and its circulation figures in Wales remained healthy right up until its final issue rolled from the press in 1748.[63] These were also months which saw the proliferation of other forms of evangelical literature. Whitefield's *Journals* remained consistently strong sellers, and the writings of Jonathan Edwards began to appear in English editions.[64] These unexpurgated editions were distinct from works produced by John Wesley.[65] They were advertised in the pages of the Calvinistic Methodist magazine and circulated among interested Methodists in Wales.[66] Efforts were also made to translate other evangelical books into Welsh; at the suggestion of Daniel Rowland, Ralph Erskine's two volumes of sermons, *Law-Death Gospel-Life* (1724) appeared in Welsh in 1743.[67] It was followed by a translation of his brother Ebenezer Erskine's sermon, *Christ in the Believer's Arms* (1726) soon after.[68] At this critical formative stage Welsh Methodism lacked the strength and perhaps sophistication to produce its own indigenous literature, and so the movement was moulded by literature produced originally in the English language. It was not until the 1760s that an indigenous theological literature began to flow from the pen of William Williams.

A steady stream of English revivalists continued to cross the border on preaching excursions into Wales as well. Whitefield was a less frequent visitor by this time, largely because of his extended absences in America, but John and Charles Wesley visited at regular intervals, and Charles's marriage to Sarah Gwynne of Garth in 1748 made the link still stronger.[69] The Moravians gained a small foothold in Wales with societies at Carmarthen and Laugharne, under the leadership of a larger parent society at Haverfordwest.[70] Howel Harris also made a concerted attempt to enthuse his Welsh brethren with the vision for the international Concert for Prayer. The brainchild of the Scottish evangelical James Erskine, and drawing in prominent colonial ministers, the project was designed to facilitate more intense and concerted prayer for fresh waves of revival throughout the North Atlantic region. Erskine was in close correspondence with Jonathan Edwards whose manifesto, *A Humble Attempt to Promote Explicit Agreement and Visible Union of God's People in Extraordinary Prayer* (1747), was heavily publicised by Harris.[71] In 1745 the Welsh Methodists recommended that a regular day of prayer should be set aside 'on account of the late work in England, Scotland, Wales & America, both to praise God for it & intercede & pray for it[s] furtherance & to be humbled for the sin that attended it'.[72] For a while it looked as though Erskine's network would lead to an impressive coming together of the main strands of the revival, recapturing the heady days of the late 1730s, but the project did not fire the imagination of enough people. It proved to be one of the last realistic opportunities for healing the rifts that had done so much to bring the revival into disrepute in the early 1740s.

In many regards the organisational structure that the Calvinistic Methodists finally set on a firm footing in January 1743 made the policy of staying within the Church of England, while jealously guarding their own separate identity and maintaining open relations with the Dissenters, increasingly difficult to sustain. Relations with the Church of England were at their most strained during the crisis surrounding the Jacobite rising in 1745, when there was a nagging suspicion amongst some that the secretive Methodist societies might be harbouring Jacobite sympathisers.[73] To combat this, Harris led the Methodists in a concerted campaign to reassert their loyalty to both the king and the Protestant religion as enshrined in the Established Church. This amounted to the holding of special days of prayer on behalf of the nation and flooding the Methodist correspondence network and the Calvinistic Methodist magazine with letters full of fervent loyalist sentiments. Harris's comments in a letter to James Beaumont in February 1744 were typical:

> We are like to be called to the field of blood soon . . . the French fleet now lay at anchor in one of our ports being come over with a firm resolution to dethrone his majesty & set the Pretenders son on the throne of England & consequently not only take away all toleration & liberty of Protestants but establish Popery again . . . Next Monday we have settled for fasting and prayer for the K[in]g & nation we all hold it our duty to preach loyalty to the King set over us by the L[or]d & as he is a Protestant & tolerates the true religion & as he is laid deeply on our hearts too.[74]

This proved to be a highly effective means of 'turning the hearts of many to the King', and staving off the most potentially damaging anti-Methodist propaganda.[75] Relations with the Dissenters, though, proved much more problematic, since the ranks of the Nonconformists remained a powerful draw for many of those who proved unwilling or unable to live with the compromises with the Established Church inherent in Methodist ecclesiology. The decisive break with the Dissenters came at a Welsh Methodist Association at Caeo in Carmarthenshire in early April 1745 at which Harris was forced into declaring publicly against them, following the tentative request of five Glamorgan exhorters for ordination.[76] The discussions that this meeting stimulated saw a reiteration of the non-secessionist policy that had been favoured by Harris and Daniel Rowland from the beginning: the Methodist movement should avoid actions that would lead to secession from the Church of England. The repeated restating of this position tended to defuse the issue.

It was not so much that the issue was resolved to everyone's satisfaction, but that there was a series of much more pressing problems afflicting the Welsh Methodist movement by this stage. The strains that had been present in the relationship between Harris and Daniel Rowland had, by the mid-1740s, begun to slip out of control. The underlying reason was undoubtedly Harris's sense of inferiority as a result of his unordained status. Although there is no evidence to suggest that Rowland thought Harris's lack of Anglican ordination was problematic, Harris regularly felt the need to pull rank on his contemporaries by reminding them that he had been 'the first of all the Brethren'.[77] Earlier disagreements had often produced heated arguments, but permanent divisions were usually avoided when Harris and Rowland stepped back and calmly considered the wider implications of their bickering for the Welsh movement as a whole. But from about 1744 onwards a new tone entered their relationship, the result, Geraint Tudur has argued, of the increasing influence of the Moravians on Harris's theological views.[78] The rapidly deteriorating relationship between Harris and Rowland, and the ill feeling that Harris's attempts to enforce discipline within the societies created, together with simmering disquiet over Harris's theology, led to an almost five-year-long power struggle for control of the Welsh revival.

Harris's new theological emphases coincided with the increasing periods he was spending in London and were a consequence of his determination to spend as much time as possible with the other factions of the revival in an effort to build bridges between them. During late 1744, infatuated by the spirituality of the Moravians, particularly their emphasis on the virtues of the blood of Christ, Harris came to the conclusion that his own weakness and powerlessness was a direct consequence of his neglect of this theme.[79] After attending a Moravian Letter Day he wrote: 'Hearing all these letters about the experience of the blood of Christ, how that it is all, I saw them gone before me far in faith and strength and the divine life.'[80] The following day he resolved that he would 'love all that preach this blood alike of all sects and countries'.[81] When he returned to Wales, he began to give the blood of Christ a much more prominent place in his sermons, a difference that did not for long go unnoticed or unchallenged. In May 1746 some of the members of Tabernacle Society in London had walked out halfway through one of Harris's sermons, citing his use of Moravian-sounding language on the blood of Christ.[82] Rowland had expressed gentle concern about Harris's theological language as early as February 1745.[83] However, it was not until the following year that the full extent of Rowland's concerns became public knowledge. At an association meeting at Trefeca in June, Rowland openly questioned Harris's orthodoxy, by accusing him of using ambiguous statements about the blood of Christ and of being an antinomian.[84] The second accusation had added bite because of the case of the exhorter James Beaumont, who by this time was also suspected of holding a heady cocktail of antinomian and Moravian beliefs. Criticising Beaumont's views on the grounds of antinomianism was a neat cover for criticising the views of the Moravians as well, and when this agenda became apparent to Harris he sprang to Beaumont's defence.[85] But, when Harris tried to defend himself by issuing a strongly worded denial of the charge that he believed that God had suffered on the Cross, the depth of suspicion was too great, and no resolution or reconciliation was reached.[86]

By October the situation had calmed somewhat, and Rowland extended the right hand of fellowship to Harris once again, but on the condition that he renounce any sympathy for Moravian teachings. Harris agreed and in his diary wrote:

> Many of the brethren, I find, despise me more and more on my infirmities and I am enabled to commit it all to God and to see to keep me in my place and to suit me with all grace and gifts.[87]

Yet this was only a temporary truce. Throughout 1747 Harris's old paranoia concerning his role in the revival re-emerged, and his language and actions again became belligerent and aggressive. He resorted once more to repeated claims about his own supremacy in Wales and sought to shore up his position by purging many of those societies under his control of members he thought lukewarm or lacking in spiritual discernment. In effect, these were those who disagreed with him or did not give him the respect he felt he deserved. Unsurprisingly, many in Wales found it increasingly difficult to work with him, and complaints about his behaviour began to mount once more. Harris continued largely oblivious, rejecting all criticism and becoming more and more isolated as he resorted to the unreasonable claim that since God had revealed new theological emphases to him directly there was nothing anybody could do to change his mind. Rowland and Whitefield, he later claimed, were carnal Christians, lacking his mature and more 'spiritual' understanding of some of the deeper mysteries of the faith.[88]

It is hard to avoid the conclusion that by the late 1740s Harris was under acute emotional and psychological pressure. As early as 1744 he had complained about being 'decayed in person and though but 30 years of age, yet look old and decaying, and have done nothing comparatively for the Lord'.[89] He had been engaged in evangelistic work for almost ten years, travelled extensively and preached on most days, often on more than one occasion. As well as leading the Welsh revival for much of the 1740s he had shouldered the onerous burden of the leadership of the English Calvinistic revival as well, something that had undoubtedly brought him to the verge of complete breakdown.[90] Always irascible, over-sensitive and prickly, these facets of Harris's personality were amplified to such an extent by the later 1740s that they clouded his judgement and seriously hampered his ability to continue to contribute positively to the revival movement.

Whitefield relinquishes leadership, and the loss of Harris

It was into a Calvinistic Methodist movement straining under these many pressures that Whitefield stepped on his return from the American colonies in July 1748. Harris was in London to meet him, and everyone expected Whitefield to pick up the reins of leadership and breathe new life into the movement once more, much as he had done in 1741. However, Whitefield had not been persuaded to return to England by Harris, but by the countess of Huntingdon who had drawn him back with the tantalising offer of a new role as her personal chaplain.[91] By this point, the countess had been inviting select individuals from among the great and the good of the land to listen to her favourite preachers. Howel Harris, for example, had been supplied with some new clothes, a wig and plenty of powder to put on it in order to make him presentable enough to preach at her salon services from 1746.[92] These occasions were certainly intended to provide gilt-edged evangelistic opportunities, but they were equally about harnessing the support of influential members of the political elite and the royal court.

This new sphere of influence had forced Whitefield to distance himself from some of the excesses of his youth. He set about revising his *Journals*, removing some of the parts where his precocious egoism had led him into harsh and uncharitable judgements.[93] However, the effect of this new version was not as significant as it might have been as it did not actually reach the printers until 1756.[94] But Whitefield's most pressing problem was the Tabernacle Society, which he now seems to have regarded as an impediment to the success of his new ministry. He adopted a servile, even sycophantic attitude to the countess,[95] which was mirrored by his criticism of the 'miserable extravagances' and 'real madness and ranticism' of his old converts in the Tabernacle Society.[96] In a letter to John Wesley in September 1748 he claimed that he had no intention of forming new societies in England and reigniting the competition for souls that had brought them into conflict earlier in the decade; but neither did he propose to hand over his converts to Wesley in a magnanimous gesture of inter-revival camaraderie, since, he maintained, 'we differ in principle more than I thought, and I believe we are upon two different plans'.[97]

Whitefield, therefore, began to cast around for somebody to take on the leadership of the Tabernacle Society on a permanent basis. Howel Harris had been doing this by default following the secession of Whitefield's preferred candidate, John Cennick, at the end of 1745; but the poor state in which he found the society, rumours about developments in Harris's theological convictions and news about tensions in Wales made Whitefield reluctant to appoint Harris immediately. He complained to John Wesley about his 'lack of proper assistants to take care' of his societies, probably a veiled reference to Harris, but in the end the lack of other suitable candidates forced him into persuading Harris to take on the role.[98] He was certainly the person of choice of the members of the Tabernacle Society itself.[99] However, Harris, possibly hurt at the reluctance with which Whitefield had approached him in the first place, began to be evasive and refused to commit himself to the role. This stalemate continued through much of 1749, and Whitefield turned instead to two of the leading lay leaders at the Tabernacle, James Relly and Thomas Adams. This move goaded Harris into action: he petulantly protested that he would with-draw from the English work entirely if he was expected to share the leadership with these more junior figures. He finally accepted the leader-ship on the basis that Relly and Adams as his assistants would step in only when he was unavoidably detained in Wales.[100] Whitefield's fear that the Tabernacle would close in less than two years, something for which Harris would have had to bear sole responsibility, may well have weighed heavily upon Harris's final decision.[101]

This new phase of Harris's leadership of the Tabernacle was not without its achievements. He quickly returned to one of his favourite projects: brokering a union between the Calvinists and the Wesleyans and, despite inauspicious circumstances, he still harboured hopes that he could 'lay a solid foundation for a lasting union'.[102] He persuaded Whitefield to attend a meeting at Bristol in August 1749 where John Wesley also promised to be present. Much to Harris's relief it turned out to be a friendly gathering, and he bullishly claimed that he felt 'nearer union in spirit in singing a hymn than ever before'.[103] Both sides reaffirmed their commitment to the Established Church, to avoid controversial subjects in their sermons and 'to come together to prevent the people's saying of either side we have changed our opinions'.[104] But in the end, once again, little positive emerged from the meeting; Harris blamed Whitefield for a lack of vision, but the real reason lay much closer to home.[105] By this point Harris had squandered any remaining trust in his leadership because of his friendship with Mrs Sidney Griffith, a married woman from Cefnamwlch in Caernarfon-shire, who had been taken in by Harris and his wife in 1749 after she had been physically abused by her husband and thrown out of the family home.

The nature of Harris's relationship with the enigmatic Mrs Griffith has aroused much prurient interest and been much debated. There is little doubt that Harris became infatuated with her very soon after first setting eyes on her, and plenty of evidence that Harris was, in Geraint Tudur's words, torn between his 'physical lust and spiritual duty'.[106] However, whether the relationship was actually adulterous is impossible to tell at this distance.[107] Harris's language at times certainly suggests adultery, especially when he began confiding in his diary that he 'felt a superior love to Mrs Griffith over all, even Anne'.[108] But it is highly probable that he meant that his spiritual love for Mrs Griffith was superior to the merely romantic love he felt for his wife.[109] Whatever the nature of his relationship with Mrs Griffith, Harris threw overboard all decorum and discretion. Nonetheless, it was not the whispers of possible immorality that led Rowland and Whitefield to take against Mrs Griffith so strongly, but the way in which Harris invested her with special prophetic gifts.[110] He began to think that she was a channel through which God communicated directly with him.[111] Harris started taking Mrs Griffith with him on some of his preaching tours and insisted that she be allowed to attend meetings at which the leaders discussed the management of the revival. Her charismatic gifts and insights, he argued, were to be given special weight in their deliberations. Yet in practice these gifts were not used to bring clarity to the discussions of the revivalists or to inject new life into the movement, but to shore up Harris's waning authority. For Rowland and Whitefield, Harris's dalliance with Mrs Griffith proved to be the final straw and the catalyst for his dismissal from the front line of the revival.

Whitefield and the London Calvinistic Methodists were the first to take action against Harris, and Whitefield's reservations about his ability to lead the Tabernacle Society soon became apparent to Harris himself. He began to criticise Whitefield for his strong line against the Moravians, and quickly came to the conclusion that Whitefield had asked him to become leader of the English Calvinists more out of necessity than choice.[112] His lack of support in London he laid squarely at the door of Whitefield himself; 'I believe Mr Whitefield', he wrote, 'thinks me selfish, and is not from his heart for my taking the care' of the Tabernacle Society.[113] Whitefield, for his part, could no longer tolerate Harris's belligerence. Following a gathering of the English Calvinists in which Harris and Whitefield publicly disagreed,

Harris withdrew from the meeting. Whitefield, it seems, had been influenced by some Dissenting friends who had counselled him that if he was serious in his intention of freeing his societies from the charge of 'enthusiasm' he would have to address the problems of Harris's leadership, the biggest issue being his reliance on the prophetess Mrs Sidney Griffith.[114]

When Harris arrived in London in December 1749 for what was to be the final time in his capacity as leader of the English Calvinistic Methodists, he was accompanied by his wife and Mrs Griffith. Whitefield's wife, Elizabeth, refused to allow Harris and his entourage the use of his usual rooms at the Tabernacle, and Whitefield himself was reluctant to meet him.[115] Harris protested at being left 'to spend my time idle after coming so far'.[116] His criticisms of Whitefield became more virulent, and Harris lashed out at Elizabeth for having undue influence over her husband. This was, of course, murky territory, since Harris had relinquished her to Whitefield in 1741. Harris had earlier chastised her for

> pride in not submitting to Mr Whitefield. My fears about her being
> prejudiced against the Moravians, and Mr Whitefield, and that she is
> to meddle no more with us and our affairs than to give her judgement
> about a thing and then leave it, not retain somewhat in her mind and
> so bring it out continually.[117]

Whitefield took conclusive action on the first day of 1750, turning Harris out of the English Calvinistic movement.[118] A few days later Harris gave up his rooms at the Tabernacle and finally parted company with Whitefield, bringing to an end a relationship that had proven remarkably fruitful for well over a decade. He stayed in London for a further three weeks but quickly discovered that wherever he went the 'rage' against him was 'amazing' on account of being 'suspected as a Moravian, my preaching Christ crucified, my catholic love to Mr Wesley, my standing ground for the authority given me and judged proud'.[119] No mention, however, was made of his relationship with Mrs Griffith: probably the overriding reason why Whitefield finally expelled him.

Harris returned to Wales, no doubt fearing that Daniel Rowland would now have the pretext for taking decisive action against him.

He tried to rally his supporters for a couple of months but quickly realised that many now treated him with suspicion, if not outright disdain. Harris and Rowland met at an association in Llanidloes in May, but Harris refused to accept Rowland's authority, which by this stage was bolstered by the support of the vast majority of the Welsh societies.[120] The Llanidloes meeting proved to be the final time Harris and Rowland met in this way for over a decade. The following month, in Harris's absence, the split was finalised at Llantrisant: Harris was expelled for holding some 'half-dozen heretical doctrines', but again little direct reference was made to the Griffith affair.[121] The members of the Methodist communities in Wales were now presented with the stark choice of whom they should follow. Harris did not withdraw immediately; he continued to travel in a slightly desperate attempt to shore up his support, particularly in south-east Wales, but to little avail. That the overwhelming majority of the Welsh Methodists sided with Daniel Rowland in 1750 is compelling evidence of Harris's isolation by this point and the extent to which his personal integrity lay in tatters.

These events really marked the end of an era in the development of Calvinistic Methodism in England and Wales. The previous fifteen years had seen the movement born in the heady atmosphere of international religious revivals, and for a while it looked as though Calvinistic Methodism would be a realistic alternative both to the Wesleyan expression of Methodism and to Moravianism. During these years the relationship between the English and Welsh wings of the movement had been substantial and multilayered, culminating in the establishment of a joint organisational and leadership structure. But with the loss of Howel Harris and the withdrawal of Whitefield from the day-to-day running of the English side of the movement that relationship was forced to evolve in new directions.

Notes

1 See Thomas S. Kidd, *The Great Awakening: The Roots of Evangelical Christianity in Colonial America* (New Haven, CT: Yale University Press, 2007), pp. 168–73.

2 Thomas Clap, *A Letter from the Reverend Mr Clap, Rector of Yale College in New Haven, to the Rev. Mr. Edwards of North-Hampton* (Boston: T. Fleet, 1745), p. 3.

3 George Whitefield, *A Letter to the Reverend the President, and Professors, Tutors, and Hebrew Instructor of Harvard-College in Cambridge* (Boston: T. Fleet, 1745), in John Gillies (ed.), *The Works of the Reverend George Whitefield* (6 vols, London: Edward and Charles Dilly, 1771–2), IV, p. 243.

4 Charles Hartshorn Maxson, *The Great Awakening in the Middle Colonies* (Chicago: University of Chicago Press, 1920), quoted in Arnold A. Dallimore, *George Whitefield: The Life and Times of the Great Evangelist of the 18th Century Revival* (2 vols, London and Edinburgh: Banner of Truth Trust, 1970 and 1980), II, p. 192.

5 Frank Lambert, *James Habersham: Loyalty, Politics, and Commerce in Colonial Georgia* (Athens, GA: University of Georgia Press, 2005), chapter 2.

6 Frank Lambert, 'Subscribing for profits and piety: the friendship of Benjamin Franklin and George Whitefield', *The William and Mary Quarterly*, 50, 3 (July 1993), 547–8.

7 George Whitefield to [Johann Martin] B[olzius], 22 March 1751, in Gillies (ed.), *The Works of the Reverend George Whitefield*, II, p. 404.

8 Boyd Stanley Schlenther, 'George Whitefield', in *Oxford Dictionary of National Biography* (Oxford: Oxford University Press, 2004).

9 Harold E. Davis, *The Fledgling Province: Social and Cultural Life in Colonial Georgia, 1733–1776* (Chapel Hill, NC: University of North Carolina Press, 1976), pp. 125–6.

10 See Stephen J. Stein, 'George Whitefield and slavery: some new evidence', *Church History*, 42, 2 (June 1973), 243–56.

11 NLW CMA Trevecka 2945 Records of Associations, I, p. 14.

12 'From Bro Howel Harris in Wales to the Society at the Tabernacle', 29 June 1745, in John Lewis (ed.), *The Christian History*, 7, 4 (1746), 15.

13 C. E. Welch, 'Andrew Kinsman's churches at Plymouth', *Report and Transactions of the Devonshire Association for the Advancement of Science, Literature and Art*, 97 (1965), 213.

14 George Whitefield to Mr S., 21 July 1744, in Gillies (ed.), *The Works of the Reverend George Whitefield*, II, pp. 61–2.

[15] NLW Trevecka Letter 1427, Elizabeth Paul to Howel Harris, 11 March 1745.

[16] Herbert Boyd McGonigle, *Sufficient Saving Grace: John Wesley's Evangelical Arminianism* (Carlisle: Paternoster, 2001), pp. 160ff.

[17] Tom Beynon (ed.), *Howell Harris's Visits to London* (Aberystwyth: The Cambrian News Press, 1966), p. 70.

[18] Ibid., p. 71.

[19] John A. Vickers, *Dictionary of Methodism in Britain and Ireland* (Peterborough: Epworth Press, 2000), p. 84; J. C. Whitebrook, 'Wesley and William Cudworth', *Proceedings of the Wesley Historical Society*, 12 (1919), 34–6. For Cudworth's subsequent trajectory, see Frank Baker, *John Wesley and the Church of England* (Peterborough: Epworth Press, 1970), p. 213; Gareth Lloyd, *Charles Wesley and the Struggle for Methodist Identity* (Oxford: Oxford University Press, 2007), pp. 167–8.

[20] Peter Gentry and Paul Taylor, *Bold as a Lion: The Life of John Cennick (1718–1755), Moravian Evangelist* (Leicester: Life Publications, 2007), p. 46.

[21] Colin J. Podmore, *The Moravian Church in England, 1728–1760* (Oxford: Oxford University Press, 1998), p. 91.

[22] Ibid.

[23] Ibid.

[24] NLW CMA 2946 Records of Associations, II, p. 9.

[25] NLW Howel Harris's Diary, 25 November 1745.

[26] NLW Trevecka Letter 1437[b], James Hutton to the Calvinistic Methodist Association [March 1746].

[27] NLW Howel Harris's Diary, 4 December 1745.

[28] Geraint Tudur, '"Like a right arm and a pillar": the story of James Beaumont', in Robert Pope (ed.), *Honouring the Past and Shaping the Future: Religious and Biblical Studies in Wales: Essays in Honour of Gareth Lloyd Jones* (Leominster: Gracewing Press, 2003), pp 133–58. For Thomas Adams, see C. E. Watson, 'Whitefield and Congregationalism', *Transactions of the Congregational Historical Society*, 8, 4 (1922), 172–80, and 5 (1922), 227–45; G. F. Nuttall, 'Rowland Hill and the Rodborough Connexion, 1771–1833', *Transactions of the Congregational Historical Society*, 21, 3 (1972), 69–73. For the Relly family, see Gomer M. Roberts, 'The Moravians, John Relly and his people', *JHSPCW*, 38, 1 (March 1953), 2–7. For Andrew Kinsman, see Welch, 'Andrew Kinsman's churches at Plymouth', 212–13, 225–36. For Herbert Jenkins, see CMA 2946, Records of Associations, II, pp. 13, 16; Garfield H. Hughes, 'Herbert Jenkins', *JHSPCW*, 32 (1947), 1–8; Geraint Tudur, *Howell Harris: From Conversion to*

Separation, 1735–1750 (Cardiff: University of Wales Press, 2000), pp. 89–90.

29 NLW Trevecka Letter 1279, Howel Harris to George Whitefield, 11 January 1745; Podmore, *The Moravian Church in England, 1738–1760*, p. 90. Jones, 'John Lewis and the promotion of the international evangelical revival, 1735–56' in Dyfed Wyn Roberts (ed.), *Revival, Renewal and the Holy Spirit* (Milton Keynes: Paternoster, 2009), pp. 24–5.

30 NLW Trevecka Letter 1372, Howel Harris to George Whitefield, 8 November 1745; Trevecka Letter 1516, Howel Harris to George Whitefield, 30 August 1746; Trevecka Letter 1522, Howel Harris to George Whitefield, 8 September 1746.

31 NLW Trevecka Letter 1595, George Whitefield to Howel Harris, December 1746.

32 NLW Trevecka Letter 1568, George Whitefield to Howel Harris, 16 November 1746.

33 NLW Trevecka Letter 1659, George Whitefield to Howel Harris, 30 May 1747.

34 NLW Howel Harris's Diary, 30 August 1741.

35 Ibid., 10 September 1741.

36 NLW Trevecka Letter 394, Howel Harris to Samuel Blackden, 14 October 1741.

37 NLW Trevecka Letter 388, Howel Harris to George Whitefield, 1 October 1741; Trevecka Letter 3329, Howel Harris to George Whitefield, October 1741; Trevecka Letter 638, Howel Harris to George Whitefield, 11 September 1742.

38 NLW Howel Harris's Diary, 3–11 March 1742; A. H. Williams (ed.), *John Wesley in Wales, 1739–1790* (Cardiff: University of Wales Press, 1971), pp. 13–15.

39 NLW Howel Harris's Diary, 'The sheet reciting points of agreement and difference between Mr Harris (and Mr Whitefield and others) and Mr John Wesley, 8 March 1742'; Tom Beynon (ed.), 'Extracts from the diaries of Howell Harris', *Bathafarn: the Journal of the Historical Society of the Methodist Church in Wales*, 6 (1951), 54–7.

40 Podmore, *The Moravian Church in England, 1728–1760*, p. 78.

41 Beynon (ed.), *Howell Harris: Reformer and Soldier (1714–1773)* (Caernarvon: The Calvinistic Methodist Bookroom, 1958), pp. 48–9.

42 McGonigle, *Sufficient Saving Grace*, pp. 153–69.

43 NLW CMA Trevecka 2946 Records of Associations, II, p. 20.

44 NLW Howel Harris's Diary, 22 January 1747.

[45] W. Reginald Ward and Richard P. Heitzenrater (eds), *The Works of John Wesley*, vol. 20, *Journal and Diaries II (1743–54)*, (Nashville, TN: Abingdon Press, 1991), p. 130.

[46] Gomer Morgan Roberts, 'Calvinistic Methodism in Glamorgan, 1737–1773', in Glanmor Williams (ed.), *Glamorgan County History*, vol. 4, *Early Modern Glamorgan: From the Acts of Union to the Industrial Revolution* (Cardiff: Glamorgan County History Trust, 1974), pp. 506–8, 531.

[47] NLW CMA Trevecka 2946 Records of Associations, II, pp. 21–2.

[48] Ibid., p. 22.

[49] Welch, 'Andrew Kinsman's churches at Plymouth', 218–20.

[50] NLW Trevecka Letter 1596, John Stevens to Howel Harris, 3 January 1747.

[51] NLW CMA Trevecka 2964 Records of Associations, II, p. 22.

[52] NLW Howel Harris's Diary, 10 February 1747; NLW Howel Harris's Diary, 14 February 1747.

[53] NLW Trevecka Letter 1614, Howel Harris to John Wesley, 14 February 1747.

[54] NLW Trevecka Letter 1621, John Wesley to Howel Harris, 3 March 1747.

[55] Beynon (ed.), *Howell Harris's Visits to London*, p. 125.

[56] Rhidian Griffiths, 'Howel Davies: Apostol Sir Benfro', *JHSPCW*, 11 (1987), 2–14; Derec Llwyd Morgan, 'Howell Davies (1717?–1770)', in *Oxford Dictionary of National Biography* (2004). Much detail on Davies's life and ministry can be found in Tom Beynon (ed.), *Howell Harris's Visits to Pembrokeshire (1739–1752)* (Aberystwyth: The Cambrian News Press, 1966).

[57] 'At the Association held at Waterford, Ap. 6 & 7 1743 when the Revd Mr Whitefield was chose Moderator', NLW CMA Trevecka 2945 Record of Associations, I, p. 13.

[58] See, for example, Eifion Evans, *Howell Harris, Evangelist (1714–1773)* (Cardiff: University of Wales Press, 1974), chapter 6; William Jacob, 'Methodism in Wales', in Sir Glanmor Williams, William Jacob, Nigel Yates and Frances Knight, *The Welsh Church: From Reformation to Disestablishment, 1603–1920* (Cardiff: University of Wales Press, 2007), pp. 178–9.

[59] Eryn Mant White, '"The world, the flesh, and the devil" and the early Methodist societies in south-west Wales', *Transactions of the Honourable Society of Cymmrodorion*, 3 (1996), 60.

[60] David Ceri Jones, '"A glorious morn"?: Methodism and the rise of evangelicalism in Wales, 1735–62', in Mark Smith (ed.), *British*

Evangelical Identities Past and Present, vol. 1, *Aspects of the History and Sociology of Evangelicalism in Britain and Ireland* (Milton Keynes: Paternoster, 2008), pp. 110–11.

61 'The Copy of a letter from Bro Howel Harris, in Carmarthenshire, to the Rev Mr Whitefield in London, 1 March 1743', in John Lewis (ed.), *An Account of the Most Remarkable Particulars Relating to the Present Progress of the Gospel*, 3, 1 (1743), 23–9.

62 Michael Watts, *The Dissenters: From the Reformation to the French Revolution* (Oxford: Clarendon Press, 1978), p. 440.

63 NLW CMA Trevecka 2946 Records of Associations, II, 6 July 1747, pp. 38–9; Frank Lambert, *'Pedlar in Divinity': George Whitefield and the Transatlantic Revivals, 1737–1770* (Princeton, NJ: Princeton University Press, 1994), p. 70.

64 NLW Trevecka Letter 1035, John Syms to Howel Harris, 5 November 1743.

65 Isabel Rivers, *Reason, Grace, and Sentiment: A Study of the Language of Religion and Ethics in England, 1660–1780*, vol. 1, *Whichcote to Wesley* (Cambridge: Cambridge University Press, 1991), p. 218; Isabel Rivers, 'John Wesley as editor and publisher', in Randy L. Maddox and Jason E. Vickers (eds), *The Cambridge Companion to John Wesley* (Cambridge: Cambridge University Press, 2010), pp. 144–59.

66 John Lewis (ed.), *The Weekly History*, 53 (10 April 1742), 4; NLW Trevecka Letter 1381, William Williams to Howel Harris, 7 December 1745; Trevecka Letter 1847, Thomas Bowen to Howel Harris, 30 January 1749.

67 Ralph Erskine, *Traethawd am Farw i'r Ddeddf, a Byw i Dduw* (trans. John Morgan), (Bristol: Felix Farley, 1743).

68 Ebenezer Erskine a Ralph Erskine, *Crist ym Mreichiau'r Credadyn: Wedi Ei Osod Allan Mewn Pregeth ar Luc. ii, 28* (Carmarthen: John Ross, 1744). For the significance of the Erskines in Wales, see Derec Llwyd Morgan, *The Great Awakening in Wales* (Peterborough: Epworth Press, 1988), passim.

69 Lloyd, *Charles Wesley and the Struggle for Methodist Identity*, pp. 90–7.

70 R. T. Jenkins, *The Moravian Brethren in North Wales* (London: The Honourable Society of Cymmrodorion, 1938), pp. 22–4, 33–4, 45.

71 Jonathan Edwards to a correspondent in Scotland, November 1745, in George S. Claghorn (ed.), *The Works of Jonathan Edwards*, vol. 16, *Letters and Personal Writings* (New Haven, CT: Yale University Press, 1998), pp. 179–97; NLW Trevecka Letter 1305, James Erskine to Howel Harris, 19 March 1745.

72 NLW CMA Trevecka 2945 Records of Associations, I, p. 145.

73 John Walsh, 'Methodism and the mob in the eighteenth century', in G. J. Cuming and Derek Baker (eds), *Popular Belief and Practice, Studies in Church History*, 8 (Cambridge: Cambridge University Press, 1972), pp. 218–19; 226–7; David Hempton, *Methodism and Politics in British Society, 1750–1850* (London: Hutchinson Education, 1984), pp. 32–3.

74 NLW Trevecka Letter 1118, Howel Harris to James Beaumont, 18 February 1744.

75 'From Howel Harris at Trevecca, near the Hay, in Breconshire, south Wales to Mr Thomas Adams, at the Tabernacle House, near Moorfields, London', in John Lewis (ed.), *The Christian History* (1747), 21–3.

76 Tudur, *Howell Harris*, pp. 112–16.

77 NLW Howel Harris's Diary, 20 January 1747.

78 Tudur, *Howell Harris*, p. 160.

79 The emphasis on the virtues of the blood of Christ was closely related to the teaching known as patripassianism. It involved confusion over the different functions of the three persons of the Trinity. Literally, the term means the suffering of the Father, and it is usually used in the case of individuals who claim that it was God the Father, the first person in the Trinity, who suffered and died on the cross as well as God the son, the second person of the Trinity. F. L. Cross and E. A. Livingstone (eds), *The Oxford Dictionary of the Christian Church* (Oxford: Oxford University Press, 1983), pp. 1233, 1434.

80 NLW Howel Harris's Diary, 3 December 1744.

81 Ibid., 4 December 1744.

82 NLW Howel Harris's Diary, 26 May 1746.

83 NLW Howel Harris's Diary, 26 February 1745.

84 Tudur, *Howell Harris*, pp. 170–1

85 Tudur, '"Like a right arm and a pillar": the story of James Beaumont', in Pope (ed.), *Honouring the Past and Shaping the Future*, pp. 141ff.

86 NLW Howel Harris's Diary, 27–8 June 1746.

87 NLW Howel Harris's Diary, 19 October 1746.

88 Beynon (ed.), *Howell Harris's Visits to Pembrokeshire*, pp. 147–8.

89 NLW Howel Harris's Diary, 6 February 1744.

90 Dallimore, *George Whitefield*, II, pp. 300–2. Others have been less prepared to take Harris's psychological condition into account during these months, preferring to see his behaviour as largely the consequence of his suspect theology. See Evans, *Howell Harris*, p. 56; Evans, *Daniel Rowland*, chapter 25.

91 Boyd Stanley Schlenther, *Queen of the Methodists: The Countess of Huntingdon and the Eighteenth-Century Crisis of Faith and Society* (Durham: Durham Academic Press, 1997), p. 39.

[92] Beynon (ed.), *Howell Harris's Visits to London*, p. 180; Geoffrey F. Nuttall, 'Howel Harris and "The Grand Table": a note on religion and politics, 1744–50', *Journal of Ecclesiastical History*, 39, 4 (October 1988), 533–4.

[93] George Whitefield to Rev. Mr S., 24 June 1748, in Gillies (ed.), *Works of the Reverend George Whitefield*, II, p. 144.

[94] George Whitefield, *The Two First Parts of his Life, with his journals, revised, corrected and abridged* (London: W. Strahan, 1756).

[95] See, for example, George Whitefield to Selina Hastings, 29 September 1748, in Gillies (ed.), *The Works of the Reverend George Whitefield*, II, pp. 185–6; George Whitefield to Selina Hastings, 27 May 1755, in Gillies (ed.), *The Works of the Reverend George Whitefield*, III, p. 120.

[96] Beynon (ed.), *Howell Harris's Visits to London*, p. 208.

[97] George Whitefield to John Wesley, 1 September 1748, in Gillies (ed.), *The Works of the Reverend George Whitefield*, II, pp. 169–70.

[98] Ibid., p. 170; Tudur, *Howell Harris*, pp. 185–6.

[99] NLW Trevecka Letter 1832, Thomas Boddington to Howel Harris, 29 November 1748.

[100] NLW CMA Trevecka 2946 Records of Associations, II, pp. 67–8.

[101] NLW Trevecka Letter 1832, Thomas Boddington to Howel Harris, 29 November 1748.

[102] NLW Howel Harris's Diary, 7 September 1749.

[103] Ibid., 3 August 1749.

[104] Ibid., 2 August 1749.

[105] NLW Howel Harris's Diary, 9 April 1749.

[106] Tudur, *Howell Harris*, p. 295.

[107] For opposing views, see Geraint H. Jenkins, *The Foundations of Modern Wales: Wales, 1642–1789* (Oxford: Oxford University Press, 1987), p. 346; Tudur, *Howell Harris*, p. 224, n. 153.

[108] NLW Howel Harris's Diary, 17 October 1749.

[109] For Howel Harris's wife's role in this debacle, see Geraint Tudur, 'The king's daughter: a reassessment of Anne Harris of Trefeca', *Journal of Welsh Religious History*, 7 (1999), 55–76.

[110] Tudur, *Howell Harris*, pp. 209–10.

[111] NLW Howel Harris's Diary, 8 October 1749.

[112] NLW Howel Harris's Diary, 12 April 1749; ibid., 7 May 1749.

[113] NLW Howel Harris's Diary, 2 September 1749.

[114] Beynon (ed.), *Howell Harris's Visits to London*, p. 240.

[115] NLW Howel Harris's Diary, 7 and 8 December 1749.

[116] Ibid., 11 December 1749.

[117] NLW Howel Harris's Diary, 14 September 1749.

[118] NLW Howel Harris's Diary, 1 January 1750.

[119] Beynon (ed.), *Howell Harris's Visits to London*, p. 257.
[120] Evans, *Daniel Rowland*, p. 279.
[121] Quoted in Evans, *Howell Harris*, p. 56.

5

'A leader is wanting': lean years in Wales, 1750–1762, tentative years in England, 1750–1765

There is little doubt that the aftermath of the separation in Wales was painful for many Methodist members, who found themselves forced to choose between the movement's two main leaders, both of whom had been held in equally high esteem. John Thomas of Rhayader, a Methodist exhorter who later became an Independent minister, recalled his distress regarding what he termed the 'unpleasant division' between the leaders, in his autobiography, *Rhad Ras*:

> Yr oeddwn o ysbryd rhydd, ac yn caru duwiolion o bob enw, ac yn casáu yr ysbryd surllyd o barti sêl pa le bynnag y gwelwn ef; yr oedd gennyf barch neilltuol i Mr. Harris, ac yn edrych arno fel fy nhad ysbrydol, ac felly yr oedd efe i lawer yng Nghymru a rhan o Loegr.

> [I was of a free spirit, and loved the godly of all names, and hated the sour spirit of party zeal wherever I saw it; I had particular respect for Mr Harris, and looked upon him as my spiritual father, and such he was to many in Wales and part of England.][1]

Thomas, despite his respect for Harris, joined the opposing party as an exhorter and expressed warm appreciation for the kind encouragement he received from Daniel Rowland.

Harris's people and Rowland's people in Wales

Many Methodists were faced with a similar quandary. Large numbers who had been recruited to the movement through Harris's preaching tours regarded him as their spiritual father, yet, at the same time, felt deep misgivings regarding his doctrine and his reliance on Mrs Sidney Griffith. With both sides casting aspersions on the other, it was hardly surprising that several members did not know which way to turn, as Robert Jones, Rhoslan, one of the first Methodist historians in the early nineteenth century, suggested.[2] A number of exhorters had been party to the decision to expel Harris and, as private exhorters and superintendents of individual societies, they were in a position to influence large sections of the ordinary membership. Harris, as general superintendent of the societies and busy itinerant, held considerable sway over the rank and file of the movement, but it was the lay preachers responsible for the constant shepherding of the Methodist membership who had the most direct influence, and this may have been telling. In addition, there was probably a sense that Daniel Rowland, Howell Davies and William Williams had a rather greater measure of status, orthodoxy and authority as a result of their position as ordained clergy in the Anglican Church. Many societies, therefore, threw in their lot with Rowland, forming what would remain the mainstream Methodist cause in Wales. Yet Harris was by no means prepared to surrender the field to his opponents in the months following the official separation.

Harris stated to John Sparks of Haverfordwest in June 1750: 'I have no party but am alone as I first went out. Only a few that know and love his flesh and wounds & blood hang on me.'[3] Yet, at the same time, Thomas William, Harris's most loyal lieutenant, was testing the allegiances of exhorters in Monmouthshire and Glamorgan in order to gauge the support for his cause.[4] At this point, Harris seemed convinced that he would be able to continue to lead a branch of the Methodist movement, with Mrs Griffith at his side. He confidently stated that the separation had simply purged the 'dross' and 'chaff' to leave a residue of true Christians in his fellowship who would help bring about a new outpouring of the spirit in Wales.[5] Those who sided with Harris formed a separate association, later referred to as a council, with twenty-five members present when they first assembled in July 1750 and a further twenty-five indicating support despite their unavoidable absence.[6] Thomas William felt that their commission to proceed might be found in the second chapter of the Book of Ezekiel, in which the prophet is sent to a rebellious Israel that is said to have transgressed against God.[7] Harris himself continued to itinerate, devoting a considerable portion of his discourse to explaining the causes of the 'Rent' as he termed it, focusing on his belief that Daniel Rowland and his associates had been attempting to undermine his authority for years, well before the advent of Mrs Griffith.[8] At the same time, his hearers learnt much of the contribution of certain scriptural women, such as Deborah and Phoebe, as models to justify Griffith's prominence.[9] The bitterness and hurt Harris felt regarding the separation and the attitude of his former colleagues is apparent in both his diary and his letters from this period. He attributed much of the blame to Rowland, in particular, believing that he had influenced Howell Davies and others in the movement. But he was also obviously angered that George Whitefield had sided with his opponents and felt that Whitefield had 'judged without hearing both sides; acted as a Bishop, and went with a curse through the country, feeding the carnal faith of the flesh and hardening souls in their security'.[10]

From the outset, Rowland's side maintained that they constituted the legitimate Methodist cause in Wales and were thus entitled to all existing funds and resources. Harris in effect acknowledged that their association represented a continuation of the official Methodist movement when he finally yielded to their demands that he transfer to them the sum of £10 collected towards legal costs in north Wales.[11] They were able to ensure the exclusive use of the chapels of ease and society houses, largely because the Methodist-inclined clergy had invariably been considered the most appropriate trustees of these buildings, enabling them to take possession of the properties which were often so valuable as centres for the ministration of the communion service. On the thorny issue of communion, therefore, Harris's group had no choice but to advise their followers to attend Anglican services, an additional problem in the light of the reluctance of some members to receive the sacrament from the hands of any but clergy sympathetic to the Methodist cause. The only property which Harris managed to retain in his grasp was the Builth society house, which became a bone of contention between the two sides. The society house was opened in 1748 with Harris and George Whitefield as trustees, although Harris argued, with some justification, that the inclusion of Whitefield's name was merely a matter of courtesy and formality and that it was Harris himself who had supervised the construction of the house.[12] Rowland's Methodists were angry at being denied its use and applied to Whitefield, who wrote to upbraid Thomas Bowen of Builth, a supporter of Harris, insisting that the building be restored to the official Welsh Methodists.[13] The mainstream movement ultimately reclaimed the house, but the arguments over its rightful ownership were indicative of the larger battle being fought in Wales.

Support for Harris was geographically limited, with none of the north Wales exhorters in his camp. He had more considerable backing in Montgomeryshire, but most of mid-Wales sided with his opponents. As might be expected, the stronghold of mainstream Methodism lay in the south-west, in Cardiganshire and Carmarthenshire, where Rowland and William Williams had particular influence. The situation was less clear cut in Pembrokeshire, where the Welsh-speaking north tended to be led by Howell Davies's example, whilst there was more uncertainty in the anglicised areas in the south of the county. The choice between the two opposing sides seems to have given rise to greater confusion and competition in areas of Monmouthshire and Glamorgan, where both had support, but neither could claim complete territorial domination during the period immediately following the separation. Thomas William of Eglwysilan was Harris's staunchest supporter in Glamorgan, and he made valiant efforts to rally exhorters and societies, with mixed results. Competition from mainstream Methodism gradually eroded the Harrisian party in the region, with Rowland himself visiting the county in April 1751 to drum up support.[14]

Increasingly, those whom Harris had anticipated would be loyal were showing a reluctance to commit themselves wholeheartedly, and supporters began to slip away. Harris's uncompromising attitude may have played a part in this process, as he continued to ascribe the causes of the division to the prejudices of the 'clergy party' and to regard both his doctrine and his championing of Mrs Griffith as above reproach. Even given the limited number of exhorters in his camp, Harris was not afraid to weaken his cause by expelling some of them for various failings, such as Thomas Meredith, who was turned out for being too worldly.[15] By April 1751, Thomas William was complaining that Henry Thomas of Gellidochlaethe was among a number of Methodists who, although claiming to be on their side, were too weak in spirit to engage actively.[16] This lukewarm attitude did not augur well for the survival of the Harrisian party, and it may well be that some of the exhorters were drifting away in this manner in order to avoid wounding Harris still further by an emphatic statement of opposition. Some of his former friends seemed to be attempting to let him down as gently as possible. John Richard, who served as superintendent over parts of Carmarthenshire and west Glamorgan, for instance, produced the subtle argument that as he was not against Harris he must, therefore, be for him, even though he no longer felt able to attend meetings of Harris's party.[17] Although Harris remained hopeful that John Richard might return to the fold, by September 1751 Thomas William was convinced that Richard's mind had been poisoned by Daniel Rowland and that he was lost to them.[18] Richard Tibbott of Montgomeryshire evidently attempted to detach himself gently by first suggesting a state of uncertainty which made it impossible for him to go forth to preach and later urging Harris to reconsider his position and to seek a reconciliation with the other Methodists.[19] Early in October 1751, Harris was moved to write to some of the exhorters with whom he had worked closely, including John Sparks, John Relly, Thomas Bowen and John Richard, pleading with them not to desert him.[20] By that time, Thomas William was the only Glamorgan exhorter remaining in Harris's camp, although even he was expelled from their associations in February 1752, pending a restoration of his spirit. Harris was obviously distressed to be, as he saw it, shunned by those whom he claimed would once have plucked out their eyes for him.[21] The death of his mother, Susannah, in January 1751 had caused further grief, despite her continued opposition to Mrs Sidney Griffith's presence at Trefeca.[22]

There is little doubt also that the Methodist cause lost a number of adherents to those existing religious groups which seemed to offer a tranquil haven to those disturbed and distressed by the turn of events. Some turned to the Dissenters, particularly the Independents, who shared a similar acceptance of Calvinist doctrine and of infant baptism. The New Inn society in Monmouthshire, for example, formed itself into an Independent church in around 1751.[23] In west Glamorgan,

Henry Thomas, whose apathy had previously grieved Thomas William, in 1752 registered his society's meeting place as a Dissenting meeting house for the use of the dozen or so members. He was listed as a Dissenting preacher, and the meeting house was served by local Independent ministers.[24] There were wide-scale desertions from the cause amongst the Pembrokeshire exhorters, where tensions had already been apparent in the years leading up to the division. The brothers William and Christopher Mends of Haverfordwest had recently left and had registered their house at Laugharne as a Dissenting meeting house in January 1750.[25] John Harris of St Kennox, who had previously served as superintendent over the Welsh- and English-medium societies in south Pembrokeshire, had clashed resoundingly with Howell Davies but continued to exhort outside the movement, causing further ruptures in the county amongst those who retained a sense of allegiance to him as their pastor.[26] David Jones seceded to join the Baptists at Moleston and later played a significant part in their mission to north Wales, becoming minister of their church in Wrexham.[27] The Moravians, who shared much of the revivalist spirit, benefited from the confusion by gaining the talents of George Gambold and John Sparks, leading to the establishment of a Moravian congregation in Haverfordwest. Yet many of these people and churches retained Methodist links and attitudes long after they had officially departed from the movement, demonstrating how evangelical influences spread through various means and to various groups in eighteenth-century Wales.

It is hardly surprising that the split between the leaders of the Welsh Methodist movement also led to further fractures at a local level, with some individuals and societies seeming to declare a plague on both Methodist houses and preferring to detach themselves from both sides in the disagreement. In 1750 the brothers James and John Relly of Jeffreston broke away from the Methodists to form a separate religious sect in the anglicised regions of south Pembrokeshire. They gained only limited support, despite recruiting the disgruntled John Harris, until he joined the Moravians in 1753, following in the footsteps of his brother-in-law, George Gambold.[28] The Rellites eventually merged once more with the Methodists after the death of John Relly in 1777. James Relly moved to England and later discarded Calvinism in favour of universalism.[29] However, a more substantial splinter group emerged in the Builth area in the following year. In January 1751, Thomas Bowen of Builth, an exhorter and cobbler who had initially supported Harris, declared his independence and, being a highly influential figure in the area, attracted the support of several societies in Breconshire and Radnorshire to form a breakaway group. It was a considerable blow to Harris's cause, particularly when the most prominent of the Breconshire exhorters, Thomas James, a former close colleague and friend, also joined the Builth Methodists. James was married to Sarah Williams of Erwood, a member of an active Methodist family, whose two brothers, John and William Williams, were also exhorters in the area. James thus commanded considerable personal and family loyalty in the region and, therefore, drew many Methodists with him when he deserted. The reason for this wholesale defection is by no means clear, especially given Harris's longstanding influence and friendships with many local Methodists. However, the explanation may well lie in Richard Bennett's suggestion that, although the Builth party did not feel that Harris was guilty of any heresy, neither could they accept the prominence of Mrs Griffith in his branch of the movement.[30] There would seem to be confirmation of this in Harris's insistence that Thomas Bowen would eventually come to a different view of Griffith's role and of Harris's relationship with her.[31] Anne Harris's connections in the locality may well have led to a certain sense of sympathy with her situation which would have increased the opposition to the woman who appeared to many to be the rival for her husband's affections. The result seems to have been the emergence of a group of Methodists who, although they did not accept that Harris was guilty of the most severe accusations levelled against him and felt sufficient loyalty towards him as a spiritual father not to side with his accusers, at the same time could not stomach the authority of Mrs Griffith.

It became increasingly apparent during the early months of 1752 that Harris's cause was dwindling. The twenty or so of his supporters who assembled for the council which met at Cantref, near Llanfrynach, Breconshire, on 20 May 1752 in effect agreed to the termination of their movement when they accepted Harris's proposal that:

> All are free to go where they will & preach as much & as little as they see right & where they will or none at all . . . & that he thinks they must come up as he did each gradually by going for the L[or]d where

He sends them . . . & that he thinks the Ld would not have them go
on with the Work as before but that each should go to the Ld & take
His Work from Him & bring to the Next Meeting his Own Round
written & so each give his paper to the other to publish.[32]

Those present each indicated an area where they felt called to serve
and where they would continue to labour, but there seems to have
been a tacit acceptance that attempts to sustain a coordinated, centralised organisation were virtually at an end. The news of Mrs Griffith's
death on 31 May arrived soon after this meeting and left Harris bereft,
doubting his ability ever to continue with his ministry and anticipating
his own imminent demise.[33] In the wake of Griffith's death, Harris
retreated to Trefeca, where his plans to establish a cooperative religious
community were already underway. For the next few years, he would
concentrate his somewhat depleted energies on acting as 'Father' to
the growing Trefeca 'Family'.[34]

Harris seems originally to have conceived the notion of establishing
a community at Trefeca upon reading of August Hermann Francke's
work at Halle in Prussia. In 1737 he noted in his diary a desire to
follow Francke's example by establishing an almshouse and school-
house.[35] This planted a seed which was to grow to fruition during the
dark days of the early 1750s. As Harris's support ebbed away and
the effort to maintain some sort of coordinated group of exhorters
wore him down, he focused increasingly on his plans for a new venture
at Trefeca. He resolved to expand the buildings to provide accommodation and to recruit craftsmen to proceed with the work. Even
before the last of his councils had met in 1752, Harris had installed
Sarah Bowen as a sort of housekeeper to oversee the new development,
with the building work beginning in April 1752. Bowen was from a
prominent Methodist family based at Tyddyn, Llandinam. She and
her sister Hannah came to Trefeca bringing with them their personal
wealth of £280, which helped finance the building programme. Apart
from his personal loss, the death of Mrs Griffith was a severe setback
for Harris's plans for the Family, as he had envisaged that she would
act as 'Mother' in conjunction with his role as 'Father'. In her stead,
he attempted to persuade Bridget Glynne, a gentlewoman Methodist
convert from mid-Wales who had moved to Shrewsbury, to assume
the task.[36] A few days' trial was, however, enough to convince Glynne

that Trefeca was not for her. Sarah Bowen thus continued as matron-housekeeper until she escaped from her quarrels with Harris by leaving to get married, thereafter spending many years in an effort to reclaim the money she had invested in Trefeca. Her role as leader of the women in the Family was then assumed for many years by her sister, Hannah. Harris was also assisted in spiritual matters by Evan Moses, with James Pritchard overseeing the building work and Evan Roberts taking charge of the Family's business affairs. The aim was a self-supporting community who would live, work and worship together. Some historians have drawn comparisons with Moravian settlements, and there were certain similarities, including the practice of dividing the occupants according to gender and marital status. Harris may well have taken some inspiration from their example, given his acquaintance with a number of prominent Moravians, but it was only well after the Trefeca community was established that he visited the Moravian settlement at Fulneck in Yorkshire for the first time in 1766.[37]

It is estimated that some 374 members in total were drawn to join the Trefeca Family during its entire history, up to the point when ownership was transferred to the Methodist Connexion in 1839.[38] There seem, however, to have been no more than 150 members at any given time. There were, nevertheless, sufficient recruits to necessitate an almost constant programme of building work to accommodate them, as well as the leasing of a number of nearby holdings, so that the total acreage farmed amounted to some 765 acres.[39] It is unfortunate that there is no accurate list of the members, although deaths in the Family were recorded, both by the community itself and in the registers of the local parish church.[40] These give a fair indication of the gender balance, suggesting that at least half the membership was female, reflecting the prevailing pattern in the wider Methodist movement. The social background of the membership was also similar to Methodism in general and, indeed, to Dissent, drawing as it did on the rural middling sorts: the section of society who were becoming more literate and more inclined to make their own choices in matters of conscience. The factors which drew them to join the Family were much the same as those which attracted converts to the Methodist movement in general, including access to fervent preaching and the sense of belonging to a close-knit society. Many of the earliest recruits were loyal supporters of Harris who seem to have preferred to make the move to Trefeca rather than to continue as members of a Methodist movement which did not contain him. As might be expected, there were very few members from south-west Wales and none at all from Cardiganshire. Quite a large proportion were drawn from mid and north Wales and, as several had been extremely active organisers in their own localities, their recruitment served to weaken Methodism in those areas for a time.

Harris's former colleagues in Wales were critical of his efforts during this period. Yet John Wesley and others in the evangelical community were more complimentary regarding the Trefeca Family.[41] Harris himself later explained to William Richard that he had found great benefits in remaining for so long in the same place, tending to the same people.[42] This was evidently the nearest Harris came to the experience of parochial ministry, and he found that, although very different to his previous itinerant work, it also had an appeal. At the same time, he managed to establish rather better relations than he had previously enjoyed with local Anglican clergy and gentry. This was partly because of the good reputation earned by the Trefeca artisans and craftsmen and also possibly because of Harris's involvement with the Breconshire Agricultural Society and the county militia. He served as a captain in the militia during the Seven Years War (1756–63), spending many months with the troops, mainly in Great Yarmouth and Devon.[43] During this period he took advantage of opportunities to preach as often as possible, finding there was less threat from the mobs when he preached in uniform with a sword at his side. These experiences may have reawakened some of his old spirit and helped convince him not to confine himself solely to his community at Trefeca.

In comparison with information regarding the Family at Trefeca, detailed accounts regarding the activities of the majority Methodist movement in Wales are frustratingly sparse for this period. Most of the records for the years prior to the division were preserved by Howel Harris, and fewer documents have survived for the period of his absence. However, it is apparent that the Methodist Association continued to meet regularly. Crucial for the survival of the movement was the fact that there were sufficient preachers available to maintain the pastoral and administrative structure built up during the 1740s. Even so, certain areas were evidently better equipped than others to continue relatively unscathed after 1750. Amongst the best served were Cardiganshire and Carmarthenshire, where the conscientious local superintendents – William Richard, James William, William John and Morgan John Lewis – remained as dedicated as ever to the welfare of their societies. Howell Davies faced a somewhat harder struggle to maintain his hold in Pembrokeshire, faced with competition from Dissenting groups. Yet, it proved possible to preserve a fairly strong presence in the Welsh-speaking north, with the assistance of John Harry of Ambleston, who emerged as one of the most diligent and trusted exhorters in the area. North Pembrokeshire also had a more natural affinity with the bordering regions of south Cardiganshire and Carmarthenshire than with the anglicised south of the county and thus was able to draw on the support provided by the close proximity of the Cardiganshire and Carmarthenshire Methodists. The south-west was also especially fortunate in the number of chapels available in which clergy sympathetic to the Methodists were able to administer communion to the membership. The practice of making use of disused chapels of ease belonging to the Anglican Church had begun during the 1740s, in an attempt to relieve the troubled consciences of members who preferred to receive the sacrament from some of the Methodist-inclined clergy rather than from parish clergy who were hostile to the evangelical movement.[44] Howell Davies and Daniel Rowland were located close at hand and journeyed regularly to chapels like Llechryd to hold services which attracted congregations drawn from the Methodist societies in the surrounding area. The chapel built at Twr-gwyn in Rhydlewis in 1752 was said to have been located on the site of an old chapel of ease, which may explain Daniel Rowland's willingness to use this building regularly for services.[45]

The diary of John Thomas, a schoolmaster and Methodist convert in Tre-main in south Cardiganshire, provides a valuable snapshot of activities in the south-west during the 1750s and depicts a thriving Methodist community.[46] For instance, on Sunday 25 March 1759 he attended two morning services: at his own parish church in Tre-main and afterwards in the neighbouring parish of Blaen-porth. In the afternoon he attended a sermon by a Baptist preacher. On the following Tuesday he heard a 'sermon from above' by Daniel Rowland at Twr-gwyn on Matthew 16: 2–4 before returning to Blaen-porth to hear Enoch Dafydd, a local exhorter, preach on John 13. On Saturday

31 March, he heard Howell Davies preach on Exodus 15: 1–3 on the theme of the God of war, at Llechryd, where he returned the next day to hear another sermon by Davies. This was by no means an unusual programme of activity for Thomas, who normally found the opportunity to attend two or three meetings during the week, in addition to his usual worship on a Sunday. This clearly demonstrates how busy lay preachers were in this area, notably the local superintendent, William Richard, a stalwart farmer from Llanddewibrefi, who had charge of the societies along the coast from New Quay to St David's. The diary also records numerous sermons and meetings conducted by John Harry of Ambleston, Dafydd William Rees, John Popkin of Tre-lech, Enoch Dafydd of Cilrhedyn and John Thomas of Nancwnlle, amongst others. Thomas also had no qualms about hearing some of the local Dissenters on occasion, especially Dafydd Thomas Rees, the minister of Cilfowyr Baptist Church in Pembrokeshire. Scarcely a fortnight went by without also a sermon from Daniel Rowland, Howell Davies, William Williams or Peter Williams, the most prominent of the Methodist-orientated clergy, with Thomas obviously setting particular store by Rowland's sermons, confirming his reputation as a preacher. In addition to taking advantage of Rowland's visits to nearby chapels, Thomas also travelled occasionally to Llangeitho, as he did at Easter 1759, noting that it was worth the journey to hear Rowland speak and to see the joy in the faces of the congregation:

> Rhyfedd yw gweld y Bobl Dduwiol sydd yn ymgynull i Langeitho – y mae dull eu hwynebau siriol oddi allan yn dangos i fod ganddunt galonnau yn Berwi o lawenydd oddi mewn.

> [It is wonderful to see the Godly People who gather at Llangeitho – the nature of their cheerful faces without show that they have hearts Boiling with joy within.][47]

Other localities probably did not fare so well and had to make do with less regular preaching and communion. Yet efforts to maintain the movement at something approaching its position prior to 1750 were more successful than might have at first been feared. To some extent it was the structure set up during the 1740s which enabled

Welsh Methodism to continue through the lean years of division. Ironically enough, many of the details of this structure had been devised primarily by Howel Harris and now proved sufficiently strong to survive his absence. The system of pastoral oversight, with each society allocated a steward, private exhorter and superintendent, continued to provide regular support for the membership.[48] Indeed, the movement owed much in this period to the steadfast commitment of the earnest, literate farmers and craftsmen who formed the majority of its lay preachers. This was a testing time for them, but they often were able to reassure their societies and maintain activities at a local level to something approaching the previous norm.

A vital ingredient in this respect was the emergence of William Williams. The son of a Dissenting farmer from Carmarthenshire, Williams was bent on a career in medicine when, at the age of twenty and as a student at the nearby Llwynllwyd Dissenting Academy, he chanced to hear Howel Harris preaching in the graveyard of Talgarth Church at some time between 1737 and 1738.[49] This experience changed the course of his life, and he never failed subsequently to acknowledge Harris as his spiritual father.[50] Abandoning his previous plans, he sought holy orders and was ordained as a deacon in the Anglican Church in 1740, becoming curate to the famous anti-Methodist author, Theophilus Evans, in his parishes of Llanwrtyd and Llanddewi Abergwesyn, Breconshire. Various complaints about his Methodist activities from Evans and his parishioners led to charges before the Bishop's Court and the rejection of his application for full orders.[51] The fact that he remained in deacon's orders restricted his contribution to the movement, since he was unable to provide the valuable service of administering communion to the members in the same way as Rowland, Howell Davies and Peter Williams. However, from 1744 onwards, with his parish duties behind him, and in his new role as Rowland's assistant, he had considerable freedom to travel. He was thus in a position by the 1750s to assume the mantle of Howel Harris as chief visitor to the societies, providing a regular connection with the leadership of the movement in a way that Daniel Rowland and Howell Davies, as parish clergymen, could not. In this capacity, Williams developed a keen understanding of the process of sharing and analysing spiritual experience through the *seiat*, the society meeting which lay at the heart of the movement. Along with Rowland and

Harris, he came to be regarded as the third of the triumvirate of acknowledged 'Methodist fathers' in Wales, a position confirmed by his growing prominence at Rowland's right hand during the period of separation and thereafter.[52]

The Welsh Methodists under the leadership of Rowland and his supporters were intent not just upon survival but also expansion, as their campaign of chapel building demonstrates. Society houses or chapels had begun to be built from the late 1740s, such as the house at Cil-y-cwm, Carmarthenshire, constructed in 1747.[53] It is calculated that seventeen chapels were built between 1751 and 1762, a sign that the movement continued to consolidate its converts, despite the challenges it faced in the wake of the division.[54] The majority were located in west Wales, reflecting the relative strength of the cause in that region. One of the earliest was Woodstock Chapel in Pembrokeshire, which was ready for the use of Howell Davies by the summer of 1751 and served as a centre for the administration of communion to the Methodists in the vicinity. George Whitefield was pressed by Daniel Rowland to attend the opening of the chapel, and his presence confirmed Whitefield's backing for the clergy's side in the division.[55] Most of these early chapels were extremely basic in design, but they served the essential purpose of providing a convenient meeting place for the members. They were generally financed by voluntary donations scraped together by local societies. In some cases, more wealthy patrons contributed the land and the bulk of the costs, as happened in 1760 when Thomas Bowen built a chapel on his estate at Waunifor, near Llandysul.[56] Some building also occurred in north Wales, including the first chapel at Bala, which apparently came into use in 1757.

Despite these developments, there is little doubt that the Methodist movement in Wales suffered during this period. William Williams probably overstated the case when he declared after the reawakening of 1762: 'till the Lord did come with these late showers of Revival, all was gone to nothing'; yet the negative effects of Harris's absence and of the division were obvious.[57] It would appear that there was widespread uncertainty regarding the actual cause of the separation, with rumours rife that Harris was an antinomian, a Moravian or an adulterer. Whilst preaching in Maenclochog, Pembrokeshire, in October 1750, for instance, Harris was jeered at by a drunkard who accused him of adultery.[58] Such a bitter rift was especially troublesome since it seemed to make a mockery of the emphasis on fellowship and mutual support, which had been part of the movement's attraction for its converts. In an atmosphere of uncertainty and internecine struggle, the Dissenters offered a welcome sense of stability. R. T. Jenkins suggested with some justification that the separation, by confining Howel Harris to Trefeca and limiting the scope for missions to north Wales in general, presented valuable opportunities for other doctrines to take root, including the teaching of the Moravians.[59] Methodism missed Harris's organisational skills in the association and his charismatic presence further afield, despite the fact that his personality was also at times prone to give rise to tensions. William Williams's elegy to Harris provides some shrewd commentary on his strengths and failings and is sharply critical of his decision to retreat to Trefeca to concentrate his efforts on the Family. Williams blamed Harris for skulking in a cave, tending to a flock of a mere hundred and neglecting the thousands in need of his guidance.[60] In all fairness, Harris can hardly be accused of dereliction of duty in this respect, since he did not decide on a whim to turn his back on the Methodist converts, but followed what seemed to be virtually the only path left to him after his expulsion from the movement. Harris's decision to quit the field and leave the clergy party to carry the day may have saved the Methodist cause from the potential injuries that might have been inflicted by further battles between the two sides for the loyalty of the membership. Had the movement been divided more equally between the two parties, the long-term damage might have been far more devastating. The fact that Rowland and his supporters gained the support of the bulk of the membership enabled Welsh Calvinistic Methodism to survive as a viable movement. The truth was that many members may have been inspired by Harris and have felt great affection for him, but they seemed to place greater trust and dependence on Daniel Rowland and his fellows to lead the movement into the future.

Tentative years in England

Not least among George Whitefield's achievements was his role in coaxing Selina Hastings, countess of Huntingdon, from her initial support of the Wesleyan 'free will' and 'Christian perfection' theology to Calvinistic predestination. As wife of the 9th earl of Huntingdon, the countess had until the late 1730s pursued a not untypical course of studied good works and charitable giving. Yet after a decade of marriage there were repeated emotional, health and financial crises, centred on her family. All seven of her children were born in that first decade, and all would be taken from her by death or rebellion against her Methodistic proclivities.

Her initial foray into Methodism focused on John and Charles Wesley: she desired that they 'might think on me as you would do on no one else'.[61] In early 1742 she had written to John Wesley that perfection was a doctrine she 'hope[d] to live and die by; it is absolutely the most complete thing I know.'[62] However, within two years she was openly speaking out against sinless perfection. This neat theological somersault dropped her into the arms of predestination, a belief, of course, famously abhorrent to the Wesleys. The clash over predestination which had so bedevilled the Methodist movement from the outset, lodged especially in the differing perceptions of John Wesley and Whitefield.[63] Indeed, the conflict over free will versus predestination would prove to be the rock upon which any hope of a united Methodist movement would be dashed. By early 1744 the countess was corresponding with Whitefield, while Wesley was accusing her of acting like a 'Luther'.[64] She met Howel Harris in the summer of 1743, and the Calvinistic-oriented Harris was visiting her frequently in London by 1744.

George Whitefield was the strongest religious influence on the countess of Huntingdon during her long life. In 1744 he had departed for what proved his most lengthy American visit, lasting four years. From Maryland he wrote that 'favour is given me in the sight of the rich and great . . . [I] sometimes think I shall never return to *England*.'[65] However, as previously noted, by 1748 he did return, attracted by the countess's desire that he become her personal chaplain. The day of his London arrival, 'fearing to offend the Countess', he presented himself at her home.[66] She indeed appointed him chaplain, and he in turn 'appointed' her as God's chosen instrument in the conversion of England to 'new birth' Christianity. The heady doctrine of predestination, or election, offered the perfect vehicle to drive her sense of personal destiny – combined with her natural sense of position. Calvinism provided her with a secure belief in election to a pivotal place in pursuing England's redemption. Whitefield bombarded her with obsequiousness. Her conduct was 'truly god-like'. God had placed her 'upon a pinnacle'. 'Tears trickle from my eyes, while I am thinking of your Ladyship's condescending to patronize such a dead dog as I am . . . He will, he will reward your Ladyship openly.'[67] 'A leader is wanting', wrote Whitefield; 'this honour hath been put upon your Ladyship by the great head of the church.' It was an 'honour to be put upon your Ladyship before men and angels, when time shall be no more'.[68]

Emerging as a focal point for the Calvinistic wing of English Methodism, at least in the first decade of this activity Lady Huntingdon believed her special mission to be the winning of the aristocracy for Christ: England would be won from the 'top down'. To carefully-staged salon services she invited the titled and wealthy to drink tea at her London home and to hear the most ardent preachers she could secure, ideally Whitefield himself, who regularly preached there twice a week 'to the Great and Noble'.[69] It has been noted that she also utilised Howel Harris at these gatherings. A basic concern was to use such influence as she could develop to seek protection for the infant Methodist movement. For some titled guests her drawing room was a hall of judgement; yet in the end blue blood ran thin in the enterprise, and the countess's aunt was her only parlour 'convert'.[70] To a sardonic Horace Walpole, Lady Huntingdon had emerged as the 'Queen of the Methodists'.[71]

A key to this programme was to soften the attitude of the bishops of the Church of England towards the itinerant clergymen who supported the movement and moreover to influence them to be willing to ordain others who were methodistically inclined. The death in 1747 of John Potter, the archbishop of Canterbury, 'a true Christian Bishop' with whom she had been on good terms for several years, robbed the circle of an important sympathetic ear.[72] In all this, the countess had strenuously attempted to cultivate the support – or at least sympathy – of Frederick, prince of Wales. However, his death in 1751 was followed immediately by Whitefield's temporary departure for America, his remarkable hopes for consecration as a bishop in the Church of England now dashed. It is possible that Lady Huntingdon had encouraged him in the belief that this would come about through her agency and influence.

An attempt at Bristol in 1749 to secure some form of union between the various Methodist factions had meanwhile proved futile. Yet, even if Whitefield's belief in predestination and Wesley's in perfectionism had not continued to widen the gulf between them, the uncomfortable fact was that Lady Huntingdon's patronage of Whitefield precluded a settlement of the dispute.[73] This was true even though she sincerely sought peace within the Methodist movement and was instrumental in establishing a rapprochement early in 1750. Yet this peace was brief, and she went on to caution Whitefield to avoid having much contact with Wesley.[74] Whitefield believed, all too correctly, that Wesley was 'jealous of me', and Whitefield's wife joined the queasy fray by accusing Wesley of 'blackening other mens c[h]aracters to exalt his own'. Wesley was mainly and publicly blackening her husband's.[75]

Lady Huntingdon's eye had remained focused on the Court. In 1749 she managed to have her elder daughter, Elizabeth, appointed lady of the bedchamber to Princesses Amelia and Caroline, the king's daughters. It was an ill-fated exercise: within months she had removed Elizabeth, horrified that she was joining in the playing of cards on Sundays. However, a far better prospect emerged when one Ann Grinfield was appointed to the same post. The countess, directing that all her letters to Grinfield be burnt, urged her to use her strategic placement to influence the princesses in private. In the event, Lady Huntingdon's agent became far too bold, and in August 1755 the princesses requested that Grinfield leave their service. She had not furthered the cause when she discussed at Court the countess's practice of holding intimate conversations with God and angels. There, it was hinted publicly that Lady Huntingdon's religion was neither sensible nor reasonable.[76] With the dramatic failure of this project to plant the gospel at the heart of the Court, Whitefield reassured his patroness that in heaven Christ 'shall hold You up before the Mighty of the Noble'.[77]

The countess of Huntingdon would continue for many years to consider herself a loyal daughter of the Church of England. Apart from anything else, she perceived this as being the fountain from which would flow England's salvation; thus all her energies were directed towards cleansing these waters: not the diverted streams of the Dissenters. She, therefore, rejoiced at news of every Church of England clergyman who adopted a stance sympathetic to the

Methodist cause. With few exceptions – most notably the leading Dissenter Philip Doddridge – the countess's ecclesiastical connections had been almost solely with Anglican clerics or with those seeking Anglican ordination. She was kept informed of the progress made by Samuel Walker, incumbent clergyman at Truro, who encouraged his people in experimental religion but who vigorously opposed the irregularity of John Wesley's lay preachers; Walker refused to condone a clergyman's preaching outside his own parish. Like most of the clergymen courted by the countess during this period, Walker was a moderate Calvinist, one who tended to hold temperate predestinarian beliefs. Notable among these men were Henry Venn, Martin Madan, William Romaine, William Bromley Cadogan, Charles Edward de Coetlogon and James Hervey.

Hervey, a writer of widely read florid religious poetry and prose, initiated a correspondence with Lady Huntingdon in 1750 at the behest of George Whitefield, and she remained supportive until Hervey's early death in 1758. He said that 'be it true or false', predestination 'makes no part of my scheme'.[78] However, Wesley certainly thought it did and attacked Hervey's writings with vigour. In 1754, Venn became curate of Clapham, which was developing into a centre for evangelicalism. The countess was charmed with the preaching of Martin Madan, a former barrister who – though converted by hearing John Wesley – had since hoisted Calvinist sails. Madan in 1750 had taken up the London post of chaplain to the Lock Hospital, a refuge for fallen women located at Hyde Park Corner. There the inmates were treated for sexual diseases and to the impassioned pleadings of Madan and other Calvinist preachers. William Romaine was the leading evangelical cleric in London during this period, indeed, the only beneficed evangelical in the capital, and was to the pulpit what David Garrick was to the stage. Later these men would forsake the countess's service and fall under her severe disapprobation – not least because unlike her they did not allow their Calvinism to override all other considerations. Yet for the present these moderate Calvinists reflected her devotion to strengthening the sinews of Calvinistic Methodism within the body of the Church of England.[79]

The theme of Lady Huntingdon's religious activities during the 1760s was to gather evangelically-minded Anglican clerics under her wing, to induce bishops to ordain more of their number and in general to promote thereby the internal invigoration of the Church of England. An important mark of her fostering such clergymen was her invitation to the Swiss-born John Fletcher occasionally to preach and celebrate communion at her house. Soon after, in 1761, she appointed William Romaine and Martin Madan to join Whitefield as her chaplains.[80] These appointments ran concurrently with a dramatic new enterprise. The countess argued that as a peeress of the realm she was entitled to attach to her private residences chapels exempt from episcopal jurisdiction. They might hold several hundred persons, but she reasoned that it would only be an extension of the principle she had followed in opening her drawing rooms to religious services. However, she was indulging in a kind of ecclesiastical subterfuge, and although she undoubtedly believed that she remained a faithful Anglican, this programme of chapel building, whatever the legal niceties, was the first, the most decisive, and the most visible stone and mortar step towards her final separation from the Church of England twenty years later.

The main chapels that Lady Huntingdon established during the 1760s were strategically sited, each at major watering places. In 1761 she built a small chapel 36 feet by 18, in the grounds of her private residence in Brighton. The second, at Bath in 1765, was much grander. Located in the Vineyards area of the expanding and fashionable 'Upper Town', it would prove to be the jewel in her crown of chapels outside London. The chapel's connection to her residence was unmistakable: the two-storey bay house with battlemented parapets fronted the chapel, which was opened for worship in October, with a copiously weeping Whitefield preaching. Howel Harris considered the Bath chapel ostentatious and on the road to 'Popery' and was particularly concerned with the countess's excessive pride in its rich ornamentation.[81] For many years this chapel would be the strongest net cast in the attempt to catch and convert the titled and moneyed classes. She had no doubt that if she could manage the chemistry of combining her favourite preachers with her most sought-after converts, it would be impossible for such people to do anything but respond to true religion just as she herself had responded. She was certain, for example, that if he could but hear Martin Madan, the king himself would be converted. In any case, the opening of her chapel in Tunbridge Wells in 1769, together with the remodelling and extension of her Bath and Brighton chapels two years earlier, underscored the need for more clerical hands.

Up to 1768 the countess of Huntingdon managed, at various times, to gather under her banner not only her three chaplains – Whitefield, Romaine and Madan – but fifteen or so other evangelically-minded Church of England clergymen. She had been successful with some of these men either in securing their ordination or in finding them livings or curates to take their parish places when they were away preaching in her chapels. Yet they were only sporadically available, and securing additional manpower through further ordination was severely limited by the few episcopal doors open to her entreaties. She held the quaint belief that by keeping her distance from Wesleyanism and Moravianism, bishops would be more ready to assist her. However, this caution made no difference: her own actions were increasing episcopal suspicion.

This period revealed a confusing ebbing and flowing of Calvinistic Methodist fortunes in both Wales and England. The personal problems faced and decisions made by Howel Harris as he retreated from the field in the early 1750s must be seen as having had a detrimental effect on the movement's progress in Wales. The baton of leadership passed from Harris to Daniel Rowland, in the process causing a real degree of momentum to be lost. In England, the increasing zeal of George Whitefield and his patroness, the countess of Huntingdon, provided a focus for a number of like-minded clergymen. However, the countess's activities, not least her commencing a programme of chapel building, led Anglican bishops to doubt her professed adherence to the Church of England.

Notes

[1] Ioan Thomas, *Rhad Ras*, ed. J. Dyfnallt Owen (Cardiff: University of Wales Press, 1949), p. 80.

[2] Robert Jones, *Drych yr Amseroedd*, ed. G. M. Ashton (Cardiff: University of Wales Press, 1958), p. 80.

[3] NLW Trevecka Letter 1944, Howel Harris to John Sparks Jnr, 23 June 1750.

[4] NLW Trevecka Letter 1943, Thomas William to Howel Harris, 23 June 1750; Trevecka Letter 1948, Howel Harris to John Sparks, 1 August 1750.

[5] NLW Trevecka Letter 1959, Howel Harris to John Gumley, 13 October 1750.

[6] NLW Howel Harris's Diary, 25 July 1750.

[7] NLW Trevecka Letter 1988, Thomas William to Howel Harris, 11 May 1751.

[8] For instance, NLW Howel Harris's Diary, 22 June 1750, 17 July 1750, 20 July 1750, 5 October 1750, 13 October 1750.

[9] For instance, NLW Howel Harris's Diary, 21 June 1750, 14 July 1750, 3 December 1750.

[10] NLW Howel Harris's Diary, 2 June 1751.

[11] Daniel Rowland, William Williams and Thomas Price signed a receipt for the money, 9 January 1751, NLW CMA Trevecka 3196.

[12] See NLW Trevecka Letter 1712, Howel Harris to Roger Jones, 17 October 1747, regarding Whitefield's involvement.

[13] NLW Trevecka Letter 1961, George Whitefield to Thomas Bowen, 19 October 1750.

[14] NLW Trevecka Letter 1984, Thomas William to Howel Harris, 20 April 1751; Gomer M. Roberts, 'Calvinistic Methodism in Glamorgan, 1737–1773', in Glanmor Williams (ed.), *Glamorgan County History*, vol. 4, *Early Modern Glamorgan: From the Acts of Union to the Industrial Revolution* (Cardiff: Glamorgan County History Trust, 1974), pp. 519–24.

[15] Richard Bennett, *Methodistiaeth Trefaldwyn Uchaf*, cyfrol I: *Hanes Cyfnod Howel Harris, 1738–1752* (Bala: R. Evans a'i Fab, 1929), p. 189.

[16] NLW Trevecka Letter 1984, Thomas William to Howel Harris, 20 April 1751.

[17] NLW Trevecka Letter 1968, John Richard to Howel Harris, 7 January 1751.

[18] NLW Trevecka Letter 2002, Thomas William to Howel Harris, 24 September 1751.

[19] NLW Trevecka Letter 1997, Richard Tibbott to Harrisian Association, 2 July 1751; Trevecka Letter 2035, Richard Tibbott to Howel Harris, 17 November 1752.

[20] NLW Trevecka Letter 2001, Howel Harris to young Welsh preachers, 13 September 1751. See also Trevecka Letter 2006, Howel Harris to John Sparks Jnr, 4 October 1751; Trevecka Letter 2007, Howel Harris to James Relly, 5 October 1751; Trevecka Letter 2008, Howel Harris

to Thomas Bowen, 5 October 1751; Trevecka Letter 2009, Howel Harris to John Richard, 5 October 1751.

21 NLW Trevecka Letter 2001, Howel Harris to young Welsh preachers, 13 September 1751.

22 NLW Howel Harris's Diary, 7–9 January 1751.

23 John Hughes, *Methodistiaeth Cymru* (3 vols, Wrexham: R. Hughes a'i Fab, 1851–6), III, pp. 373–6.

24 Gomer M. Roberts, 'Henry Thomas, Gelli Dochlaethe', *Y Cofiadur*, 17 (1947), 72–7; Gomer M. Roberts, 'Pobl Rowland yn ystod yr Ymraniad 1750-1763', in Gomer M. Roberts (ed.), *Hanes Methodistiaeth Galfinaidd Cymru*, cyfrol I: *Y Deffroad Mawr* (Caernarfon: Llyfrfa'r Methodistiaid Calfinaidd, 1973), pp. 390–1.

25 Carmarthenshire Record Office, Quarter Session Records, QS I/1, p. 57.

26 Eryn M. White, *Praidd Bach y Bugail Mawr: Seiadau Methodistaidd De-orllewin Cymru* (Llandysul: Gwasg Gomer, 1995), pp. 59–60.

27 Joshua Thomas, *Hanes y Bedyddwyr* (Carmarthen: John Ross, 1778), pp. 154–60, 447; T. M. Bassett, *The Welsh Baptists* (Swansea: Ilston House, 1977), pp. 95, 101.

28 Gomer M. Roberts, 'William Gambold a'i Deulu', *Y Genhinen*, 22 (1972), 194–6.

29 Jones, *Drych yr Amseroedd*, p. 90; Gomer M. Roberts, 'The Moravians and John Relly and his people', *JHSPCW*, 38 (1953), 2–7.

30 Richard Bennett, *Methodistiaeth Trefaldwyn Uchaf*, cyfrol I: *Hanes Cyfnod Howel Harris, 1738–1752* (Bala: R. Evans a'i Fab, 1929), pp. 187–9.

31 NLW Trevecka Letter 2008, Howel Harris to Thomas Bowen, 5 October 1751.

32 NLW CMA Trevecka 2997 Records of Associations, 20 May 1752.

33 See, for instance, NLW Trevecka Letter 2031, Howel Harris to anon., 18 June 1752.

34 See Alun Wyn Owen, 'A study of Howell Harris and the Trevecka "family" (1752–60) based upon the Trevecka letters and diaries and other Methodist archives at the NLW' (unpublished MA thesis, University of Wales, 1957); K. Monica Davies, 'Teulu Trefeca', in Roberts (ed.), *Y Deffroad Mawr*, pp. 356–77; Eryn M. White, 'Women, work and worship in the Trefeca family 1752–1773', in Peter Forsaith and Geordan Hammond (eds), *Religion, Gender and Industry* (Eugene, OR: Wipf and Stock, 2011), pp. 109–22.

35 NLW Howel Harris's diary, 10 January 1737.

36 NLW Trevecka Letter 2052, Bridget Glynne to Howel Harris, 21 March 1753; Trevecka Letter 2247, Howel Harris to Bridget Glynne, 25 March 1753; Trevecka Letter 2249, Howel Harris to Bridget Glynne, 11 April 1753; Trevecka Letter 2250, Howel Harris to Bridget Glynne, 15 April 1753; Bennett, *Methodistiaeth Trefaldwyn Uchaf,* pp. 169–70, 230–1, 244.

37 See R. T. Jenkins, *The Moravian Brethren in North Wales* (London: Honourable Society of Cymmrodorion, 1938), 14; Geoffrey Nuttall, *Howel Harris 1714-1773: The Last Enthusiast* (Cardiff: University of Wales Press, 1965), pp. 24–7; J. C. S. Mason, *The Moravian Church and the Missionary Awakening in England 1760–1800* (Woodbridge: The Boydell Press, 2001), p. 50.

38 Alun Wyn Owen, 'A study of Howell Harris and the Trevecka "family", 241.

39 John Davies, 'Howell Harris and the Trevecka Settlement', *Brycheiniog*, 60 (1963), 105.

40 NLW CMA Trevecka 3140; CMA Trevecka 3141. These manuscripts were written, in Welsh, by Evan Moses and record the deaths of members of the Family between 1752 and 1804.

41 See, for instance, A. H. Williams (ed.), *John Wesley in Wales 1739–1790* (Cardiff: University of Wales Press, 1971), pp. 63–4.

42 NLW Howel Harris's Diary, 3 December 1763.

43 See Tom Beynon (ed.), *Howell Harris, Reformer and Soldier (1714–1773)* (Caernarvon: The Calvinistic Methodist Bookroom, 1958), pp. 58–146; Griffith T. Roberts, *Howell Harris* (London: Epworth Press, 1951), pp. 68–70; Gomer M. Roberts, *Portread o Ddiwygiwr* (Caernarfon: Llyfrfa'r Methodistiaid Calfinaidd, 1969), pp. 140–4.

44 White, *Praidd Bach y Bugail Mawr*, pp. 12–16.

45 Gomer M. Roberts, 'Methodistiaeth Gynnar Gwaelod Sir Aberteifi', *Ceredigion*, 5 (1964), 7.

46 NLW MSS 20515-6C; R. G. Gruffydd, 'John Thomas, Tre-main: Pererin Methodistaidd', *JHSPCW*, 9–10 (1985–6), 46–68; E. M. White, '"A breach in God's house": the division in Welsh Calvinistic Methodism, 1750–63', in Nigel Yates (ed.), *Bishop Burgess and his World: Culture, Religion and Society in Britain, Europe and North America in the Eighteenth and Nineteenth Centuries* (Cardiff: University of Wales Press, 2007), pp. 95–6.

47 NLW MS 20515C, 15 April 1759.

48 White, *Praidd Bach y Bugail Mawr*, pp. 50–60, 130–41.

49 Gomer M. Roberts, *Y Pêr Ganiedydd (Pantycelyn)*, cyfrol I: *Trem ar ei Fywyd* (Aberystwyth: Gwasg Aberystwyth, 1949), pp. 32–6.

50 William Williams, *Marwnad er coffadwriaeth am Mr. Howel Harries... 1773* (Brecon: E. Evans, 1773), p. 3.
51 Roberts, *Y Pêr Ganiedydd*, cyfrol I, pp. 42–69; Derec Llwyd Morgan, *Y Diwygiad Mawr* (Llandysul: Gomer, 1981), pp. 87–90.
52 John Morgan Jones and William Morgan, *Y Tadau Methodistaidd*, I (Swansea: Lewis Evans, 1895), pp. 141–76. For a recent biography of Williams in English, see Eifion Evans, *Bread of Heaven: The Life and Work of William Williams, Pantycelyn* (Bridgend: Bryntirion Press, 2010).
53 NLW Trevecka Letter 1471, William Williams to Howel Harris, 5 June 1746; NLW Howel Harris's Diary, 22 July 1747; CMA Trevecka 3054, 30 April 1748.
54 Roberts, 'Pobl Rowland', pp. 383–8; Evans, *Daniel Rowland*, p. 288.
55 Roberts, 'Pobl Rowland', pp. 384–5; Rhidian Griffiths, 'Howel Davies: Apostol Sir Benfro', *JHSPCW*, 11 (1987), 8.
56 Thomas, *Rhad Ras*, p. 94; Leslie Baker-Jones, *Princelings, Privilege and Power: The Tivyside Gentry in their Community* (Llandysul: Gwasg Gomer 1999), pp. 246–7.
57 NLW Howel Harris's Diary, 3 August 1763.
58 NLW Howel Harris's Diary, 10 October 1750.
59 Jenkins, *The Moravian Brethren in North Wales*, pp. 33–43.
60 Williams, *Marwnad...Mr. Howel Harries*, p. 5.
61 Selina Hastings to John Wesley, 24 October 1741, in Frank Baker (ed.), *The Works of John Wesley*, vol. 26, *Letters II, 1740–55* (Oxford: Oxford University Press, 1982), p. 6.
62 Selina Hastings to John Wesley, 15 March 1742, *Methodist Magazine*, 21 (1798), 643.
63 'Wesley brought to the Revival a High Church tradition that preserved the notion of man's free will, while others, Anglicans as well as Dissenters, had inherited a reformed theology in which predestination served to emphasize God's free grace at work in man's salvation.' Alan Harding, *The Countess of Huntingdon's Connexion: A Sect in Action* (Oxford: Oxford University Press, 2003), p. 232.
64 Howel Harris's Diary, 12 June 1744, in Tom Beynon (ed.), *Howell Harris's Visits to London* (Aberystwyth: The Cambrian News Press, 1966), p. 146.
65 George Whitefield to Mrs L____, 26 August 1746, in John Gillies (ed.), The *Works of the Reverend George Whitefield* (6 vols, London: Edward and Charles Dilly, 1771–2), II, p. 83.
66 Howel Harris's Diary, 5 July 1748, in Beynon (ed.), *Howell Harris's Visits to London*, p. 201.

67 George Whitefield to Selina Hastings, 24 February 1749; 27 May 1749; 27 May 1755, in Gillies (ed.), *Works of George Whitefield*, II, pp. 238, 258; III, p. 120.

68 George Whitefield to Selina Hastings, 30 November 1749, in Gillies (ed.), *Works of George Whitefield*, II, p. 294.

69 George Whitefield to Mr B___, 10 March 1749, in Gillies (ed.), *Works of George Whitefield*, II, p. 244.

70 Edwin Welch, *Spiritual Pilgrim: A Reassessment of the Life of the Countess of Huntingdon* (Cardiff: University of Wales Press, 1995), p. 70; Paul Langford, *A Polite and Commercial People, England 1727–1783* (Oxford: Oxford University Press, 1989), p. 254.

71 Horace Walpole to Horace Mann, 4 March 1749, in W. S. Lewis (ed.), *Horace Walpole's Correspondence*, vol. 20 (New Haven and Oxford: Yale University Press, 1937–83), p. 33.

72 Drew A98, Selina Hastings to Theophilus Hastings, n.d.

73 Henry D. Rack, 'Survival and revival: John Bennet, Methodism, and the old dissent', in Keith Robbins (ed.), *Protestant Evangelicalism: Britain, Ireland, Germany and America, c.1750–c.1950* (Oxford: Basil Blackwell, 1990), pp. 12–13.

74 Howel Harris's Diary, 29 April 1749, in Beynon (ed.), *Howell Harris's Visits to London*, p. 224; W. Reginald Ward and Richard P. Heitzenrater (eds), *The Works of John Wesley*, vol. 20, *Journal and Diaries II (1743–54)* (Nashville, TN: Abingdon Press, 1991), p. 319 (28 January 1750); George Whitefield to Selina Hastings, 22 December 1752, in Luke Tyerman, *The Life of the Rev. George Whitefield* (2 vols., London: Hodder and Stoughton, 1876), II, p. 289.

75 George Whitefield to Charles Wesley, 22 December 1752, in Gillies (ed.), *Works of George Whitefield*, II, p. 464; Rylands PLP 113.2, 3, Elizabeth Whitefield to John Bennet, 21 November 1751.

76 Boyd Stanley Schlenther, *Queen of the Methodists: The Countess of Huntingdon and the Eighteenth-Century Crisis of Faith and Society* (Durham: Durham Academic Press, 1997), pp. 48–9.

77 Drew B6, George Whitefield to Selina Hastings, 11 July 1755.

78 James Hervey to Lady Frances Shirley, 9 January 1755, in Luke Tyerman, *The Oxford Methodists: Memoirs of the Rev. Messrs. Clayton, Ingham, Gambold, Hervey, and Broughton, with biographical notices of others* (London: Hodder and Stoughton, 1873), p. 290.

79 Schlenther, *Queen of the Methodists*, pp. 50–1.

80 Lambeth Palace Library, Registers of Peers Chaplains, FV/1 Calendar, vols XII and XIII.

81 NLW Howel Harris's Diary, 6 and 7 October 1765.

6

'I will once more shake the heavens': a new revival for Wales, 1762–1779

After the lean years of the 1750s, Welsh Calvinistic Methodism experienced a much needed renewal of vigour in the early 1760s, which marked the beginning of a period of gradual but sustained growth. The crucial development was the new revival of 1762–4 that spread throughout much of south Wales, but which began in Daniel Rowland's own parish of Llangeitho in the county of Cardiganshire and is thus frequently referred to as the Llangeitho revival.

The 1762 Llangeitho revival

The revival's origins are shrouded in obscurity, but it seems to have been the result of a combination of Daniel Rowland's preaching ministry and William Williams's success as a hymn writer.[1] There is ample testimony to Rowland's famous ability to move a congregation with the power of his preaching, making Llangeitho a highly likely location for such a revival. However, when explaining the origins of the revival, William Williams informed Howel Harris that 'this was not by any man but by the Lord Himself, or by some of the meanest of all the exhorters', which suggests the involvement of someone other than Rowland himself.[2] One who seemed to claim to have been present at the very beginning of the revival was William Richard of Llanddewibrefi, Cardiganshire, a lay exhorter who was superintendent over the societies along the southern stretch of the Cardigan Bay coastline, from St David's in Pembrokeshire to Llwyndafydd, near New Quay, in Cardiganshire. He later recounted to Harris that 'when the first cried out at Llangeitho' he had been forcefully reminded of the verse: 'I will once more shake the heavens' (Hebrews 12: 26).[3] This would indicate a realisation at the time that something more significant was afoot than the usual enthusiastic responses to Methodist preaching. Frustratingly, Harris did not record any further details he may have been told about when and where this occasion took place. William Richard's words have been interpreted as suggesting that he was one of the 'meanest of exhorters' to whom Williams attributed the outbreak of revival. Considering how prominent William Richard had become in Welsh Methodism, as an active preacher, as super-intendent of a number of societies and, as will be seen, as one of the six who signed the letter inviting Harris to return to the movement in 1763, it is highly doubtful whether Williams would have referred to Richard in that light. It may well be, therefore, that the early sparks of renewal were lit during meetings overseen by relatively obscure local exhorters, none of whom could claim sole responsibility for a single event which began the revival. A number of exhorters had been fostered in the area under Rowland's ministry, including William Richard Lloyd, Griffith Lewis Siôn, Evan Dafydd Jenkin and Dafydd Lewis.[4] In some sense their influence could be attributed to that of their spiritual father and the religiosity developed in the area under his guidance, so that Rowland undoubtedly deserved a share of the credit for the renewed enthusiasm evident in 1762.

One of the earliest printed accounts of the revival came in the history of early Methodism published in 1820 by Robert Jones, who had been active in the movement long enough to have heard the recollections of many of those affected by the revival. He declared that it was:

> y dydd y daeth Mr. W. Williams â'r llyfr hymnau a elwir '*Y môr o Wydr*' i Langeitho, y torrodd y diwygiad allan, ar ôl yr hir aeaf a fuasai yn gorchuddio yr eglwysi, yn achos y rhwyg . . .

> [the day that Mr. W. Williams brought the hymnbook called '*Y môr o Wydr*' to Llangeitho the revival broke out, after the long winter which had enveloped the churches, because of the division . . .][5]

If this was the case, the indications that the printing of this particular volume of hymns was actually completed at the end of 1761 suggest a date very early in the new year for the outbreak of revival.[6] Williams himself made no mention in subsequent prose work of his own possible influence on the start of the revival, but that may well have been as a result of reluctance to blow his own trumpet. *Caniadau y Rhai sydd ar y Môr o Wydr* ('The Songs of those who are on a Sea of Glass') is generally regarded as one of Williams's finest collections, demonstrating his increasing maturity as a hymn writer.[7] Some of his previous hymns had been criticised for requiring, in order to be sung with genuine conviction, a level of assurance of faith beyond many newer or weaker members. Williams quite consciously took this into account when writing the 1762 collection, declaring in the foreword that there were few hymns that could not be sung by all, regardless of their spiritual strength and maturity.

There may be some uncertainty about how William Williams's literary outputs contributed to the revival, but there is greater consensus over the question of how the revival affected Williams. The year 1762 is regarded as a milestone in his literary career, marking his emergence as a more mature and rounded writer.[8] Its immediate effect was to inspire Williams to embark on the publication of a series of prose works specifically for the Welsh Methodists. His first work, *Llythyr Martha Philopur* ('The Letter of Martha Philopur') (1762) was written from the perspective of Martha, a young woman influenced by the 1762 revival, who described her experiences in the form of a letter to her spiritual mentor, Philo-Evangelius. It is probably significant that Williams chose a female character to represent the archetypal convert, given that women formed the majority in most of the early societies.[9] It was equally appropriate, however, that the wise mentor whose advice she sought was a father figure, since the early exhorters and society stewards were invariably male. His next work, *Ateb Philo-Evangelius* ('The Answer of Philo-Evangelius') (1763), as the title suggests, was the fictional response to Martha's letter, the two volumes forming a dialogue regarding the nature of conversion and revival. Williams experienced something of a creative resurgence in the wake of 1762, going on to produce in addition the epic poem *Theomemphus* (1764), along with further volumes of hymns and prose works aimed at providing guidance for the members of the movement.[10] The structure of the dialogue or exchange of letters first employed in 1762–3 would be repeated frequently thereafter in Williams's publications, following in a long tradition in Welsh literature of using this device to convey information in a more engaging fashion than a more obviously didactic work. In *Drws y Society Profiad* ('The Door of the Experience Meeting') (1777) he provided valuable guidelines regarding the most appropriate way to conduct a society meeting, what questions to ask to encourage constructive self-examination and which to avoid.[11] Although already gaining respect as a hymn writer prior to 1762, it was the productivity and creativity of the years following the Llangeitho revival which confirmed Williams's pre-eminent role as literary spokesperson for the Methodist cause in Wales. His works did much to assist converts to recognise and interpret their own spiritual condition and to realise that often they were neither alone nor unique in their experiences.

The Llangeitho revival set the pattern not just for the emergence of Williams's creative talents, but also for Welsh Methodism as a whole, as periodic awakenings became a recurring feature of the movement. In *Ateb Philo-Evangelius*, Williams suggested that the whole of Christian history could be interpreted as a continuous cycle of revival and decline.[12] Within the history of the Methodist movement, it was hardly surprising that a spell of intense religiosity tended to be followed by a more restrained period of consolidation. From time to time, concern arose that these quieter times teetered on the brink of lapsing into stagnation, and thus they frequently provoked a conscious desire for a renewal of piety, which might well evolve into the early stirrings of fresh revival. Further awakenings followed at fairly regular intervals, leading to the assumption by the nineteenth century that a revival could be expected every ten years. Some of these resurgences of enthusiasm were local in their impact, whilst others achieved a broader influence throughout Wales, emulating the spread of 1762. In 1780–1, for instance, there was a widespread awakening which was apparently sparked off at Llangeitho when Daniel Rowland recited verses from the Gospel according to Matthew during his sermon: 'I thank thee, O Father, Lord of heaven and earth, because Thou hast hid these things from the wise and prudent, and hast revealed them unto babes; even so, Father, for so it seemed good in Thy sight'.[13] During the eighteenth century, each revival served the dual purpose of revitalising the existing adherents and of winning new converts to the cause, doing much to ensure the steady growth of the membership.

Many of the features evident in 1762 would be repeated in later revivals, primarily the centrality of preaching, the importance of hymnody and the enthusiastic response to both. Preaching had of course been an essential element of Calvinistic Methodism from the outset, but the other two factors in the revival came to be regarded as especially characteristic of Welsh Methodism. It was the 1762 revival which seemed to establish the reputation of the Welsh Methodists as enthusiasts and 'Jumpers', a tendency which discredited them in the eyes of many Anglican and Dissenting contemporaries. John Wesley looked askance at this kind of fervour, believing it to be the result of Satan working on honest, but inexperienced, Christians in order to bring discredit on God's work.[14] By 1764 the Independent minister, Thomas Morgan, was concerned that the awakening had spread to north Wales and that the Methodists there were 'Stark mad & given up to a Spirit of Delusion to the great Disgrace & Scandal of Christianity. May the Lord pity the poor Dissenters there: I am afraid some of them will fall away by that Strong Wind of Temptation.'[15] A large part of William Williams's motivation for writing *Llythyr Martha Philopur* in 1762 was his wish to defend the Methodists against such misgivings. Martha was made to cite a number of scriptural examples of rejoicing and dancing which seemed to offer justification for the joyous behaviour of those affected by revival.[16] Even so, Williams insisted at the same time that converts during revivals should be subject to the same rigorous procedure for acceptance as full members which had been in place since the 1740s, to ensure that they were sincere in their professions. Harris also defended the exuberance, but likewise sounded a note of caution, suggesting that it was essential for joy and sorrow to grow together in one's religious experience.[17] Robert Jones acknowledged that in the heady atmosphere of 1762, with the jubilant response to the offer of free grace predominating, there had been a danger of forgetting the vital importance of also preaching sober morality, the need to demonstrate the 'fruits of the spirit'.[18] The fear was that in the midst of such unrestrained enthusiasm the unwary and uninformed might fall prey to the lurking peril of antinomianism. There was always a danger too that the spontaneous emotion generated in the atmosphere of revival could give rise to a more contrived emulation, as 'jumping' was perceived by some to be an expected characteristic of true revival. Although the leadership remained generally wary of the sort of rampant emotionalism which could lead to accusations of mindless hysteria, they continued to defend the right of the Methodists to rejoice over genuine spiritual experiences.

It could also be said that 1762 confirmed the vital connection between revivalism and hymn singing. When Howel Harris first learnt of the 1762 awakening, he referred to it in his diary as the 'spirit of singing', indicating the general perception that communal singing was intrinsic to the phenomenon.[19] From the 1740s onwards, Methodism had increasingly developed the use of hymns as a means of expressing the emotions experienced by the converted.[20] The first published rule book for the Welsh societies advocated songs of praise as a crucial part of Methodist activity and contained a number of hymns as examples, including early works by Howel Harris and Daniel Rowland.[21] Williams published the first part of his initial volume of hymns, appropriately entitled *Aleluja*, in 1744, with further collections following in the 1750s.[22] Although Williams was the most famous, the evangelical revival produced several other acclaimed hymn writers, including Morgan Rhys and Ann Griffiths. Their contribution, along with the continued development of Nonconformist hymnody throughout the nineteenth century, ensured that the exuberant singing which characterised 1762 became a common feature of future revivals in Wales.

The return of Howel Harris

It was while the wave of revival was still surging through south Wales that Howel Harris formally returned to the movement. Despite the emphasis on Harris's heretical tendencies as the major cause of the rift, it would seem that Mrs Sidney Griffith's demise in 1752 actually removed the greatest stumbling block for his colleagues, who began to make tentative moves towards rapprochement as early as 1754. Daniel Rowland and William Williams visited Harris at Trefeca that year on 16 September, a significant step forward, considering the painful and intensely personal nature of the separation.[23] Representatives of the two sides had met by chance on previous occasions, but this was the first time that Harris and Rowland had encountered each other face to face since before Harris's expulsion. Despite this visit, it took several years before full reconciliation was achieved, partly because of Harris's poor health in the first instance and latterly because of his activities and prolonged absences with the Breconshire militia. Increasingly, friendly relations were established, and Williams, accompanied by Peter Williams, called at Trefeca on 12 June 1759.[24] However, in a meeting with Rowland, Williams, Peter Williams, William John, John Popkin and Thomas Bowen at Trecastle on 4 September, 'the Enemy came down' and they failed to reach agreement. Harris feared at the time that his reinstatement would stir up fresh hostility towards him from some within the Methodist movement.[25] Indeed, some diplomacy seems to have been necessary within Rowland's group in order to reassure those exhorters who may have felt disquiet at the prospect of Harris resuming his dominant role over them. William Williams apparently played a key role in these negotiations, according to a letter sent by him to Harris, in which he claimed to have assured his colleagues that Harris had no authoritarian designs in seeking to return, and 'as soon as I put things in that light before them . . . all with one voice expressed a hearty consent to desire you to come among us'.[26] Williams, although not without criticism of some of Harris's behaviour, always regarded him as a spiritual father and was evidently one of the keenest to achieve a reconciliation. He freely acknowledged that Harris's organisational skills had been missed.[27] But he was probably also aware that there was some concern in the movement more generally that the price to pay for those abilities was the tension Harris's personality could create. By 1762, however, the future of Calvinistic Methodism in Wales seemed rather more assured in the light of the renewed revival. As a result, it was perhaps easier for the doubters to invite Harris to return to a more confident, reinvigorated movement rather than to one in desperate need of his assistance.

A formal letter was sent by Rowland, William Williams, Peter Williams, William Richard, David Williams and John Harry on 19 May 1762, inviting Harris

once more to fill up your Place among us, which we sensibly acknowledge has been long vacant. We have followed you with our prayers

---

thro' your various tours, and are satisfied you generally appeared double armed, to the furtherance of the Gospel: Glory be to free sovereign Grace: and we unanimously conclude that your inclination to visit our several counties again is the voice of Heaven, and we doubt not but all animosities will and must subside and a spirit of love take place.[28]

The letter offered no apology for the expulsion and seemed rather to indicate that the content of Harris's preaching was now deemed to be acceptable, enabling his reintegration into the movement. Judging by some of his diary entries, Harris himself seemed to interpret the reunion as his colleagues tacitly owning that they had been mistaken in condemning his religious views and his friendly attitude to the Moravians, especially as it was his colleagues who had approached him about a possible return.[29] Both sides, not unnaturally, seem to have reserved the right to view the end of the division from slightly different perspectives, to provide some justification for their previous actions. Even so, all seemed agreed that the breach should be closed, for the good of all, since, as Harris acknowledged: 'Sure they suffer for want of me and I for want of them.'[30] Harris resigned his commission with the militia at the end of 1762 and was formally welcomed back to the Methodist fold shortly afterwards. He met Rowland on 15 February 1763, when the pair discussed the causes of their previous disagreement.[31] They then accompanied each other to the association meeting the next day at Llansawel, Carmarthenshire, where Harris addressed the exhorters for two hours. On 29 March, he set out for his first preaching tour of Carmarthenshire for many years, attended by substantial crowds, surely partly because of the novelty of his return to the south-west and the Methodist cause. He claimed to speak with 'the old and uncommon freedom', but also yearned for the 'fire and life' apparent among those affected by the recent revival.[32] Another milestone was reached when, at Rowland's urging, the first association to be held at Trefeca since the separation met on 18 May 1763, with most of those present seemingly determined to heal old wounds rather than to open them afresh.[33]

Harris continued to demonstrate the organisational talent which had provided the movement with its abiding structure and which had been one of the reasons why the others had been so eager to seek his return. Harris himself felt that one of the factors behind the separation was that the Methodist leaders had not appreciated the need for discipline as he had always done. He thus perceived their 'crying for discipline' by the time of the reconciliation as confirmation that they had erred against him in the past.[34] He offered some sound advice on how to organise the societies efficiently, including the suggestion that issues decided by the association should not subsequently be altered by individuals but referred back to the association. To a large extent, Harris was simply reiterating principles that had long been accepted, such as the wisdom of allocating roles within the movement which best suited an individual's talents. Yet, there may well have been a need to re-establish some of these basic procedures which may have become somewhat neglected during the strain of the years of separation. It was generally acknowledged that the Methodist leaders had struggled with the organisation of their cause during this period and that Rowland in particular found he had little talent or taste for administration. As Williams explained to Harris: 'Mr Rowland did shine in the pulpit, but was not fit for any other place or work.' As for administration, Rowland's approach had been 'but huddling of things over in a hurry'.[35]

Yet Griffith T. Roberts rightly suggests that the reunion was 'never complete'.[36] Tensions almost inevitably remained, as was occasionally evident in some heated exchanges in association meetings. One barrier to full reconciliation was the fact that the Trefeca Family was never truly accepted by the Welsh Methodists, which must have seemed to Harris to belittle his achievements during the division. Too much time had passed for him to be accepted fully on the same terms as previously, as a new generation of exhorters had emerged who did not necessarily have any special sense of respect for Harris. These were likely to have been among those who needed to be appeased by Williams prior to the reunion. One in particular who seemed to needle Harris was John Popkin of Swansea, an exhorter of gentry background who had risen to prominence during the 1750s.[37] His name figured frequently in the diary of John Thomas of Tre-main, Cardiganshire, as one of the exhorters who visited the area regularly at a time when he was based in Tre-lech in Carmarthenshire.[38] His had already been something of a dissenting voice at the Trefeca association in May 1763, offending Harris by uttering some criticism 'under pretence of

Brotherly Love'.[39] At an association at Llangeitho in August 1763, he again clashed with Harris, who threatened to leave rather than submit to 'his having any authority over me, or his speaking as a Bishop, that he is but a young preacher'.[40] Williams intervened to quieten matters, although he himself was to disagree vehemently with Popkin during a subsequent meeting of the association in 1764, as the exhorter veered increasingly towards Sandemanianism, publishing a number of works described by Gomer Roberts as 'soulless, long-winded and slippery'.[41]

Popkin was not the only Methodist who continued to regard Harris with some misgivings. Harris's tendency to seek fellowship with all who called themselves Christian had increased during his years adrift from the formal Welsh Methodist movement. He yearned for greater union between the separate sections of the evangelical revival and continually renounced the term 'Methodist', refusing to espouse any name but 'Christian' since it was the most inclusive and least divisive.[42] He had, for instance, attended the Wesleyan Conference in 1759 and 1760 and would do so again in 1763 and 1767.[43] It is probably to his credit that he did not forget the comradeship shown him by the Wesleys and the Moravians at a time when the Calvinistic wing of the revival shunned him, but it was an attitude not likely to endear him greatly to his colleagues. Condemnation of the Wesleyan Methodists invariably annoyed him as displaying pride and narrowness of spirit. This almost inevitably led to confrontation with his old friend, Howell Davies, who faced competition from both Moravians and Wesleyans in Pembrokeshire. Davies resented John Wesley's visits to the county, leading Harris to accuse him of seeking to establish a monopoly in the area and to exclude all other preachers.[44]

Harris did, however, find common ground with the leading Methodist-minded clergy in their continued efforts to resist any argument in favour of secession from the Established Church. They may, indeed, have been glad to have him add his voice to theirs on a matter which continued to cause tension and disagreement within the movement. Harris had come to be on better terms with his own parish clergyman, Pryce Davies, the vicar of Talgarth, during the years of separation and had always insisted that the Family attend church services regularly.[45] Yet, relations with the Church in general were not so cordial for all Methodists at this time, as demonstrated by Daniel Rowland's ejection from his curacies. For years, Rowland had served as curate to his brother, John Rowland, who had been rector of Llangeitho from 1730 until his death in 1760. At that time, Daniel Rowland had rather pointedly been overlooked for preferment, in favour of his son, another John Rowland. It has been suggested that this may have been a useful compromise for Bishop Anthony Ellis of St David's, as a means of acknowledging Rowland's support in the parish without being seen to reward his Methodist activities.[46] It was, however, Bishop Samuel Squire who was in charge of the diocese at the time of the Llangeitho revival, and he seems to have been less inclined to compromise. In July 1763, at a time when Methodist fortunes seemed on the rise as a result of revival and internal reconciliation, Rowland was expelled from the curacies of Llangeitho and Nancwnlle.[47] Precisely how this was enforced remains uncertain, as the records of the Church in the diocese of St David's shed no light on the matter. It has frequently been reported that representatives of the bishop intervened at a Sunday service to bar Rowland from the pulpit.[48] A rumour which reached Glamorgan was that Rowland had been excluded during the bishop's summer visitation since he refused to comply with the demand that he refrain from itinerant preaching for a period of three years.[49] However it came about, this was a decision which ultimately did the Church little good, as the parishioners of Llangeitho deserted their parish church to receive communion from Rowland in a new chapel built for him nearby. The expulsion also served to strengthen the hand of those who argued that the Welsh Methodists should leave the Church, although the leadership continued to reject such importunings. Rowland met with considerable support and sympathy, sometimes from unexpected quarters. By the 1770s he was appointed chaplain to the duke of Leinster as a result of the influence of the countess of Huntingdon, who had a high opinion of Rowland's abilities as a preacher.[50] He was also offered the rectorship of Newport, Pembrokeshire, in 1769 by John Thornton, an affluent and philanthropic London merchant who was a leading member of the 'Clapham Sect', seeking regeneration of the Church of England by securing the right to appoint evangelical clergymen to local parishes. Yet Rowland was obliged to decline the Newport rectorship, as he could not bind himself to be resident and leave behind his former parishioners in Llangeitho who were distraught at the thought of his departure.[51]

The 1760s was, therefore, a period of change and adjustment for the Methodist leaders. It undoubtedly marked the beginning of a new phase in the history of the Welsh movement, with the effects of the 1762 revival leading to a renewal of energies and to Methodism gaining ground gradually during the decade. The informative diary of William Thomas of Michaelston-super-Ely in Glamorgan, for instance, is sprinkled with references to Methodist preachers and adherents as a common feature of daily life in the area.[52] The first signs appeared also of the emergence of a second generation of leading Methodists, including the appearance of a young Nathaniel Rowland at the association meetings by 1763.

The 1770s brought further significant changes, with the loss of both Howell Davies and Howel Harris. Davies's death on 13 January 1770, aged 53, marked the passing of the first of the early Methodist leaders, although Davies never gained the same prominence as Harris, Rowland and Williams, perhaps because he was hampered by ill health and also because he tended to be confined to a particular area of the country. Regarded as 'the Apostle of Pembrokeshire', he had been the driving force for Methodism in that county.[53] From his parish of Llys-y-frân near Haverfordwest, Davies had established a following in both the Welsh-speaking north and the more anglicised south, visiting a number of chapels to provide regular preaching and communion for his Methodist flock. A staunch Calvinist, who was incensed at the incursions of the Wesleyan Methodists into his territory, he had a reputation as a stirring preacher and obviously commanded considerable loyalty among the Pembrokeshire Methodists, despite the challenges from other religious groups. He was in an advantageous position to operate with some freedom as a result of the authority which arose from his situation as an ordained clergyman, along with the financial independence he had acquired as a result of the comfortable estate left to him at the death of his first wife. Despite concentrating his efforts on Pembrokeshire, he also travelled to north Wales on several occasions, when his health allowed, and preached in a number of English chapels at the invitation of Lady Huntingdon.

Howel Harris died on 21 July 1773, aged 59, and was buried in Talgarth Church three days later, in a service attended by an estimated twenty thousand people.[54] Whatever the exact figure, the large numbers who gathered for his funeral gave a clear indication of the abiding respect felt for him by many of the ordinary members of the Methodist movement. Many of the crowd doubtless would have felt inclined to concur with William Williams's injunction, in his elegy to Harris, to voice no further criticism of the deceased.[55] Despite the frequently fraught nature of his relationship with his fellow Methodists, he did much to establish the character of the movement, through the indefatigable itinerancy of the early years, the insistence on order and method and the unswerving allegiance to Calvinist theology and the articles of the Church of England. At times a divisive figure in his native land, he often proved a more conciliatory presence beyond its borders. Although his irenic inclinations brought their own problems, Howel Harris, perhaps more than any of the other early evangelical leaders, sought tolerance and collaboration between the separate streams of the revival.

Even as the Welsh Methodists mourned the passing of two of their early leaders, a new generation nurtured under the continued guidance of Daniel Rowland and William Williams was coming to the fore in Wales. After Howell Davies's death there were concerns about the future of the movement in Pembrokeshire, in light of continued competition from the Moravians and Wesleyans.[56] The invitation issued to Howel Harris to visit the county within days of Davies's death in January 1770 probably reflected this mood of uncertainty and the need for consultation.[57] As a fully ordained Anglican priest, Davies had been in a position to administer communion regularly, not only in his only parish, but in a number of chapels of ease and in new Methodist chapels in the surrounding area of north Pembrokeshire and south Cardiganshire. There was no doubt that the loss of his contribution as both preacher and pastor would be keenly felt. At the time, there was no obvious immediate successor to Davies's role in the area, but the position eventually fell to Nathaniel Rowland, who married in 1776, Margaret, Davies's sole daughter and heiress, moving to the family home at Parciau, Henllan Amgoed. A graduate of Christ Church, Oxford, Nathaniel Rowland had been ordained as an Anglican cleric in 1773 and resigned a curacy in the Chelmsford area to return to Wales. Unlike his older brother John, Nathaniel adhered to the Methodist cause and quickly gained prominence in the movement, largely as a result of the respect felt for his father Daniel.[58] Once established in Pembrokeshire, Nathaniel Rowland became a frequent visitor to the new Tabernacle at Haverfordwest and, by 1778, was confirmed as its pastor by the association, in the same meeting in which he was appointed secretary to the association, a position he continued to fill for nearly twenty years.[59]

Information regarding the Welsh Association is sparse for the period between the death of Howel Harris and the time that Nathaniel Rowland's record-keeping began. There is, however, evidence that the movement continued to grow steadily during the 1770s, with over forty chapels being constructed throughout north and south Wales.[60] Yet, perhaps the most significant development in this period was the growing prominence of Llangeitho as a destination for Methodist pilgrims, seeking both to hear Daniel Rowland preach and to receive communion from his hands.[61] The monthly communion Sunday at Llangeitho in particular was attended by hundreds of Methodists, some from as far afield as Caernarfonshire and Anglesey.[62] One Methodist sympathiser from among the Pembrokeshire minor gentry, James Bowen of Llwyngwair, calculated that on one of his visits some fourteen thousand communicants waited on Rowland and his son Nathaniel.[63] Such estimates are probably a considerable exaggeration, although there are indications that over a thousand received communion regularly in the 'New Church' built for Daniel Rowland at Capel Gwynfil, Llangeitho, after he lost the use of the parish church. [64] Sermons were frequently conducted outside to accommodate the numbers, but the chapel was designed to deal with what amounted to a production line of communicants, with four different doors so that a constant stream could enter and then depart having received the elements. A large communion table which spanned the width of the building was lowered on ropes and lifted out of the way when not in use. Llangeitho became accustomed to crowds, and contemporary commentators described how the surrounding hills rang with hymn singing as the travellers wound their way home.[65]

During this period, Calvinistic Methodism in Wales had proven strong enough to survive a testing time of dispute and division. Not only that, but it had emerged as a reinvigorated movement as a result of the first fresh wave of revival it had experienced since its early years. Harris's return to the fold had certainly helped confirm the impression that Methodism had overcome its difficulties and was looking to the future with renewed confidence. Whilst Harris was never quite able to regain his previous authority in the movement, his death left Daniel Rowland as undisputed leader of the Welsh Methodists, a group who could increasingly be regarded as Rowland's people, even if the structure of the movement still owed much to Harris's careful planning.

Notes

1   See R. Geraint Gruffydd, 'Diwygiad 1762 a William Williams o Bantycelyn', *JHSPCW*, 54, 3 (1969), 68–75; 55, 1 (1970), 4–13; Eryn M. White, '"I will once more shake the heavens": The 1762 Revival in Wales', in Kate Cooper and Jeremy Gregory (eds), *Revival and Resurgence in Christian History*, Studies in Church History, 44 (Woodbridge: Boydell, 2008), pp. 154–63.
2   NLW Howel Harris's Diary, 3 August 1763.
3   Ibid., 29 November 1763.
4   John Hughes, *Methodistiaeth Cymru*, cyfrol II (Wrexham: R. Hughes a'i Fab, 1851–6), pp. 1–3; Gomer M. Roberts, (ed.), *Hanes Methodist-iaeth Galfinaidd Cymru*, cyfrol I: *Y Deffroad Mawr* (Caernarfon: Llyfrfa'r Methodistiaid Calfinaidd, 1973), pp. 259–60, 262.
5   Robert Jones, *Drych yr Amseroedd*, ed. G. M. Ashton (Cardiff: University of Wales Press, 1958), p. 86. The hymn book referred to is William Williams, *Caniadau, (y rhai sydd ar y mor o wydr yn gymmysgedig a than, ac wedi cael y maes ar y bwystfil) i Frenhin y Saint* (Carmarthen: John Ross 1762). The title draws on a reference in the Book of Revelation to those who had conquered the beast singing praises and playing God's harps whilst on a sea of glass mixed with fire, an image which may have been considered appropriate to the early Methodists. Revelation 15: 2–3.
6   Gomer M. Roberts, *Y Pêr Ganiedydd (Pantycelyn)* cyfrol II: *Arweiniad i'w Waith* (Aberystwyth: Gwasg Aberystwyth, 1958), p. 250.
7   Derec Llwyd Morgan, *William Williams Pantycelyn* (Caernarfon: Gwasg Pantycelyn, 1983), pp. 17–9, 54–65; Glyn Tegai Hughes, *Williams Pantycelyn* (Cardiff: University of Wales Press, 1983), pp. 75–124.
8   Kathryn Jenkins, 'Williams Pantycelyn', in Branwen Jarvis (ed.), *A Guide to Welsh literature c.1700–1800* (Cardiff: University of Wales Press, 2000), pp. 256–64.
9   Eryn M. White, '"Myrdd o Wragedd": Merched a'r Diwygiad Methodistaidd', *Llên Cymru*, 20 (1997), 62–74; Eryn M. White, 'Women in the early Methodist societies in Wales', *Journal of Welsh Religious History*, 7 (1999), 95–108.

[10] English translation available in Eifion Evans, *Pursued by God: A selective translation with notes of the Welsh religious classic Theomemphus, by William Williams of Pantycelyn* (Bridgend: Evangelical Press of Wales, 1996).

[11] William Williams, *Templum Experientiae apertum; neu, Ddrws y Society Profiad Wedi ei agor o Led y Pen* (Brecon: E. Evans, 1777); English translation by M. Lloyd Jones, as William Williams, *The Experience Meeting – an introduction to the Welsh Societies of the Evangelical Awakening* (Bridgend: Evangelical Movement of Wales, 1973).

[12] Garfield H. Hughes (ed.), *Gweithiau William Williams Pantycelyn, cyfrol II: Rhyddiaith* (Cardiff: University of Wales Press, 1967), pp. 21–4.

[13] Matthew 11: 25–6; Eifion Evans, *Daniel Rowland and the Great Evangelical Awakening in Wales* (Edinburgh: The Banner of Truth Trust, 1985), p. 352.

[14] Quoted in Gruffydd, 'Diwygiad 1762', 72.

[15] NLW MS5453c, 13 March 1764.

[16] Hughes (ed.), *Gweithiau William Williams*, pp. 5–11.

[17] NLW Howel Harris's Diary, 2 April 1763.

[18] Jones, *Drych yr Amseroedd*, pp. 86–7.

[19] For instance, NLW Howel Harris's Diary 15 February 1763; 29 March 1763; 2 April 1763.

[20] Derec Llwyd Morgan, *The Great Awakening in Wales* (Peterborough: Epworth Press, 1988), pp. 267–97; E. Wyn James, 'The Evolution of the Welsh Hymn', in Isabel Rivers and David L. Wykes (eds), *Dissenting Praise: Religious Dissent and the Hymn* (Cambridge: Cambridge University Press, 2011) pp. 229–68.

[21] *Sail, Dibenion a Rheolau'r Societies neu'r Cyfarfodydd Neilltuol a Ddechreusant Ymgynull yn Ddiweddar yng Nghymru* (Bristol: Felix Farley, 1742), pp. 4, 17–23.

[22] William Williams, *Aleluja, neu, casgljad o hymnau ar amryw ystyriaethau* (Carmarthen: Samuel Lewis, 1744); *Hosanna i fab Dafydd, neu gasgliad o hymnau* (Bristol: Felix Farley, 1751); *Rhai hymnau a chaniadau duwiol ar amryw ystyrjaethau* (Carmarthen: Evan Powel, 1757).

[23] NLW Howel Harris's Diary, 16 September 1754.

[24] NLW Howel Harris's Diary, 12 June 1759.

[25] NLW Howel Harris's Diary, 4–5 September 1759.

[26] NLW Trevecka Letter 3325, William Williams to Howel Harris, n.d. Although undated, the content of the letter suggests it was composed at around the same time as Harris was invited to return to the movement. See also Roberts, *Y Pêr Ganiedydd*, cyfrol I, pp. 131–7.

27 NLW Howel Harris's Diary, 3 August 1763.
28 NLW Trevecka Letter 2472, William Williams, Daniel Rowland, Peter Williams, William Richard, David Williams and John Harry to Howel Harris, 19 May 1762.
29 See NLW Howel Harris's Diary, 12 May 1763.
30 NLW Howel Harris's Diary, 3 August 1763.
31 NLW Howel Harris's Diary, 15 February 1763.
32 NLW Howel Harris's Diary, 29 March 1763.
33 NLW Howel Harris's Diary, 18 May 1763.
34 NLW Howel Harris's Diary, 21 September 1763.
35 NLW Howel Harris's Diary, 3 August 1763.
36 Griffith T. Roberts, *Howell Harris* (London: Epworth Press, 1951), p. 73.
37 Roberts, *Y Pêr Ganiedydd, I*, pp. 137–48; D. Emrys Williams, 'The Popkin family', *Carmarthenshire Antiquary*, 7 (1971), 120–34; Gomer M. Roberts, 'Pobl Rowland yn ystod yr Ymraniad', in Roberts (ed.), *Hanes Methodistiaeth Galfinaidd Cymru*, cyfrol I, p. 396.
38 NLW MS 20515-6C.
39 NLW Howel Harris's Diary, 18 May 1763.
40 NLW Howel Harris's Diary, 3 August 1763.
41 Roberts, *Y Pêr Ganiedydd, I*, p. 145. Sandemanianism aimed to restore a pure New Testament church free of any connection with the state and tended to reject religious emotionalism.
42 See Eryn M. White, 'The eighteenth-century evangelical revival and Welsh identity', in Mark Smith (ed.), *British Evangelical Identities Past and Present*, vol. 1, *Aspects of the History and Sociology of Evangelicalism in Britain and Ireland* (Milton Keynes: Paternoster, 2009), pp. 86–7.
43 Roberts, *Howell Harris*, p. 76.
44 NLW Howel Harris's Diary, 12 May 1763 and 3 August 1763.
45 For improved relations with Davies, see NLW Trevecka Letter 2044, Howel Harris to Pryce Davies, 29 January 1753; NLW Trevecka Letter 2242, Pryce Davies to Howel Harris, 11 December 1758.
46 Evans, *Daniel Rowland*, p. 324. E. D. Jones also regarded it as an 'amicable settlement made locally'. 'Report of the centenary meeting held at Aberystwyth', *Archaeologia Cambrensis*, xcix, part 1 (1946), 154.
47 Evans, *Daniel Rowland*, pp. 323–6.
48 John Morgan Jones and William Morgan, *Y Tadau Methodistaidd* (2 vols, Swansea: Lewis Evans, 1895), I, pp. 54–5; Raymond L. Brown, 'The expulsion of Daniel Rowland from his curacies: an oral tradition?', *JHSPCW*, 20 (1996), 31–5.

49 R. T. W. Denning (ed.), *The Diary of William Thomas of Michaelston-super-Ely, near St Fagans Glamorgan 1762–1795* (Cardiff: South Wales Record Society, 1995), p. 119.

50 The title first appears on the title-page of a collection of Rowland's sermons in 1775. Daniel Rowland, *Tair Pregeth a bregethwyd yn yr Eglwys Newydd, gerllaw Llangeitho* (Carmarthen, John Ross, 1775).

51 NLW Trevecka MS 2842a, 30 November 1769; Gomer M. Roberts, 'Trannoeth yr Aduniad', in Roberts (ed.), *Hanes Methodistiaeth Galfinaidd Cymru*, II, pp. 40–1.

52 For instance, Denning (ed.), *The Diary of William Thomas*, pp. 33, 38, 42, 52, 72, 75.

53 Hughes, *Methodistiaeth Cymru*, I, pp. 80–4; Jones and Morgan, *Y Tadau Methodistaidd*, pp. 128–40; Rhidian Griffiths, 'Howel Davies: Apostol Sir Benfro', *JHSPCW*, 11 (1987), 2–14.

54 Hugh J. Hughes, *Life of Howell Harris: The Welsh Reformer* (London: James Nisbet & Co., 1892), pp. 434–6; Jones and Morgan, *Y Tadau Methodistaidd*, p. 430; Tudur, *Howell Harris*, p. 233.

55 William Williams, *Marwnad er coffadwriaeth am Mr Howel Harries* (Brecon: E. Evans, 1773), p. 8.

56 Roberts, 'Trannoeth yr Aduniad', pp. 43–4.

57 NLW Trevecka Letter 2677, Thomas Davies to Howel Harris, 18 January 1770.

58 See J. Trefor Lloyd, 'Nathaniel Rowland (1749–1831)', *JHSPCW*, 45 (1960) 60–6; 46 (1961), 10–16; Eifion Evans, 'Nathaniel Rowland's ordination and curacy at Stock, Essex', *JHSPCW*, 45 (1960), 67–70; Euros Wyn Jones, 'Nathaniel Rowland', *JHSPCW*, 7 (1983), 35–42.

59 NLW CMA Trevecka 2999, Journal of the Welsh Association, 1778–1797; D. Myrddin Lloyd, 'Nathaniel Rowland and the Tabernacle, Haverfordwest', *JHSPCW*, 36, 2 (1951), 33–41.

60 Roberts, *Hanes Methodistiaeth Galfinaidd Cymru, II*, p. 534.

61 See Derec Llwyd Morgan, 'Daniel Rowland (?1711–1790): Pregethwr Diwygiadol', *Ceredigion*, 10 (1991), 217–37; Eryn M. White, '"Gwnaeth ei farwnad yn ei fywyd": Cofio Daniel Rowland, Llan-geitho (1711?–1790)', *Y Traethodydd*, 166 (October 2011), 250–67.

62 Derec Llwyd Morgan, *Pobl Pantycelyn* (Llandysul: Gomer, 1986), pp. 1–19.

63 NLW Llwyngwair MS 16986a.

64 D. J. Odwyn Jones, *Daniel Rowland Llangeitho (1713–1790)* (Llan-dysul: Gomer, 1938), pp. 59–61.

65 NLW Llwyngwair MS 16986a; William Williams, Marwnad y Parch. Daniel Rowland, Llangeitho', in N. Cynhafal Jones (ed.), *Gweithiau*

Williams Pant-y-celyn (2 vols, Holywell: P. M. Evans and Son, 1887), I, pp. 586–7; George Eyre Evans (ed.), *Lloyd Letters (1754–1791)* (Aberystwyth: William Jones, 1908), p. 52.

7

'You are only going to a few simple souls': new English Calvinistic groupings, at mid-century

The heady exuberance of the countess of Huntingdon's activities began in the 1760s and reached a height during the 1770s and 1780s. By the mid-1760s she was ready with dynamic plans to revamp the whole Church of England, but believed that it was not yet ready for it.[1] Her expanding enterprises called for far more manpower than she was able to attract naturally. She was secretly involved in supporting six students at St Edmund Hall, Oxford, who were famously expelled in 1768 for their Methodistic activities and their Calvinistic orientation. With Whitefield rushing into print in the students' support, John Wesley offered no criticism of his university. Viewing the event not as the expulsion of Methodists, but of Calvinists, Wesley was pleased that the Oxford authorities had cleared the Church of England of official belief in predestination; it was a doctrine, in his view, inconsistent with its teaching.

The expulsion fell neatly into place with a plan the countess had been nursing for four years. Whatever hopes she may have entertained for the easy passage of evangelicals through the universities to Anglican ordination were tempered by bitter experience. As she boldly extended her activities during the early 1760s she had seen the doors of episcopal palaces and university colleges increasingly bolted close. For academic training, the Dissenting academies were no option: that would lead to non-episcopal ordination, and her mission was to reform the Church of England. The only alternative she saw was to establish her own institution of learning. By remaining a professing Anglican, she reckoned that she could find at least some bishops willing to ordain the products of such an establishment. 'I wish we had a nursery' for preachers, she wrote in 1764 and early the following year was already discussing plans for a 'college' to be 'established in the true and full primitive spirit'.[2] She reasoned that its location should also be 'primitive'; thus she turned to Howel Harris and his mountain retreat in the Breconshire hills of Wales – where her 'college' would be safe from the prying eyes and interfering hands of bishops. There, 200 yards from Harris's religious 'Family' of artisans at Trefeca – without whose assistance it could never have been built – she would establish an institution to train young men to carry the gospel throughout England and parts of Wales.

While, of course, bitterly opposed to the Oxford expulsion, the countess always relished the sense of occasion, and this moved her to establish what would be known as 'Trevecca College'. Thus Oxford's loss would be Trevecca's gain: she hoped that those students would become the first fruits of her 'college'. Upon their expulsion, she immediately invited them all to become her students, although only two accepted – the least academically qualified of the six – and remained only briefly. Neither apparently found the exchange of Oxford for Trevecca to his taste. The deliberate christening of her institution as a 'college' was a provocative gesture: no Dissenting academy made so bold until 1786. Moreover, from the outset Lady Huntingdon was determined to give her 'college' as many physical academic trappings as was practical. From the day of its opening, students were dressed in caps and gowns supplied by their benefactress, a practice that created much outside opposition, since it was 'assuming one of the privileges of the university'.[3] As she made final plans for its opening on 24 August 1768, she reflected – not without a *frisson* of excitement – that she 'must expect fires on all sides kindled for me . . .[The] universitys & the bishops with all the outward clamo[u]r of order will be employed against me.'[4]

In Dissenting eyes, Trevecca 'formed a body of more injudicious Calvinists than England had ever before seen'.[5] Its lack of commitment to intellectual endeavour cast 'an unfavourable light upon the whole evangelistic movement'.[6] Indeed, the countess insisted on an education that distanced her students from the earlier Dissenting emphasis on a learned ministry. 'Did you ever see anything more queer than their plan of institution', wrote John Wesley: 'Pray who penned it, man or woman?'[7] The countess had secured John Fletcher, now the vicar of Madeley, Shropshire, to serve as occasional visitor and overseer, but she never found any truly qualified man to conduct a sustained programme of learning. In fact, Trevecca can be seen much more accurately as a missionary organisation rather than as a college.

Often in residence for long periods, the countess, as one former student recollected, was 'a stern disciplinarian, in the government of her students – as they all found – in the domestic as well as the scholastic arrangements of the college'. She laid great stress on the students' cleanliness and neatness and 'claimed implicit obedience'.[8] She also undertook to organise all their far-flung preaching assignments. Over the years they roamed every English county, especially through the south-east (focusing on Kent and Sussex), the west (especially Somerset, Gloucestershire and Worcestershire), the north (primarily Yorkshire and Lancashire), and Cornwall, Berkshire, Hertfordshire, Staffordshire and Norfolk, as well as London and the anglicised areas of south Wales.

During its twenty-four-year existence, over two hundred men were enrolled at one time or another at Trevecca, yet only twenty ever secured episcopal ordination. The bishops' anxiety over the quality of their education was justified, and it proved decidedly difficult to find an adequate master: during some periods there was none. Students often complained that they were not students at all, but inexperienced preachers sent to far-flung places. One said that in three years he had not been at the 'college' more than a total of three months, wisely observing that 'altho learning do not make ministers, it is necessary for ministers to have it'.[9] At one point the tutor reported that with only two exceptions all the students were 'exceedingly ignorant in scripture history . . . little better versed in this . . . than they are in Mahomet's Koran'.[10] But the countess's real aim for this institution was that it gather a group of young men who would constantly scour the nation proclaiming a simple message. As she told them: 'Come, come . . . you are only going to a few simple souls: tell them concerning Jesus Christ, and they will be satisfied.'[11] Such an approach to ministerial training may well have fitted the Methodism of the eighteenth century; it was far removed from what Calvinism had traditionally insisted upon.

Most Trevecca students were from England, but with those from Wales who spoke little or no English the countess insisted they become proficient in that language, since the proclamation of the gospel was not to be impeded by any local considerations. Her vision was to reach out to the whole nation, and to fulfil that she reasoned English to be necessary for all her men. Her preachers must be able to roam as far and wide as possible. To one such she wrote as early as 1772:

> I hope you will not lose your English too much [by his preaching in north Wales], as I am not satisfied unless all my Welch students are English preachers. Our calls are so extensive . . . I dread nothing so much for any of you as sitting down in some poor narrow limit the littleness of your faith might make for you. Give the Lord your youth & strength over the whole world. [She has had one Welsh student staying with her in Sussex in order to improve his English.] If I succeed with him I intend to have one of the Welch students in their turn with me for this purpose till they all are masters & have it made easy to them in both Languages.[12]

The countess later observed that 'the Welch students are great trials to me, yet the Welch will be set hard to give us quite up'.[13]

The countess's enterprise was but one of the Calvinistic groups to surface in the Methodistic stream. When Lady Huntingdon began attending George Whitefield's London Tabernacle in the mid-1740s, the chapel had been in existence for only three years. The Tabernacle became the seedbed for further splintering and acrimony, especially during Whitefield's absence, once again in America, from 1744–8. Many members left to join the Moravians. Howel Harris jousted with several other chapel leaders and found himself accused of being unable to control the warring factions. The Tabernacle became notorious for its antinomianism: the belief that by virtue of being under the rule of grace Christians are released from the obligations of moral law. Harris was accused of tolerating terrible practices amongst chapel members. There were leaders of the Tabernacle who got 'in to Men's Houses . . . adulterating their Wives, fornicating their daughters, sodomitically abusing their Boys'.[14] It was not long before James Relly, one of Whitefield's most trusted preachers at the Tabernacle, took a mistress, while assuring his wife that it was 'no sin before God'.[15] Relly went on to perform a total theological inversion by becoming a leading universalist, and his disciple John Murray became the founder in America of that creed, diametrically opposed to Calvinism. John Wesley's rejection of the Calvinistic version of Methodism was not a little influenced by what he perceived as its resulting indifference to moral laws.

From 1741, for four decades Whitefield's Tabernacle was the centre of Calvinistic Methodist organisation in England. As the preaching missions expanded, the Calvinistic Methodists were strongest in Gloucestershire, parts of Essex, around Birmingham and in Chatham, Portsmouth and Plymouth. There was at least an informal system that enabled groups of local adherents to exchange preachers. John Cennick was perhaps the first Methodist lay preacher and sided with Whitefield early-on over predestination and was, therefore, expelled by Wesley in March 1741. Cennick, as previously noted, had erected a Calvinist Tabernacle in Kingswood, near Bristol, that June. In Wiltshire, he was attacked by mobs in Swindon, Stratton and Lyneham, yet converts were formed into the first Calvinistic Methodist organisation, the Wiltshire Association. However, this was short-lived, as Cennick shifted his allegiance to the Moravians, and with him went these Wiltshire Association societies.[16] Such defections and disjunctures would continue to undermine any orderly progress of organised Calvinistic Methodism within England during the eighteenth century.

There are minutes for the Calvinistic Methodist Association in England only from 1745 to 1749, and it is possible that the formal organisation ended then, with the total breakdown of relations between Whitefield and Howel Harris at the end of 1749. After Whitefield's departure for America in 1744, meetings of Calvinistic Methodist Associations were held not only at the Tabernacle but in Bristol, Gloucestershire, Wiltshire and Abergavenny. At an association held in Bristol on 20 March 1745, with twenty preachers attending, it was 'agreed that infant baptism was truly scriptural and that none should minister in the sacraments but such as are [episcopally] ordained'.[17] The same meeting adopted a series of theological statements that clearly hammered home Calvinist teachings. The scriptures were declared 'the written word of God and . . . what is written was wrote by holy men of God as they was moved by the holy ghost'. After a person 'receives Jesus Christ in his heart and becomes one with him

. . . the union between Christ and that soul is never dissolved afterwards, world without end'. Works

> shall be rewarded in the last day openly before men and angels! Yet are they in no wise any part of our salvation, neither are we beloved the more for them by the Lord, but we are loved freely, justifyed freely, without respect to any work done by us or in us or by any other save Jesus Christ.[18]

Two years later, again meeting at Bristol, it was stated: 'Of man's salvation being all of God and his damnation all of himself.'[19] This is a clear and crucial rejection of so-called 'double predestination', the belief that God not only chooses those who will be saved, but those who will be damned as well. Yet 'double predestination' had by no means been permanently silenced.

There is but one comprehensive listing, dated 1747, of the societies and other preaching locations in England associated with Whitefield, together with the names of his preachers.[20] Two of these men, Howel Harris and James Beaumont, also had responsibilities for serving in Wales, but on such occasions not under the aegis of the English Association. Harris was certainly active in England beyond the Tabernacle. One woman wrote from Essex, imploring him once again to visit her local Calvinistic Methodist society; and she noted that it was their practice to cry aloud 'gogoniant [glory] through the heavens'. Howel Harris appears to have taught more than religious language to the English groups he visited.[21]

In reality, the organisation of Calvinistic Methodism in England was chaotic in the extreme, especially with Whitefield's frequent absences. This was particularly true of his four years away in America until 1748, which led to the splintering of the work, particularly that which was centred on his London Tabernacle. After the departure of large numbers of members and preachers to the Moravians in 1745 the situation was desperate, and the perceived remedy was painfully revealed at the association, convened on 20 July 1748, only a fortnight after his return. With Whitefield in the chair, the association minutes record that he was distressed that so many of the young preachers had gone 'rashly out beyond their line'. He was 'determined not to labour with any that would not shew a teachable mind and willingness to submitt' to means to improve their talents. 'He hated to affect to be head . . . yet he must see everyone acquainted with their own places and to look on themselves as candidates or probationers.' Each agreed to this, 'and look on themselves as helps and on him as a father'.[22] Yet within nine months Whitefield was disengaging himself from being 'head'. On 27 April 1749 it was determined 'that Mr [Howel] Harris will take the oversight of the Tabernacle and other English societies and preachers. And that Mr Whitefield will do all he can to strength[en] his and their hands, consistent with his going about preaching the gospel either at home or abroad.'[23] All this was put more forcefully four months later:

> Having declared his conviction to go about preaching the gospel over the nation at home and abroad as he is called and not to take the immediate care of any place, but having committed the care of his labours in England to Brother [Howel] Harris, and the other brethren to assist each according to his ability, he [Whitefield] owns himself in connexion with the brethren in this branch and to do all he can to help car[ry]ing on the work here suitable with his general plan.[24]

Whitefield rebuilt his Tabernacle at Moorfields in 1753 and in 1756 opened a second London chapel. Tottenham Court Road, designed for a higher class of auditor than the Tabernacle, was much extended three years later and was the largest nonconforming church building in Britain and probably in the world. In many ways a Puritan *redivivus*, Whitefield re-energised the Calvinist message, and he had long desired to position himself in London's West End, close to its theatres. For this purpose Tottenham Court Road was perfectly situated. Throughout his ministry Whitefield was especially vigorous in condemning public amusements of all kinds: musical concerts, dances, card playing and the theatre. On one occasion he upbraided an eminent Dissenting minister for singing in a London tavern a song in praise of old English beef. Towards the end of 1759 Whitefield preached a sermon threatening London theatregoers with damnation. This was reciprocated with a vengeance by numerous satirical productions, based on the premise that Whitefield was himself a consummate actor. As early as 1746 he was introduced as the adulterous Doctor Preach Field in the production of Charles Macklin's *A Will and No Will*. Now, in 1760, he was treated by the leading theatrical satirist, Samuel Foote. In *The Minor*, White-field was called Squintum, occasioned by the severe squint in his left eye. Squintum was thenceforward the satirists' usual appellation, suggesting that Whitefield focused on the carnal while gazing heaven-ward. Indeed, he was the target of most of the satirical writing directed against the Methodist movement as a whole.

By 1763, in addition to his distress at these satirical attacks, White-field was wearied with overseeing his two London chapels. Returning to America for the penultimate of his seven visits there, he left their management to laymen, with instructions not to 'consult me in any thing, unless absolutely necessary', later adding that he could not 'bear the[ir] cares' even when in London.[25] Whitefield never acquired a taste for organisation or administration, and after his death all chapels in his 'Connexion' soon went their own ways, most joining the Independents (Congregationalists). In truth, what cohesion White-field's groups of followers had was basically through Whitefield himself. His frequent absences and general disinclination to engage in day-to-day administration meant that their organisation was more aspiration than reality.[26] According to one contemporary source, in 1748 John Wesley had 12,000 adherents in England, while Whitefield had 20,000.[27] If this be so, it only underscores how serious was the effect on the further developments of Whitefield's chapels in England of his disengaging himself from the organisational leadership of these groups. This was in stark contrast to the very 'hands-on' approach of the countess of Huntingdon regarding her enterprises.

Apart from the activities of the countess and Whitefield, there were other, minor, players, who inhabited England's Calvinistic Methodist world during these years. Andrew Kinsman had been converted to Methodism by Whitefield and aligned himself with a group of White-field's followers in Plymouth, where he became the recognised leader, by 1748 assuming regular preaching there. He expanded his work by establishing another chapel, in Devonport. It was not until 1763 that he was ordained, by a group of Methodist and Nonconformist preachers. He continued to maintain his chapels as Calvinistic Methodist and encouraged the preaching of the countess's Trevecca students; but at his death Kinsman's two chapels, as so frequently happened, embraced Nonconformity.[28] There was infrequent contact between the countess and the very few chapels in England of her Scottish counterpart,

Willielma Campbell, Viscountess Glenorchy. While living in Staffordshire, Lady Glenorchy came into contact with the Hill family of
Hawkstone Park, Shropshire, and in 1765 fell under the influence of
Rowland Hill. Thus did her Scottish Presbyterianism become blended
with Calvinistic Methodism. The chapel she established in Edinburgh
created tensions with the Church of Scotland, and in 1776 she moved
to England. From there she sent English Calvinistic Methodist preachers to fill her Edinburgh chapel, thus solving the problem caused by
a lack of Church of Scotland ministers willing to undertake that task.
Her first chapel in England was at Exmouth, followed by ones at
Carlisle; Matlock Bath, Derbyshire; Workington, Cumberland; and
the Hope Chapel, Bristol. However, Viscountess Glenorchy's death
in 1786, at the age of 44, cut short her work, and all her chapels soon
disappeared.[29]

Besides the Whitefield Connexion and Lady Huntingdon's chapels
the most important Calvinistic Methodist grouping was that led by
Rowland Hill. After graduating from Cambridge in 1769, Hill spent
four years preaching throughout England and Wales. Refused ordination by six bishops because of his irregularities, in 1773 he was
ordained deacon by the bishop of Bath and Wells and appointed to
the curacy of Kingston, near Taunton. Nonetheless, he continued to
itinerate and, therefore, was never ordained priest – thus passing
through life, he said, wearing only one ecclesiastical boot. He settled
at Wotton under Edge, Gloucestershire, where he built a chapel,
followed in 1783 by his Surrey Chapel, Blackfriars, London. Surrey
Chapel was the largest of its kind in London and could seat 3,000;
attached to it were Sunday schools for over 3,000 children. He promoted a floating chapel on the Thames, and there were also a number
of relief societies connected to Surrey Chapel.[30] In the early 1770s
Hill was the darling of the new generation of evangelicals and preached
regularly in the countess of Huntingdon's chapels.[31]

There was in addition a small group of settled Anglican clerics who
during this period could be counted as supporters of the Calvinistic
Methodist cause. Perhaps we should pass by the Reverend Richard
Thomas Bateman, rector of St Bartholomew the Great, London, who
for a time in the 1740s actually attended London meetings of Whitefield's association and appears to have preached on occasion at his
London Tabernacle. A native of Haverfordwest, Bateman was thought

for a time by Howel Harris and others to be a magnificent addition to their work. However, this positive impression was quickly dispelled when Bateman was discovered copying word for word a published sermon on the new birth and passing it off as his own. That and some other things about Bateman's conduct had given Harris 'a stab . . . in my soul'.[32] Mention has already been made of Samuel Walker, James Hervey, Henry Venn, Martin Madan and William Romaine. Among others of note, there was William Grimshaw, vicar of Haworth, who, though a Calvinist, maintained close personal relations with the Wesleys.[33] He also was a link between Methodism and the later evangelical presence within the Church of England. Then there was the delightfully provocative and eccentric vicar of Everton, Bedfordshire, John Berridge. Ever ready to puncture pomposity, Berridge was perhaps the only cleric who could – and did – refuse to cater to the countess of Huntingdon's need for deference. Deeply committed to the work of his own parish, he frequently fended off imperious demands to drop everything to fill her chapels' pulpits. For example, he refused to obey her '*Vatican Bull*' to come to Brighton:

> You threaten me, Madam, like a Pope, not like a Mother in Israel, when you declare roundly, that God will scourge me, if I do not come . . . Verily, you are a good piper, but I know not how to dance. I love y[ou]r scorpion-letters dearly, tho' they rake the flesh off my bones . . . All marching officers are not general officers . . . and my instructions, you know, must come from the Lamb, not from the Lamb's Wife.[34]

Thus, during the middle decades of the eighteenth century several stages were being built to present Calvinistic Methodism to the English public, occupied by a colourful and often disparate cast of would-be leaders. The personalities and theologies of these and Wesleyan Methodism's main actors meant that the lively hope once held for a truly unified movement was rapidly fading. Indeed, the simmering cauldron of differences was about to boil over into lasting acrimony and permanent division.

Notes

1. Selina Hastings to Howel Harris, 15 January 1765, in Edward Morgan, *The Life and Times of Howell Harris* (Holywell: W. Morris, 1852), p. 238.
2. Rylands, Black Folio 75, Selina Hastings to Charles Wesley, 9 June 1764; Selina Hastings to Howel Harris, 15 January 1765, in Morgan, *Life and Times of Howell Harris*, p. 237.
3. NLW Howel Harris's Diary, 30 March 1769.
4. Duke, Frank A. Baker Collection, Selina Hastings to Mrs H. Leighton, 11 March 1768.
5. D. Bogue and J. Bennett, *History of Dissenters from the Revolution in 1688 to the Year 1808* (4 vols, London, 1808–12), III, p. 79.
6. Deryck W. Lovegrove, *Established Church, Sectarian People: Itinerancy and the Transformation of English Dissent, 1780–1830* (Cambridge: Cambridge University Press, 1988), p. 70.
7. John Wesley to Charles Wesley, 14 May 1768, in John Telford (ed.), *The Letters of the Rev. John Wesley* (London: Epworth Press, 1931), V, p. 88.
8. Thomas W. Aveling, *Memorials of the Clayton Family* (London: Walford and Hodder, 1867), p. 17.
9. Cheshunt E4/4/12, Thomas Suter to Selina Hastings, 14 September 1782.
10. Cheshunt F1/706, John Williams to Selina Hastings, 21 February 1788.
11. John Henry Meyer, *The Saint's Triumph*, (London: n.p., [1791]), p. 40.
12. Rylands, Black Folio 139, Selina Hastings to Thomas Jones, 3 August 1772.
13. Dr Williams's Library, Congregational Library II, c.7/21, Selina Hastings to Thomas Wills, 6 August 1784.
14. NLW Trevecka Letter 1306, James Erskine to Howel Harris, 20 March 1745.
15. Howel Harris's Diary, 16 January 1750, in Tom Beynon (ed.), *Howell Harris's Visits to London* (Aberystwyth: The Cambrian News Press, 1966), p. 261.
16. Colin J. Podmore, *The Moravian Church in England, 1728–1760* (Oxford: Oxford University Press, 1998), pp. 88–95.
17. Edwin Welch (ed.), *Two Calvinistic Methodist Chapels, 1743–1811: The London Tabernacle and Spa Fields Chapel* (London: London Record Society, 1975), item 54.

18 Ibid., items 54–6.
19 Ibid., item 82.
20 For the societies and preaching locations see Appendices A and B of this present work. For the preachers see Welch (ed.), *Two Calvinistic Methodist Chapels*, item 49.
21 NLW Trevecka Letter 1904, Mary Biggs to Howel Harris, 18 December 1749.
22 Welch (ed.), *Two Calvinistic Methodist Chapels*, item 96.
23 Ibid., item 100.
24 Ibid., item 104.
25 George Whitefield to R[obert] K[een], 26 March 1763 and 4 May 1765, in John Gillies (ed.), *The Works of the Reverend George Whitefield* (6 vols, London: Edward and Charles Dilly, 1771–2), III, pp. 290, 326.
26 David W. Bebbington, *Evangelicalism in Modern Britain* (London: Unwin Hyman, 1989), p. 30.
27 Cited in Podmore, *The Moravian Church in England, 1728–1760*, p. 120.
28 C. E. Welch, 'Andrew Kinsman's churches at Plymouth', *Report and Transactions of the Devonshire Association for the Advancement of Science, Literature and Art*, 97 (1965), 212–36.
29 Edwin Welch, 'Willielma Campbell, Viscountess Glenorchy (1741–1786)', in *Oxford Dictionary of National Biography* (Oxford: Oxford University Press, 2004).
30 'History of Surrey Chapel', *Evangelical Register*, February 1837, 37–42.
31 For Hill's life and ministry see P. E. Sangster, 'The life of the Rev. Rowland Hill (1744–1833) and his position in the Evangelical Revival', D.Phil. thesis, University of Oxford, 1964.
32 NLW Trevecka Letter 1737, Howel Harris to Richard Thomas Bateman, 3 December 1747.
33 George G. Cragg, *Grimshaw of Haworth: A Study in Eighteenth Century Evangelicalism* (Norwich: Canterbury Press, 1947).
34 Countess of Huntingdon Connexion Archives, Rayleigh, Berridge letters, no. 12, John Berridge to Selina Hastings, 26 December 1767.

8

'My Lady's society': the birth and growth of the Countess of Huntingdon's Connexion, 1770–1791

From Methodism's earliest days, a yawning theological gap increasingly defined these two branches of the movement. Indeed, the clash over predestination bedevilled it from the very beginning, lodged especially in the differing perceptions of George Whitefield and John Wesley. It had marked out a terrain of conflict that over the ensuing years would ultimately change from jousting-ground to battlefield. By definition, the Calvinists held to predestination: that from the beginning of time God had designated who would be saved. This ensured that no Christian could earn salvation through good works. To the Wesleys the notion that God had chosen, from the beginning of Creation, who would be saved, was a truly shocking doctrine that totally negated human free will and responsibility. This pulsating conflict precluded any possibility of raising a united Methodist voice. Although initially accepting the Wesleys' position, the countess of Huntingdon soon had negotiated a startling theological volte-face after Whitefield bombarded her for over two hours with arguments in favour of predestination. He had, she said, a more vigorous commitment to the doctrine than anyone she had encountered and had expressed that commitment with 'a command of words & smoothly put together'.[1] It was not long before she had begun attending Whitefield's London Tabernacle Chapel, supported in this by Howel Harris.

An attempt at Bristol in the summer of 1749 to secure some form of union between the various Methodistic factions had proved futile. Whitefield felt that John Wesley was 'monopolising the name of

Methodist to himself only'.[2] Over the coming years this continued to rumble beneath the surface, occasionally creating visible fissures. In the early 1760s Wesley wrote to the countess that many of the Calvinistic clergy she supported, including Whitefield, seemed to be saying 'down with him, down with him, even to the ground'.[3] A few years later still Wesley restated with vigour his belief that Christians could be perfected from sin in this life, and with equal vigour his detestation of predestination. For her part, the countess judged Wesley 'as an Eel, no hold of him and not come to the truth' – that is, Calvinistic election and predestination.[4]

Continued controversy over Calvinism in England

This tension was significantly increased in 1768 by the expulsion of six Methodistic Oxford students, which, as previously noted, contributed to the establishing of Trevecca 'college'. The countess had been intimately, if quietly, involved in nurturing several, if not all, of these young men for possible ordination. Those involved with her in planning for the enlargement of the evangelical witness at Oxford were committed to strict secrecy. In their defence of the expelled students Lady Huntingdon's supporters were intent not only to present the young men as innocent victims of harsh and arbitrary treatment but also to support a particular theological orientation. 'What I mean to insist upon', wrote Richard Hill, 'is that the Church of <u>England</u> is certainly calvinistical'.[5] This was a position emphatically rejected by Oxford's vice-chancellor. To John Wesley predestination was a doctrine 'utterly inconsistent' with the teaching of the Church of England.[6] In any case, the expulsion of the six students reopened the ever-present theological fault-line within Methodism, which two years later would lead to a convulsion of seismic proportions.

The claim that Calvinistic predestination had no part in official Anglican teaching was fiercely challenged in the pamphlet war surrounding the Oxford expulsions, most especially by the rigid Calvinist polemicists Richard Hill and Augustus Toplady, who gladly dug their chisels into Wesleyan Methodism's most jagged fissures.[7] For some time past Wesley's Arminian views had become even more fixed, and he reflected that 'a pious churchman who has not *clear conceptions* even of *justification by faith* may be saved'.[8] Since the countess had raised the stakes in their personal and theological contest, Wesley threw caution to the wind: in August 1770, at his movement's annual conference, the official minutes asserted that, in effect, continuing good works are a condition of a Christian's salvation.[9] By intent and result these minutes loudly slammed the door against any possible accommodation between the Wesleyan and Calvinistic wings of English Methodism, while throwing open a wide door through which the ecclesiastical furies sprang free. Once the minutes of Wesley's conference were published, events tumbled forward at a frantic pace. Their public proclamation was aimed directly at the countess's theology, and Wesley followed this by writing to her a 'bitter' and provocative letter, 'charg[in]g her w[it]h self and having fall[e]n to Pride'.[10] Wesley said that for several years he had felt he ought to confront her with these failings. It was his '*business*' to do so, 'as none else either c[oul]d or w[oul]d to it'. He told her that 'you think yourself of *more importance* than you are'. He said that she replied,

> in effect; 'Nay, you think *yourself* to be of more importance than *me*.' Indeed I do; to be of ten times more, yea an hundred times more . . . I *know* her perhaps better than any other person in Engl[an]d does. And I c[oul]d do her more good. But she rewards me evil for good. So fare her well.[11]

Her first action upon reading the minutes was to weep copiously, next to proclaim publicly that she 'abhorred' Wesley 'worse than any creature in the creation, repeating it again and again'.[12]

Lady Huntingdon was stung into action, seeing her most urgent task to cleanse Trevecca of any lingering Wesleyan influences. From its founding, students had been carefully and ardently examined regarding their commitment to Christian belief couched in Calvinistic terms. Now they were compelled to produce in writing a renunciation of Wesley and all his works, a requirement she proved endlessly thorough in enforcing. She watched, hawk-like, for any hint of wording that she could construe as sympathetic to Wesley's despised doctrine.[13] Perhaps too angry to think clearly, the countess addressed her students and denounced his teachings, calling the 1770 conference minutes '*horrible, abominable* and *subversive*'. She said that 'she must *burn*

1. George Whitefield

2. John Wesley

3. John Cennick

4. Howel Harris

Painted by R. Bowyer

Engraved by I. Fittler.

5. Daniel Rowland

6a. William Williams

6b. 'Y Sasiwn Gyntaf' [The First Association]

7. The countess of Huntingdon

8. Thomas Charles

against' all who did not exuberantly reject those views, and that 'who-ever did not fully disavow them should quit the College'.[14] It was a turbulent and painful process for many of her students. In this testing theological period she not only lost her tutor, Joseph Benson, but also the superintendent of Trevecca, the Reverend John Fletcher, who had faithfully and arduously made frequent visits and had been received by the students 'as <u>an Angel of God</u>'.[15] Fletcher wrote to Wesley that he had told his 'mind to our Deborah, about bigotry, partiality, prejudice . . . I have insisted and do insist . . . if every Arminian must quit the college, I am discharged for one.'[16] Fletcher told her that her action 'may appear to many zeal for truth &c but seems to <u>me</u> a spirit of prejudice and needless divisions'.[17]

Both Fletcher and Benson shared the Wesleyan belief in the possibility of salvation for all. Therein lay the roughest theological rub. Lady Huntingdon had fallen under the sway of England's most vociferous exponents of full-blooded predestinarianism. Wesley's conference minutes had indeed gone far beyond his and Whitefield's earlier juggling of this theological time bomb. In fact, Whitefield's sudden death, a month after the conference, removed a moderating Calvinistic voice from the ensuing conflict. When the countess had altered her theological orientation during the mid-1740s, she imbibed Calvinism from those whose views, particularly on predestination, were expressed with a degree of moderation. Men like Whitefield and Harris, while adherents of the doctrine, had refused to let it dictate their religious enterprises.[18] Yet now, with Whitefield dead and Harris on the verge of exclusion from her presence, the countess was subjected to the full blast of those who blew no uncertain predestinarian trumpets. Moreover, at Trevecca, Harris was horrified by the antinomianism he perceived in some of the students.

Only days after learning of Whitefield's death, Lady Huntingdon enrolled her cousin, Walter Shirley, as one of her chaplains, and Shirley was thrust to the forefront of the conflict with the Wesleyans. She and Shirley joined in preparing a remarkable composition, sent widely throughout England. With her hand 'at the head of the opposition', this printed letter called on Calvinistic supporters, in either the Church of England or Dissenting denominations, to descend upon Bristol en masse on 6 August 1771, the date of Wesley's next conference: this group was to 'insist upon a formal recantation of the said minutes'.[19]

In the event, the Calvinistic troops failed to muster at Bristol; yet, led by Shirley, a tiny delegation to the conference believed they had secured the Wesleyan recantation they demanded. It was a belief quickly dispelled by Wesley's publication only a few days later of a 100-page pamphlet by Fletcher vindicating Wesley's theology and attacking Shirley. The next month Shirley leapt into print with a rebuttal, its introduction and conclusion composed by Lady Huntingdon herself.[20]

A highly acrimonious pamphlet warfare, which lasted many years, had been launched into already turbulent waters. Further expanding the printers' trade, Wesley commenced a revision and republication of his previous works. From the other side, the provocatively titled *Gospel Magazine*, supported by Lady Huntingdon and edited by the virulent Calvinist, Augustus Toplady, turned its guns on Wesley, railing against his 'apostasy from the genuine faith of the gospel, an awful proof that evil men and seducers wax worse and worse'. Wesley's teachings were 'the very doctrines of Popery'.[21] Wesley went on to establish his even more provocatively titled *Arminian Magazine.* Methodist publications, which had previously been directed towards fostering general tenets of the evangelical revival, had now become narrowed organs broadcasting the propaganda of warring camps. Rival chapels served as distribution centres for these unhappy outpourings.

Augustus Toplady was a young Anglican cleric whose full-throated espousal of the doctrine of presdestination invited no competitor. He had published *The Doctrine of Absolute Predestination Stated and Asserted* in 1769, and his decisive influence over the countess during the 1770s is the clearest indication of the freezing of her Calvinistic orientation. Unlike the Calvinism espoused by Whitefield's Association in 1747, which clearly opted for only 'single predestination' (God's choosing the elect for heaven), Toplady propagated 'double predestination' (God's choosing both those who are to be saved and those who are to damned). Lady Huntingdon was delighted by Toplady's militantly vituperative proclamation of the Calvinist doctrine, particularly when he publicly labelled John Wesley 'the most rancorous hater of the gospel system that ever appeared in England'.[22] Toplady preached regularly in the countess's chapels, and the two maintained a regular correspondence. After his death, Toplady's influence continued through her avid reading of his printed works.

Lady Huntingdon's convictions were further undergirt by ultra-predestinarian laymen. Rowland Hill's brother, Richard Hill, who had proved his Calvinistic credentials during the pamphlet war over the 1768 Oxford expulsions, now sharpened his pen against Wesley and John Fletcher in a number of vitriolic productions. Bolstered by some of England's most outspoken defenders of a rigid predestination, the countess's commitment to the doctrine became total. What previously had served as personal consolation now became for her not only a badge of orthodoxy but also a litmus test of loyalty. Moving ahead to build further chapels, she issued a firm instruction that 'no Ministers are to be admitted . . . but such as preach the pure Gospel, & the true Calvinist Doctrine'.[23] Indeed, all ministers and students who preached for her were thrown on the defensive, for fear that she would receive report of their not toeing a clear Calvinist line. Many evangelical clergymen who previously had moved with some degree of freedom between Methodism's two camps, attempted to keep their heads down to avoid the direct volleys fired from both sides. One such was Vincent Perronet, the venerable vicar of Shoreham, Kent, who earlier had stood on friendly ground with the countess. Horrified by the virulence of her reaction to the 1770 Wesleyan minutes, he was even more aghast at the vehemence of her predestinarianism: 'May God give repentance to the broachers of such blasphemies!'[24]

For Lady Huntingdon there were painful personal implications in these partings of Methodist ways. Her theological cleansing could not even stop short of her affection for Charles Wesley. She foolishly provoked this old friend by sending him a copy of the circular letter ('the first sent out by me to any one') together with a personal covering message. Here she re-emphasised her belief that the 1770 minutes were properly described as 'Popery unmasked': all 'ought deservedly to be deemed papists who did not disown them'. She concluded by telling Charles that she had laid all this before him 'in order that with the greatest of openness your Brother might be informed by you'. Charles's reaction to this bold attempt to drive new wedges was to scrawl on her letter an endorsement: 'L. Huntin[g]don's LAST.' 'Unanswered by J.W.'s Brother!'[25]

Charles Wesley's hymns now became an obvious target for the Calvinists. Since hymns often are written with the purpose of driving home and maintaining the author's particular theological position either directly or more subtly, a hymn could mould and maintain a singing congregation's theological bent. In the year of its opening, 1765, Lady Huntingdon had authorised – and probably had taken an active hand in preparing – a hymn book for her Bath chapel. Not surprisingly, the collection contained several of Wesley's hymns, with which she had long been 'charmed'.[26] But now that the Methodistic streams had permanently divided, such inclusions as Charles Wesley's were no longer possible, at least not without careful theological vetting. As the countess's doctrine sharpened, so her hymnody narrowed, and she demanded the publication of a new hymn book. Wesley's hymns either must be excised from the new collection or at the very least severely altered, since all her 'Ministers oppose this [Wesleyan] doctrine to a Man'.[27] In the event, Lady Huntingdon now exercised total control over 'omitting or adding any' hymns.[28] Over the next decade a number of different collections appeared, prepared for use in various of her chapels, culminating in a general collection published in London in 1780: *A Select Collection of Hymns to be universally sung in all the Countess of Huntingdon's Chapels, Collected by her Ladyship.*

Although the printed warfare that produced upwards of fifty pamphlets trailed off following Toplady's death in 1778, the practical effects of the controversy bit deep into the Methodistic cause in England. It was a conflict in which claims had been pitched at their highest and the language of denunciation stretched to its limits. Her Trevecca 'college', now narrowly affixed to the Calvinistic camp, was thereby greatly crippled in its potential to serve the whole evangelical enterprise and was to limp from crisis to crisis over the following years. Lady Huntingdon denounced Wesley as 'a papist unmasked, a heretic, an apostate'.[29] Preachers in her chapels dutifully followed suit: 'I could not profitably labo[u]r with any one that's tainted with Wesleyism, for I believe it to be the bane of Religion', one assured her.[30] She and Wesley sent out their preachers as soldiers girt for battle. In the process, and given the urgency, it may be supposed that her students occasionally were less than clear as to whose service she had called them: 'I have fully secured and taken the place in her Ladyships name', one wrote.[31] Often the targets of her activities were not areas previously untouched by the Methodist message but those where Wesley's men had been active. At Dover, Wesley recorded in his journal that her 'preachers had gleaned up most of those whom we had discarded.

They call them "My lady's society" and have my free leave to do them all the good they can.' Again, Wesley at Dover: 'The raw, pert young men, that lately came hither (vulgarly, though very improperly, called "students"), though they have left no stone unturned, have not been able to tear away one single member from our society.'[32] In London, Wesley's followers 'speak very disrespective of your Ladyship, and say your Ladyship must shut up some of your chapels very soon for nobody will preach for you because of [your] opposing Mr Wesley'.[33] Wesley opined that her preachers were 'wholly swallowed up in that detestable doctrine of Predestination, and can talk of nothing else'.[34]

By 1776, though unrepentant, Lady Huntingdon apparently was distressed by the seemingly unending and unquenchable combustibility of the conflict as its flash points spread across the country. She wrote to Wesley to assure him of her strenuous efforts to ensure that her students, when on their preaching rounds, avoided casting aspersions on the Wesleyans. He immediately replied, 'persuaded your Ladyship is not sensible of the manner wherein many of the students have treated me. But let that pass. If your Ladyship will be so good as to give them a caution on that head, I know it will not be in vain.'[35] Yet in vain it proved. What she told Wesley may have been true but, if so, the countess had lost control of a conflict that had taken on a life of its own. Too many had been cut by the sharp crystals of this theological disputation. In fact, her assurances rang rather hollow, since it was not long before Wesley was once again observing that 'those who styled themselves "my Lady's preachers", who screamed and railed and threatened to swallow us up, are vanished away. I cannot learn that they have made one convert – a plain proof that God did not send them.'[36] Elsewhere they apparently were more effective. At Grimsby 'and many other parts of the kingdom, those striplings who call themselves Lady Huntingdon's Preachers had greatly hindered the work of God . . . Wherever we have entered . . . they creep in and by doubtful disputations set everyone's sword against his brother.'[37]

Into the 1780s it continued, with one of her preachers boasting in print that wherever he preached he had given the Wesleyans a black eye, while from Norwich she was informed triumphantly that forty of Wesley's followers had converted to her chapel.[38] It seems that the Wesleyans could give as good as they got. One of the countess's chapels pleaded for an able minister 'to keep our little Flock from being stolen' by Wesley, whose 'preachers make it Rule to preach against us almost every where'.[39] Wesley himself, it was reported, had delivered at Penzance an 'extraordinary Harangue & Exhortation' in which he spoke 'very disrespectful[ly] of Mr Whitefield . . . and of your L[adyshi]ps. College & Collegians'.[40] In lulls between battles over the succeeding years, both she and Wesley engaged in a programme of pushing and probing one another's ecclesiastical defences. They eyed one another either bitterly or warily across a divide they themselves had done not a little to create. And Wesley wrote to an acquaintance: 'From the time I heard you were rejected by Lady Huntingdon, I have had a tender regard for you.'[41]

The countess and slavery

The jarring conflict within Methodism reverberated across the Atlantic. As has been noted, on his first visit to Britain's colonies in America George Whitefield had established his orphanage in Georgia. Over the years it had proved a financial and emotional burden for him, and when he died in 1770 he left this establishment to the countess, with the injunction that she attempt to convert it into a college. With inter-evangelical warfare at its height in England, establishing an unmistakably Calvinistic college in Georgia could exact revenge against Wesley, who had just revealed his true theological colours. In October 1772 Lady Huntingdon dispatched Trevecca students to man Bethesda. William Williams wrote:

> Bethesda thrive under SELINA'S wing,
> Teach Georgia wild to love the eternal King.[42]

The students arrived boasting that 'they w[oul]d soon drive all the [Wesleyan] Meth[odis]t Preachers from the [American] continent'.[43] On the contrary, the enterprise proved a total disaster, with Georgians burning down Bethesda shortly after her group of students arrived. Nonetheless, Wesleyan preachers in America anticipated that at the very least the countess's men in America 'will sow the seeds of discord and make a breach in the rising [American Wesleyan] Societies'.[44]

Although the countess attempted to resurrect Bethesda over the following two decades, in the end there was nothing to show for her American efforts.[45] However, one aspect of her activities there sharpened the edge of her conflict with Wesley. Initially, Whitefield had vacillated over black slavery but soon concluded that Bethesda must have it to prosper. Becoming one of the most outspoken defenders of the institution, he exclaimed: 'Blessed be God for the increase of the negroes.'[46] He had emerged as perhaps the most energetic, and conspicuous, evangelical defender and practitioner of slavery. The countess inherited from Whitefield both this philosophy and his Bethesda slaves, to which she added substantial numbers over the following years. She even wrote to her agents in Georgia: 'I must . . . request that a woman-slave may be purchased . . . and that she may be called SELINA, after me.'[47] For several years one can trace in the lists of the Bethesda slaves this black Selina.

Lady Huntingdon's deliberate extension of slavery sharpened the pen of its most articulate opponent in colonial America. The Philadelphia Quaker Anthony Benezet wrote to her in 1774 'from a persuasion that thy love to mankind . . . would induce thee to give what assistance is in thy power . . . of putting a stop to this iniquitous Traffick'. She replied that it is 'God alone, by his Almighty power, who can and will in his own time bring outward, as well as spiritual deliverance'. A further letter from Benezet told her of his dismay at Whitefield's support of slavery, as well as enclosing copies of 'a late publication on this interesting subject by my esteemed friend, John Wesley', which called the institution a 'villainy'.[48] This open criticism of Whitefield and hearty praise of Wesley's unequivocal denouncing of slavery may very well have helped to ensure that the countess of Huntingdon persisted in the ownership and trade of slaves right to the end of her life.

Not only Lady Huntingdon's dogged devotion to George Whitefield blocked any challenge to slavery; she also was hindered by her theology. Wesley and his branch of Methodism emphasised individual free will: they tended to call for emancipation largely because slaves by definition could not exercise the free will necessary to achieve salvation. The countess's Calvinism demanded no such freedom. Struggling to be relieved from the logic of cause and effect, she ever sought to throw on to God the responsibility for any social action. As a further example,

163

she came totally to reject any financial giving to charities. This was occasioned not only by a threadbare purse but by a philosophy of giving. Providing preaching, she said, was the 'greatest of all charitys I know on earth'. When approached to aid a distressed family, she replied that she was sorry but could not help: 'I am obliged to be a spectator of miseries, which I pity but cannot relieve.'[49] One could pursue a comparison of Wesleyan and Calvinist Methodism based on John Wesley's affection for the poor and dislike of the rich; and Wesley severely castigated the countess for her refusal to contribute to charities. In a broader sense, Calvinistic Methodism in general and the countess of Huntingdon in particular were intent not on planting and nurturing, but harvesting. This was her contribution to the new-birth movement, and in full and fervent flow it might hold for a period all the excitement of a virgin enterprise. But it was also a toxic contribution, since her impulsive heart and hand turned from one new project to another. When these schemes faltered, as assuredly they did, she had neither the inclination nor the ability to organise the unexciting means by which they might have been maintained. Thus her religious zeal did not direct her or her people towards works of charity; if anything, the reverse was true. Such solid yet unspectacular achievements as some might make in daily practical service did not impress her. At least they were not the stuff of Christianity as she understood it. She had not been converted from a profligate life to one of good works, but from good works to one of wrestling faith. At its worst, this produced a religion that lacked the discipline of ethics.

Building Calvinist chapels

The chapels the countess of Huntingdon had built during the 1760s were visible indications of an impatience with the progress of her brand of evangelicalism within parish churches. She insisted that she was a faithful daughter of the Church of England, but this chapel building, together with Trevecca and the itinerating of its students, certainly called the claim into question and in reality reinforced her ecclesiastical irregularities. The Church's bishops became increasingly uneasy and far less likely to consider the young men she presented for ordination. By the late 1770s it was clear to her that episcopal doors were being closed and that it would be nearly impossible any longer to find bishops' hands to rest upon her students' heads. In 1777 the archbishop of Canterbury wrote to her that though he was certain her intentions were good, Trevecca was not 'likely to send forth very able or judicious Divines'.[50]

Whatever her professed principles in upholding Anglican theological orthodoxy, the countess of Huntingdon's practice spoke in a different voice. Here was a leader who, together with her men and her movement, appeared ever at loggerheads with the church she claimed to serve. The small number of Calvinistically-minded Church of England clergymen who actively engaged to assist her by occasional chapel preaching had to tread carefully lest episcopal feathers were ruffled. Her chapels were stone and mortar witnesses that the countess was outside the Church of England. Her initial chapels, during the 1760s, had dwelling-houses attached, and she maintained that these places of worship were merely extensions to her private residences.[51] This tendentious claim could hardly be made for the new chapels erected throughout the kingdom in the following decade, in places she had never seen and often would never visit, let alone reside. However, she hoped that by granting them her patronage, even these would thereby be protected from official censure or interference.

The Toleration Act of 1689 had called for all places of non-Anglican worship to be registered with the proper ecclesiastical or civil authorities. Registration clearly marked out such a building as a Dissenting chapel. The countess's negative attitude to Dissenters, combined with her positive claim to be working from within to save the Established Church, had precluded her even contemplating sheltering under the Toleration Act. Since her chapel building had commenced in the provinces, it was inevitable that London would stand at the apex of her plans. In 1772 she took responsibility for the chapel of William Piercy in Woolwich Ropeyard. She had appointed Piercy head of her mission to Georgia, and when that project collapsed he and she became bitter enemies. But she now had gained a tenuous London toe-hold. Two years later the Princess Street Chapel, Westminster, was taken over and opened by Henry Peckwell. The countess's preachers assisted at the chapel, and for a time she granted it her patronage.[52]

The Wesleyans had long had chapels in London, and John Wesley's opening of an additional one in the spring of 1777 very likely acted to spur her in that direction. Her Mulberry Gardens Chapel was built some months later at Wapping, provocatively adjacent to that of a Dissenting minister fervently opposed to Methodistic enthusiasm. Indeed, her chapel was so close that his preaching was being drowned out by their loud singing.[53] The voices raised within this Mulberry Gardens Chapel were discordant, and the fits and starts surrounding the establishing of the enterprise resulted from bitter internal strife among and between the people and various ministers. By 1778 Lady Huntingdon had fully exerted her authority, with the 'Lord's appearing for me in so wonderfull a manner at the Mulbury Gardens'. The iniquitous people she had put to rout there 'make the wicked as ashes under the soles of my feet'.[54]

Mulberry Gardens quickened the countess's pulse regarding large-scale London plans. Already her eye had fallen on the Pantheon, a large amusement house in Clerkenwell. Built some years earlier as a place for genteel conversation, the taking of tea, coffee and wine in pleasure gardens or galleries in the rotunda – mostly on Sundays – it was not long before the establishment proved attractive to prostitutes. After its promoter went bankrupt in 1777, two Anglican evangelical clerics spent a great deal of money to embellish the interior of the building and then opened what they called Northampton Chapel as a registered Dissenting meeting house. However, the incumbent of the parish challenged the project by citing the two clerics before the Consistorial Court of the bishop of London for preaching in a Dissenting chapel. The court found in the incumbent's favour, whereupon Lady Huntingdon made her move and set out from Bath 'to take possession'.[55] The round brick structure of three storeys, with a large tiled dome, was quickly altered and refitted according to her taste. The interior contained two complete circular galleries which incorporated an organ, box pews and an elevated pulpit fronted by a huge black eagle. Hard against the building stood a three-storey private dwelling, where she immediately took up residence and had a door knocked into the wall between house and chapel.

As with former such enterprises, the countess hoped that her presence and her peerage would protect from ecclesiastical challenge what she now called Spa Fields Chapel. Supposing it best to force the issue at once, she initiated a correspondence with the bishop of London. Her argument was that by taking the chapel under her wing she was preventing it from defecting to the Dissenters. Thus she had 'agreed to take it, & to protect it regularly under the church', which would be ensured by its being 'a regular chapel of my own'. To put the bishop's mind at rest she assured him that 'nothing has ever caused any unhappy unchristian differences wherever she has been'.[56] The countess had moved with great speed: the bishop wrote that he had been informed of 'the impropriety of your Ladyship's interposition in this affair' by reopening the now rechristened Spa Fields Chapel only a fortnight after it had been closed by the Consistory Court.[57] Indeed, the bishop was justified in perceiving her action as ecclesiastical legerdemain.

Events now followed an inexorable course. The incumbent immediately took the matter back to the court, where Lady Huntingdon persisted in the claim that Spa Fields, in spite of being capable of seating over 2,000, was her private chapel. After a year of legal squabbling the decision went against her, and even before this inevitable outcome her attitude had changed from optimism to truculence. She arrived at the conclusion that 'unless they allow me my right I will secede being resolved that Christ shall be magnified . . . If they are permitted to turn us out woe woe be to them. Death & Hell will flow fast upon' them.[58] Seeing that the only alternative to breaking the law or giving up all her work was to leave the church and register Spa Fields as a Dissenting chapel, she chose the latter, thus becoming the first English Methodist to secede from the Church of England.

In the event, only two Anglican clerics agreed to join her in withdrawal from the Established Church, one being her niece's husband, Thomas Wills, who had been serving at Spa Fields for several months. He registered as a Dissenting minister and signed the chapel's application for registration as a Dissenting chapel on the same day, 12 January 1782. The other was William Taylor, one of the two clerics who had set up the abortive Northampton Chapel. The countess applied astonishing personal pressure on a number of other men to follow, but they all refused and were treated with her fastidious contempt. All turned their backs on her, to which she responded by describing them as 'plausible pleaders for Satan only', driven from her purse and presence.[59]

Many advised her against a general secession: it should just be Spa Fields, since that was the only one of her chapels to face legal challenge. Yet once having made her decision, she forced the wheels of secession forward and pinned her final hopes on securing a mass exodus of Welsh evangelical clergy: 'The whole association of Wales was to offer their all in supporting my cause', she believed, remarkably. [60] However, the Welsh clergy reported that it would be as possible 'to perswade the *Pope* to become *Lutheran*' as to get them to agree to secede from the Church of England.[61] It was not clear to some of her English ministers why she was so intent on involving the Welsh clergy:

> why Madam so anxious for the concurrence of the Welch Ministers? I don't see any assistance they [can] give your Ladyship in your english work, w[h]ether you have, or have not their Approbation. I think it will be quite immaterial – your seceding will not frustrate their work in Wales, nor will it prevent any one of them (if they are dispos'd to assist us) preaching in your English Chapels.[62]

Any hope of maintaining, let alone expanding, her work depended upon securing new ministers. With further Anglican orders now impossible, the countess and her advisers laid plans for their own connexional ordination. As with most new religious denominations, this event marked her church's true birth. It took place at Spa Fields on 9 March 1783, when during a five-hour service Wills and Taylor ordained six Trevecca students as ministers of what was called the 'Countess of Huntingdon Connexion'. The attending congregation were told that the 'right of setting such apart . . . is not only the work of Bishops, now so called' but by faithful ministers of Christ, 'who are exactly described by the Presbytery deputed by the Holy Ghost, for such work, in the days of the Apostles'.[63] But the secession was not to produce a clean cut with all things Anglican. The Book of Common Prayer was used in the countess's leading chapels, such as Bath, Brighton, Tunbridge Wells and Spa Fields, and even in a number of smaller chapels. After secession this practice continued, but it was made clear that parts of the Prayer Book were not theologically compatible with Calvinistic Methodism. The service of baptism was amended, since the Prayer Book referred to every child being 'regenerate'. At the burial service, the reference to 'a certain hope of a resurrection unto eternal life' was excluded. However, in the main, the usual services of matins and evensong continued to be used virtually unaltered.

For a formula of doctrine, candidates were obliged to sign publicly a newly drafted Confession of Faith, consisting of fifteen articles resting on a firm Calvinistic foundation and maintaining, in article two, 'the infallible truth' of the scriptures. Roughly one-third of the confession was derived from the Thirty-Nine Articles of the Anglican Church and a half from the Westminster Confession of Faith – the thoroughly Calvinistic statement of faith drawn up during the Puritan revolution of the seventeenth century.[64] A significant divergence from the Thirty-Nine Articles is the connexion's clearly Calvinist statement in its article ten, 'Of Justification', that fallen and sinful human beings are made righteous by the imputation of Christ's 'obedience and satisfaction'.[65]

Despite the fact of its having scrupulously excluded those portions of the Thirty-Nine Articles that did not appear to validate a Calvinistic position, the Countess of Huntingdon's Connexion continued to affirm that its secession had changed nothing theologically and that its fifteen articles were totally in doctrinal tune with the thirty-nine. The connexion remained resolutely firm in its commitment to the baptism of infants and clearly believed that any theological distance that had been placed between it and the Anglican Church was infinitesimal compared with the chasm thus placed between it and Baptists.[66]

A year after the countess took over Spa Fields, London experienced the turmoil of the Gordon Riots. In 1779 a 'Protestant Association' was formed in Scotland to protest at the proposed limited repeal of penal laws there against Roman Catholics, repeal that had been peacefully accomplished for England the preceding year with the Catholic Relief Act. This association was successful, through rioting and civil disobedience, in having the proposal abandoned in Scotland; and, savouring this success, the association turned its attention to the south, seeking to force repeal of the freshly passed English legislation. To that end, the eccentric young Lord George Gordon was dispatched to London at the end of 1779, where he commenced gathering signatures for a petition. He told Parliament that the 'indulgences given to Papists have alarmed the whole country'. If Parliament needed any persuading, Gordon said that they 'will find 120,000 men at my back'.[67]

By June 1780 he had collected a petition containing 44,000 signatures. More ominously, he had collected in St George's Field 60,000 supporters of his Protestant Association. Over the next several days London was thrown into chaos, with Catholic chapels and homes destroyed to the piercing cries of 'No Popery'. The mob violence spilled over into the successful freeing of prisoners from several gaols, and unsuccessful attacks on Lambeth Palace and the Bank of England. At one point, well over thirty fires raged in the City alone. Ten thousand troops were poured into the capital, turning Hyde Park into an armed camp. During that dreaded first week in June, 300 people were killed in the London rioting, twenty-five eventually executed for their roles and substantial property damage sustained. Between the Great Fire and the Blitz it was London's most devastating destruction.

Although the rioters were active in Clerkenwell, they took deliberate care that no damage be done to Spa Fields chapel when one of their leaders announced that his mother worshipped there. The chapel was spared, it was said, because it was deemed to be a 'No Popery place'.[68] The countess of Huntingdon was by no means unusual in her abhorrence and fear of Roman Catholicism, but her intensity in the matter brooked no competition. The countess's words against Catholics were harsh.[69] When they built a chapel and school in Bath she was beside herself: 'Papists over England threaten terrable days against this land & the Church of God', although she would find some hope in the prophecy that 'Popery and Babylons downfall will be in the year of 1790'.[70]

At his trial in 1781 Gordon's serving barrister was his cousin, who was also brother to Lady Huntingdon's permanent companion, Lady Anne Erskine. Gordon's chief defence witness was the Reverend Erasmus Middleton, one of the six students expelled from Oxford in 1768 and a protégé of one of the countess's chief clerical supporters, Thomas Haweis. Middleton had been preaching at the countess's Mulberry Gardens Chapel in Wapping. Moreover, he had just taken over as editor of the periodical she supported, the *Gospel Magazine*, on the death of Augustus Toplady. A member of the Protestant Association committee and related to Gordon by marriage, Middleton argued that any thought of creating violence had been absent from their intentions. In spite of the prosecution's serious questioning of Middleton's veracity, for lack of any hard evidence Gordon was found not guilty.

Immediately following the riots the *Gospel Magazine* published a hearty defence of the Protestant Association, while distancing all concerned from the depredations of the rioters. This they published along with a lurid description of how 200,000 'inoffensive' Protestants in Ireland during the reign of Charles I had been 'inhumanly butchered' at the instigation of 'Romish priests'. That 'was but a little above a century ago, and . . . Rome is still the same . . . Her bigoted zealots would not shudder at the like cruelties, if their priests required them at their hands.'[71] A month following the Gordon Riots the countess wrote that 'Popery, if ever established, must involve the body of the Church in all its absurdities of faith & practice'.[72] It is clear that Calvinistic Methodists tended to be in the vanguard of what might be called 'anti-Catholicism'. Its theology pushed it further in this direction than that of any other religious body of the day. However, with ecclesiastical authority bearing down on her as the secession crisis at Spa Fields reached its head just at this time, Lady Huntingdon hardly wished to incur the additional wrath of civil authority: the riots had made her extremely fearful of guilt by association. While she implied that Gordon had been among 'our best friends', she now instructed her Spas Fields Committee to arrange a secret meeting with the Mulberry Gardens Committee '& inform & enforce caution & care in publick matters . . . I consider this way in private to you to be most effectual that the pulpit may be kept for the Lords services, & not as the medium of Politics.'[73] How her London pulpits had been used during the recent crisis can only be imagined.

Whichever way she now turned the countess saw the crumbling of certainties. The Church of England had been worth fighting for, worth saving, since it had stood as a bulwark against the Church of Rome. Yet now even the bishops appeared willing to contemplate religious toleration, while at the same time 'fall[ing] on me with such violence, [I] that contended all her life for the Church'. This toleration was simply too much for her to grasp, let alone contemplate: it was 'against the truth itself'.[74]

Rival English Calvinistic Methodist connexions

The solidarity displayed in their reaction to the Wesleyan Conference minutes of 1770 did not ensure the maintenance of harmony within the Calvinist camp. The 1770s and 1780s witnessed the gradual estrangement of the countess of Huntingdon's collection of chapels from a number of groups to which it was doctrinally close. Of these, it might well be expected that following Whitefield's death in 1770 the countess would assume a significant role in guiding the work of his 'Tabernacle Connexion' – perhaps even to the extent of merging its work with hers. This might have appeared particularly appropriate, since there was no figure who took over Whitefield's role within that grouping. However, although there never had been, never would be, any minister able to approach him in her esteem ('My heart was unalterably attached to him & I trust ever will be') she had no illusions regarding his interest in and capacity for detailed organisational leadership.[75] Indeed, she became increasingly suspicious of some of the ministers and laymen who endeavoured to carry on Whitefield's work.

In 1777, when the London Tabernacle trustees offered help in the planning of her chapel in Mulberry Gardens, Wapping, she was highly apprehensive: there clearly now was a permanent gulf between her work and that of the Whitefieldite connexion. By that October, congregations in Wiltshire faced a choice between preachers of Whitefield's Tabernacle Association and hers, while at the same time it seemed that the Tabernacle trustees were attempting to interfere with her chapel in Norwich.[76] By the early 1780s she totally rejected any connection with the London Tabernacle and its broader association of chapels:

> The Tabernacle Connection & Mr Hills [Rowland Hill] both universally to be rejected. A clergyman told me lately that they were watching to get Plums for themselves out of our Puddings, & they are Laying wait for any of my able & faithfull ministers or students, & have made their offers.[77]

She now determined that

> we stand alone never entering into any ones labours, & being remarkably carefull [not] to have any with us we cannot be fully answerable for, lest the young men [her students] suffer from any supposed union which may not be altogether in life & doctrine what I require from them.[78]

Yet problems rumbled on, as with conflict between the countess's Bristol Chapel and the Whitefieldian Tabernacle there.[79] Lady Huntingdon also began to fancy that Lady Glenorchy was plotting to undermine her work.

Gloucestershire had provided a fertile ground for Calvinistic Methodism from its early period, not least perhaps because of Whitefield's early years there and also because it served as a crossroads for preachers coming and going between England and Wales. Over the years the Gloucestershire societies and the chapels that followed Whitefield developed their own association, known as the Rodborough Connexion. It was named after a village near Stroud where Whitefield's convert Thomas Adams had founded a 'Tabernacle' chapel in 1750. This Rodborough chapel assumed a central importance in the area during the early years of Calvinistic Methodism, with a number of chapels in its vicinity established by preachers sent out from this chapel.[80] The connexion actually was composed of Calvinistic Methodist societies in Gloucestershire and neighbouring Wiltshire, where, for example, the Tabernacle Chapel in Chippenham owed its origin to exhorters, especially Whitefield, who were active in the area from as early as 1742.[81]

Until 1770, the societies and chapels of the Rodborough Connexion, including those at Rodborough, Dursley, Painswick, Stroud, Ebley, Wotton under Edge, and many others were ministered to by preachers closely connected with Methodism. The death that year of a number of them, including Whitefield, began the process that would accelerate over the coming decades of these groups becoming Independent. However, the leadership of Rowland Hill from his chapel at Wotton under Edge would for a number of years maintain the connexion's identity as an important centre of Calvinistic Methodism in England.[82]

In 1774 a chapel had been opened at Haverfordwest, called the 'Tabernacle' out of reverence for George Whitefield and erected mainly by the labours of his English connexion. Though the members of the Tabernacle always considered themselves to be in a special relationship with Whitefield's London Tabernacle, they desired cordial alliance with their Welsh-speaking neighbours. However, because of the language difference they needed ministerial supplies from England. By 1780 this Tabernacle had been in 'a state of flux' with regard to its affiliations with the Welsh Association, English Whitefieldian Methodism (centred on the Rodborough Connexion) and the Countess of Huntingdon's

Connexion.[83] To deal with these uncertainties and consequent conflict an agreement was adopted on 26 June 1781 between the Welsh Association and the Rodborough Connexion where each would respect the other's preachers and forego any interference in the other's sphere of interest. To effect all this, there were to be quarterly meetings, with six members of each connexion serving as delegates. However, nothing came of the plan, because there was a basic provision stipulating that the Rodborough Connexion 'deliver up to the Welsh Association all right power or influence in Haverfordwest or elsewhere in Wales held by them'.[84] By his actions, Rowland Hill, titular head and ruling spirit of the Rodborough Connexion, clearly considered Haverfordwest to be in his bounds, directed from Wotton under Edge. This infuriated Lady Huntingdon, and she and Hill were at serious variance over the matter. Moreover, Hill had previously raised her ire by attempting to have a number of his Rodborough Connexion societies in Gloucestershire ordain some of her students without any prior reference to her.[85] Some of these students also accused Hill of trespassing on their preaching in the Bridgwater, Somerset, area; moreover, they complained about his facetiousness in preaching, which was true enough. All in all, this further jarring discordance undermined any hope of maintaining a coordinated Calvinistic Methodist movement in England.

Another colourful Calvinist character of the time was Torial Joss, a former sea captain who had become one of Whitefield's assistants in 1766 and preached regularly in Gloucestershire. Aiding Hill there and in his Haverfordwest activities, Joss became tainted with the same brush with which the countess blackened Hill. There was sharp discussion about some of the Gloucestershire chapels and an especially angry controversy over the Haverfordwest Tabernacle. The countess held that all Methodist chapels and societies in the principality should be under the control of the Welsh Association; however, the Tabernacle congregation preferred to be allied with Gloucestershire, which was the nearest of the English associations.[86]

In all this turmoil, Lady Huntingdon supported Nathaniel Rowland, who was in charge of the Haverfordwest chapel and was in frequent conflict with its members. All this uncertainty rumbled on for a number of years, with Rowland complaining about Hill's 'unbecoming Conduct' regarding Haverfordwest. Rowland wrote to the countess that he had told the people that if we could obtain a new Chapel I did not doubt but your Ladyship would spare some of your Ministers occasionally, particularly those who can preach both Languages. My dear Lady H. I have my hands so full I know not which way to turn. [David] Griffiths will not preach but in Churches, our other faithful Ministers have no English, Lord send more English labo[u]rers into the Harvest.[87]

Moreover, 'the Welsh', said Rowland, 'are well off having . . . preachers among themselves that visit them frequently'.[88]

In other ways did the countess of Huntingdon establish the distinctiveness of her enterprises. The Whitefieldites were closer to Dissent than was the countess's work, largely because, as has already been noted, she maintained the use of the Anglican liturgy in the central services of worship in a number of her chapels. Generally, the Wesleys followed the practice of maintaining their chapels as places of preaching, not worship. Therefore, Wesleyan Methodists were expected to attend their local parish churches, and to receive communion there. This procedure was retained by the Wesleys until the 1780s, when the pressure from members meant that the sacrament began to be celebrated in their chapels. However, as long as John Wesley lived, such occasions were infrequent, because he held fast to the belief that only ordained men could celebrate communion, and there was a decided lack of such clergymen. In contrast, Lady Huntingdon made no attempt to persuade her congregations to worship in parish churches, nor did she show any reticence at the administration of the sacraments in her chapels. In the 1770s, for example, there is evidence of weekly celebrations at Bath. In 1782 the norm for the connexion's congregations was perhaps communion every two months, though this was not always maintained. The constraint – certainly prior to the institution of the connexion's own ordination in 1783 – was lack of ministers. Unlike Wesleyan Methodism, there is no indication of pressure in the countess's connexion for laymen to be allowed to conduct such rites.

What ministers wore also set the countess's connexion apart from other non-Anglicans. The use of a black gown and preaching bands appears to have been the normal practice amongst both ministers and students of the connexion. Moreover, they were worn out of doors as well as in chapel. Like the use of the Book of Common Prayer, the wearing of clerical dress added a degree of authority, and respectability, to the connexion.[89] As for her providing the students with caps and gowns, as already noted it, was a practice that made bishops and clergy 'murmur against' Trevecca; and, unsurprisingly, John Wesley joined in bitterly criticising the practice.[90] One senior Trevecca student wrote to his fellows with stunning candour: 'Those that the gospel won't draw the college gown will.'[91]

Despite the usual image of genteel attendance at her chapels, in practice the presence of those of high birth was unusual enough to warrant special mention.[92] The only countess of Huntingdon chapel during the eighteenth century for which lists of members have been preserved is Lewes, Sussex.[93] In 1776 there were thirty-seven men and twenty-two women. Very little evidence survives regarding the occupations of members, but those in remote places such as Ely tended to be 'but very poor', while at Chichester 'there is a good spirit for hearing, tho' it is mostly among the poorer sort of people'.[94] However, the backbone of her chapels appears to have been formed of artisans and small business entrepreneurs. There are registers for Norwich chapel in 1788 and 1789 which record the following for the fathers of children being baptised: baker, bricklayer, gauze-weaver, haberdasher, manufacturer, mason, staymaker, weaver, woolcomber, worsted weaver. At London's Mulberry Gardens during the same period there were: glasscutter, hatter, linen draper, sailor, tallow chandler.[95] At the Birmingham Chapel, leaders were a cabinet-maker, a grocer, a plater, a gilder and a leather box-maker. Even at Bath the leading men were a builder, a currier, a tallow chandler and a haberdasher.[96] For many upwardly thrusting artisans, being associated with one of her chapels provided a degree of vicarious social standing. They could claim membership in the 'Countess of Huntingdon Connexion'. This meant that they were usually unhappy to see seats provided for worshippers who could not pay. At one chapel, where 'the poorest' were attracted, the leading men in the congregation 'oppose . . . and abuse the poor people that come'.[97] Such men proceeded in their chapel life with a zeal fuelled largely by their own ambitions.

The countess insisted that seating at her main chapels be by ticket only. This means of reserving seats was a technique designed to provide a constant source of local finance. The use of chapel tickets was hardly unique but, whereas Wesley's societies issued them as badges for those deemed worthy of continued membership, for the countess their use was purely a money-raising device, or on special occasions an inducement to notables to attend by supplying them gratis.[98] Lady Huntingdon took personal responsibility for preparing the copper plates used to print these tickets, either for individual chapels, or, alternatively, as a special 'season ticket' whereby those subscribing money to purchase a seat in any one chapel could gain admittance to services in all. Many people, especially in London, paid for seats in order to hear particular preachers and complained bitterly if those men did not appear in the pulpit.[99] Her Bath chapel tended to make clear-cut distinctions in their seating arrangements and even in the nature of the services provided. There the general practice was to limit admission at morning services to the higher ranks of society, while the humbler classes attended in the evening. Only the best preachers were booked for the former, while those of lesser talents held forth in the latter.[100]

Thus in many and diverse ways did the Countess of Huntingdon's Connexion attempt to maintain its distinctive nature, especially against various Dissenting groups. Ideally, the countess could hope that if she had to be a dissenter it would be as a dissenter with a difference. She feared, with some justification, that Dissenters – mainly Independents (Congregationalists) – would prove incapable of holding to orthodox Calvinist doctrines. In addition to this possibility of theological impurity, Dissenting chapels used settled ministers, and the countess never relented in her insistence on a constantly mobile ministry. Nonetheless, the countess of Huntingdon's arrival at Spa Fields, the subsequent secession and her increasing triumphalism also dug a wide chasm between her and the emerging evangelical wing of the Church of England. Some of these men 'have set their faces in open war against me & will join heartily with any evil adversary. But my cause is in the Lords hands.'[101] Others, such as John Berridge, Henry Venn and John Newton, pursued their courses more quietly, redoubling efforts to invigorate the parish life of the Established Church. Thus the philanthropic 'Clapham sect' of evangelicals, centred round the layman John Thornton, developed apart from Lady Huntingdon. Her active support of slavery further widened the division. Hannah More took pains to show that she had never attended services at any of the Huntingdon chapels.[102] The countess's correspondence with Thornton ended soon after the secession, when he informed her that his efforts must continue to be directed towards the work of parishes; and soon after she had most bitterly dismissed one of her ministers, Thornton befriended him.[103]

The antinomian label: charged with immorality

The secession crisis contributed significantly to a bunker mentality, yet Lady Huntingdon's belief that she was being persecuted from many directions was worn as a badge of pride. Her Spa Fields cathedral became for her a castle. Over the life of Spa Fields Chapel the countess brooded with commanding eye. Ever refusing to allow any of her ministers to settle in one place, to the end of her life with an increasingly shaky hand but deep well of ink she continued to write letters, exercising a meticulous control over their movements. Indeed, believing that any unpregnant moment was a faithless one, if nothing else was to hand she wrote her letters, frequently devoting six or seven hours a day to the task. 'I have been writing since ten this morning & so fatigued I am ready to faint.'[104] Spa Fields, in Clerkenwell, received her special care regarding preaching. She ensured that the people heard such sermons as that preached by a former Trevecca student, now a minister in her connexion:

> How will you, gospel despisers, who have heard Christ preached in Spa-Fields Chapel, and elsewhere, be alarmed to see Jesus sitting upon his judgment throne, in the clouds, preparing vengeance for you who have despised his word, neglected his gospel, and blasphemed his name! . . . you daring sinners [with] your secret sins, and midnight impurities; your sins committed in the dark . . . How will the presumptuous soul be alarmed to see the bottomless pit open its insatiable mouth; and with an horrid visage and greedy eye looking, gaping, yawning, to swallow him up!

Warming to this theme, the preacher described what awaited them:

> Rivers of fire, in which wicked spirits are plunged, rolled, tormented, and burned after death . . . You have heard from this pulpit many

times, by many of God's ministers, that the day of account will come
. . . It is at the peril of your souls that you speak one word against the
things which you have heard.[105]

The preacher alludes to one of the basic charges levelled against
Calvinists of any stripe: antinomianism, the belief that by virtue of
being one of God's 'elect' a Christian is released from the obligations
of moral law. John Wesley's rejection of the theological position of
the Calvinistic version of Methodism was not a little influenced by
what he perceived as a resulting indifference to moral laws. Referring
to some of the ministers most intimately involved in the countess's
preaching plans, including Whitefield, Wesley had lamented their
'amorous' ways of praying to Christ in public.[106] Lady Huntingdon's
drawing room services during the 1750s and 1760s had attracted some
'scented beaus', who were 'hoping to see a young wench in a religious
frency'.[107] Trevecca students presented special problems. One revival
meeting there saw male and female displaying 'unruly Passions'.[108] In
nearby Cardiganshire it was observed in 1778 that two young Methodist women who 'did jump & keep a noise above the rest are now
turned whores, to the great scandal of jumping'.[109]

It was when away from Trevecca that the most serious difficulties
arose. Peripatetic preachers with a lively message of divine love on
their lips had far greater temptations, and opportunities, for misdeeds
than a man rooted in his local charge. As with most mobile Methodist
exhorters during this eighteenth-century formative period, they tended
to be 'sexually active preachers on the move'.[110] One student on his
preaching rounds had 'most shamefully formed such a connection'
with a member of one of the countess's chapels 'as to be wicked with
her for almost all the time he was there'. For a while it had been
hushed up,

> but at last it had vent, and out it came to the wide world, to the no
> small reproach of the Gospel at that place. He did not promise to
> marry the girl at any time, but persuaded the deluded creature that
> there was no manner of sin in Fornication.

On his return to Trevecca the young man informed the master that
'your Ladyship . . . maintained the same sentiments'.[111] Towards the

end of her life, the countess received news that one of her students had become a rank antinomian. The student wrote to her that he considered this teaching 'the simple Truth, and the Old Light of the Prophets and Apostles and that which Jehovah Jesus himself Taught'.[112] A man not unsympathetic to the countess remarked on the great 'immodesty' of her students.[113] The impressionable young men had been seduced by example, some apparently believing that they had been licensed for mischief.

Either through the ridicule or incomprehension of those outside the movement, or through the heady excitement that drew together those who had experienced what others had not, the correspondence of countless Methodists bespoke a love for one another that could leap the bounds of propriety, or at least of good judgement. Over the years the chapel at Bath provided more than its share of heartache for the countess of Huntingdon. Not least among the trials were remarkable reports she received in 1788. She had recently appointed a new member of the chapel committee, one P. A. Saxby. Yet Saxby had been keeping a young mistress, who was already carrying his child, and his appointment had been a 'matter of astonishment to most people of the Chapel'. When Saxby began openly parading his mistress about the Pump Room, his wife upbraided him, upon which he 'beat her unmercifully so that the whole street was in an uproar crying out: "These are Lady Huntingdon's People"'.[114]

The countess's enterprises were hindered not only by misconduct heterosexual. In the last year of her life she found it necessary to initiate investigations into the activities of a preacher she had prided herself in having induced to leave Wesley. 'He has in time past', she was informed, 'too near approach'd a Line of Conduct, unnatural in itself, and too indelicate to mention. Rom[ans]. 1.27.'[115] She probably took special pains in securing the truth, given the dreadful uncovering some years earlier of the activities of one of the leading laymen in her Spa Fields Chapel. As a member of the chapel committee, Morris Hughes held power of attorney for Lady Huntingdon and was superintendent of the chapel society which met weekly. Claiming that he had been 'made free', Hughes 'exposed his person' to a chimney sweep, a baker, a plumber and a cabinet-maker. Moreover, he had engaged in 'playing at blindmans-buff with the boys in the neighbourhood, and in making a barber's boy thrust his curling irons up his nostrils to make his nose bleed'. Most serious, all this had become common fame, gleefully reported in the press. The hapless man was stripped of all his chapel responsibilities and, excommunicated, fled London.[116]

It is little wonder that Lady Huntingdon was herself charged with being an antinomian. Even Charles Wesley, who despite their increasing differences sought to see her in the best possible light, concluded that 'her Ladyship approaches too near the Antinomian extream'.[117] When one member of her connexion was accused of living an openly wicked and profane life, he replied: 'Don't preach your legal stuff to me. I am not in Bondage. I am for my Lady's Gospel.' When asked if he thought he was behaving correctly, he answered: 'No. Yet it cannot hurt me; for I know that I have a finish'd salvation a complete Righteousness.' In other words, the countess was counselled, her twist on Calvinistic theology was producing 'pernicious' fruits.[118] Indeed, in one of the sermons preached on the occasion of her death it was reported that Lady Huntingdon 'was almost cried down as an Antinomian; but none could prove her one in her practice: and as to the law, she felt, from long experience, that she could neither get life nor comfort from it'.[119] At the very outset of her Calvinistic orientation, she had been advised that there was a

> pipe of faith . . . which reaches from the soul of the true believer up into the highest heavens from whence God is pleased to communicate all his gifts & graces . . . Whoever is thus born of God cannot committ sin because [of] the Holy Ghost.[120]

Over the years the countess encountered a cascade of problems from those who found in her gospel what they considered an open invitation to disregard moral restraint. They enjoyed the comfortable conviction that whatever they did could not hinder their election to salvation. It was a mischievously attractive doctrine, and it was precisely the Wesleyan theological concern that brought matters to a head in 1770. Perceived widespread moral laxity among Lady Huntingdon's branch of Methodism was driven home by her erstwhile Trevecca superintendent, John Fletcher, who vigorously defended Wesley's 1770 conference minutes in his six *Checks to Antinomianism* (1771–5). One of her leading students at Trevecca, who like so many others later departed her connexion to settle as a Dissenting minister, reflected on her itinerant preachers 'wandering from county to county, and from diocese to diocese', preaching 'in meeting-houses, and fields, and barns, the flesh-pleasing doctrines of the antinomian error'.[121]

To the end of her life, Lady Huntingdon found it impossible to shake off this label. On one occasion at Trevecca, when her birthday and the anniversary of the founding of the 'college' were being celebrated, the festivities suffered an electrifying interruption by a man screaming that she was 'a whore'.[122] Her former clerical supporter, the incisive John Berridge, felt impelled to write to her words of strong caution:

> Though Believers are under the teaching of God's Spirit, they often fall into their own; and thereby slide into sad doctrines, and sometimes into sad practices; and how must you deal with such people if there is no rule of life to appeal to? You may tell them that Jesus, by his Spirit, teaches you so and so; and they will tell you that Jesus teaches them quite the contrary. And if they are led by their own spirit, they will be more violent for their mistake, than you can be for the truth. If there is no written Rule of Life of allowed authority, you can never deal with deluded Christians; they will plead inward teaching for the worst doctrine, and godly motives for the worst practices.[123]

The internecine conflict between Wesleyan and Calvinistic Methodism was a theological dispute over the source of salvation. But in practical terms, and on good authority, it is not beliefs but fruits that can be judged in this life. The basic problem was that passionate Christians found it decidedly difficult to respond to only one set of emotions.

The countess's Welsh connections

Following the formal establishing of the countess's connexion in the early 1780s, Lady Huntingdon began to despair of the products her 'college' at Trevecca was producing. She was, of course, desperate for preachers for the connexion's chapels, and as with everything else regarding Trevecca she had total control over which young men would be admitted. Indeed, one tutor criticised her for admitting, in effect, almost anyone who applied; he appealed that future prospective candidates should be 'properly examined, & tried respecting their characters, abilities, motives'.[124] This suggests that it was not always intellectual qualities that were wanting. One chapel bitterly complained about those sent from Trevecca to preach: the 'vilest of all R[asca]ls falsely call'd Students, for I declare from my heart, nine out of ten deserve that name'; and it is evident that a number of the students were emotionally immature. Many left after a brief time, one citing 'the Strife and Contention that is dayly at College'.[125] Moreover, given her unwavering demand for them to act as travelling preachers, it is not difficult to understand why a growing number of her students left her service to plough ecclesiastical furrows of their own with Independent Dissenting chapels. She viewed 'with grief' ministers 'confined to chapels, while thousands of souls are perishing'.[126]

In any case, Lady Huntingdon's retirement to Spa Fields, 'quite fatigued out of my life', put further miles between her and Trevecca.[127] By 1784 she was receiving plaintive letters: 'We are not ready to con-clude you have forgotten your little, poor, afflicted Family, at the College.'[128] When she departed Trevecca in the spring of 1787 after a six-week stay, it was for the last time. In fact, as early as 1782 she was thinking of uprooting the institution, to move it either to London or to a site adjoining her chapel in Swansea.[129] Meanwhile, Trevecca was left to wither on the vine. Apart from the raw quality of most of the students, their constant displacement to pursue itinerant preaching throughout the kingdom wreaked havoc with any sense of academic continuity. Even the countess came to reflect, looking back over all the students 'under my hands' since the founding of Trevecca, that 'I have been offended' with them.[130] In fact, during the late 1780s she virtually abandoned them. Numerous letters begged her to pay the long overdue accounts of local tradesmen clamouring for their money.[131] Rent for the 'college' building and lands had not been paid for two years; the tax authorities were threatening to seize its goods; and the countess had made not a single reply to urgent letters from the 'college'. The ten students in 1788 were virtually in rags. The 'college' was down to two horses, one lame the other totally blind. Effectively, the 'college' had been hobbled.

Beyond her 'college', the countess had several Welsh interests and connections. It may come as a surprise that there was a countess of Huntingdon chapel in Swansea, yet there were others: at Monmouth,

Llangattock Lingoed and Brecon; and, of course, she had taken a keen interest in the one at Haverfordwest. Apart from these, all the countess's chapels were in England except for one in Guernsey and one in Dublin. Swansea chapel was established in about 1774 when one of her students wrote to her that 'we have got a good Room intirely to ourselves at Swansea for preaching in. Mr Wesley's preachers had turned their backs upon it.'[132] In 1786 she visited the town and engaged a local architect, William Jernegan, to build a chapel and to find her a house with a sea view. By the 2 August 1788 the chapel was ready, but Jernegan was still seeking a proper house for the countess, which never materialised.

In one way Wales proved vital to Lady Huntingdon's enterprises. Although any notion of Welsh secession from the Church of England had been firmly scotched, during the 1780s the countess secured periodic preaching from some Calvinistic Welsh Anglican leaders at Spa Fields, and occasionally at other of her major chapels. The most prominent of these were David Jones, vicar of Llan-gan, Glamorgan; David Griffiths, vicar of Nevern, Pembrokeshire; and Thomas Charles of Bala, Merionethshire. Jones wished that: 'I had much more time to spend in the Connection. Your Ladyship knows how I am tied among the poor Welsh.'[133] On one occasion Griffiths wrote that despite the great inconvenience involved, he could not refuse her urgent request to come to preach at Spa Fields.[134] Thomas Charles had preached for a season at the Bath chapel as early as 1781.[135] Although ordained and having served curacies in Somerset, after his marriage in 1783 he settled in Bala and sustained the Calvinistic Methodist cause in several ways. His lack of a parish post gave him unusual flexibility and meant that he was able to preach at Spa Fields for a few summer Sundays during the last two or three years of the countess's life and probably was the most frequent Welsh cleric to visit her chapels.[136] In addition, Charles made valiant yet unsuccessful efforts to find Lady Huntingdon a replacement for John Williams as head of her Trevecca 'college'.

The countess also had the services over a number of years of Nathaniel Rowland, who is presumed to have held Anglican ordination. Long the mainstay of the Tabernacle in Haverfordwest, he also frequently preached in the countess's chapels in Bristol and Bath. From Bath he wrote that: 'I am still astonish'd that the most gay, polite, etc. instead of walking out and deserting the Chapel on account of my *Welchy* unpolish'd Language should burst into Tears and attend as ever on Week Nights.'[137] In 1790 the countess wrote to Thomas Charles one of her constant appeals for him to continue coming to London to fill her pulpit: 'Don't forget us . . . Spa Fields is now styled the Welsh Society . . . It much rejoices & honours me by its title.'[138] There is no doubt that she was relieved when able to secure the preaching of all these men, but she complained that they seemed less than eager to prolong their tours of duty. Lady Huntingdon confided to a correspondent that the 'Welch ministers are so slippary that I cannot keep them one day longer than they agree to stay'.[139]

In 1790 David Jones wrote to the countess that on 20 May the Association of Welsh Calvinistic clergy had recorded a resolution to persuade all people 'of that sweet harmony which Subsists between our Association & your Ladyship's Connection':

> That the Welsh Association wish from the Ground of their hearts to cultivate & maintain a christian & friendly Connection with the Right Honourable the Countess of Huntingdon: & that they wish to further & promote . . . her Ladyship's work at Swansea & everywhere else.[140]

Indeed, it was David Jones who delivered the sermon at her funeral at Spa Fields the following year. Several years later it was observed that the connexion's major chapels were being served by clergy 'especially from Wales'.[141]

The clash over predestination finally produced a 'break' between Calvinistic and Wesleyan Methodism. Given their diametrically opposed theologies over the matter, not to mention the personalities of the countess and John Wesley, this was virtually inevitable. The importance of maintaining the doctrine of predestination meant that Trevecca became a focus of attention. Moreover, the countess's adherence to this belief, and her personal devotion to George Whitefield, contributed firmly to her unquestioning support of American slavery. At the same time her programme of chapel building continued apace, the zenith of which was Spa Fields in London – which led directly to her secession from the Church of England and her establishing of a new denomination. Her connexion sought to maintain some aspects of Anglicanism while at the same time attempting to remain as distinct as possible from Nonconformist bodies. It is worthy of note that at the end of her life the countess of Huntingdon seems to have found her greatest support from Welsh clergymen.

Notes

1 Rylands, Black Folio 3, Selina Hastings to John Wesley, 18 February 1742.
2 Howel Harris's Diary, 2 August 1749, in Tom Beynon (ed.), *Howell Harris's Visits to London* (Aberystwyth: The Cambrian News Press, 1966), p. 229.
3 John Wesley to Selina Hastings, 20 March 1763, in John Telford (ed.), *The Letters of the Rev. John Wesley* (8 vols, London: Epworth Press, 1931), IV, p. 206.
4 Howel Harris's Diary, 4 November 1763, in Tom Beynon (ed.), *Howell Harris, Reformer and Soldier (1714–1773)* (Caernarvon: The Calvinistic Methodist Bookroom, 1958), p. 205.
5 [Richard Hill], *Pietas Oxoniensis* (2nd edn, London: J. and W. Oliver, 1768), p. 82n.
6 W. Reginald Ward and Richard P. Heitzenrater (eds), *The Works of John Wesley*, vol. 22, *Journals and Diaries V (1765–75)* (Nashville, TN: Abingdon Press, 1993), p. 164.
7 For a discussion of a number of these publications, see James E. Hull, 'The controversy between John Wesley and the countess of Huntingdon' (unpublished Ph.D. thesis, University of Edinburgh, 1959), 229–30.
8 Ward and Heitzenrater (eds), *The Works of John Wesley*, XXII, p. 114.
9 *Minutes of the Methodist Conferences*, vol. 1 (London, 1862), p. 96.
10 NLW Howel Harris's Diary, 12 October 1770.
11 Duke, Wesley Family Papers, item 18-H, John Wesley to Joseph Benson, 30 November 1770.
12 Rylands, John Fletcher Letter Books, John Fletcher to Joseph Benson, 10 January 1771.
13 Cheshunt F1/2202, William Aldridge to Trevecca students, 20 April 1774.
14 'An account of John Fletcher's case', in Luke Tyerman, *Wesley's Designated Successor: The Life, Letters and Literary Labours of the Rev. John William Fletcher* (London: Hodder and Stoughton, 1882), p. 184.

15 Rylands, PLP 7/8/13, Joseph Benson to [John Wesley], 15 October 1785.
16 John Fletcher to John Wesley, 20 February, 24 June 1771, in Luke Tyerman, *The Life of the Rev. John Wesley* (3 vols, 4th edn, London: Hodder and Stoughton, 1878), III, p. 88.
17 Cheshunt E4/7/1, John Fletcher to Selina Hastings, 7 March 1771.
18 'Doctrines, (I am more and more convinced) are of no service to believers.' George Whitefield to Selina Hastings, 10 November 1755, in John Gillies (ed.), *The Works of the Reverend George Whitefield* (6 vols, London: Edward and Charles Dilly, 1771–2), III, p. 150; 'I am betw[ee]n Calvin[is]m & free will'. NLW Howel Harris's Diary, 19 January 1767.
19 Cheshunt F1/1386, Richard Hill to [Walter Shirley], 10 January 1772; circular letter, [June 1771], in Tyerman, *Life of John Wesley*, III, pp. 93-4.
20 Walter Shirley, *A Narrative of the Principal Circumstances relative to the Rev. Mr. Wesley's Late Conference* (Bath: W. Gye, 1771), pp. 3, 24.
21 *Gospel Magazine*, August and May 1771, quoted in Tyerman, *Life of Rev. John Wesley*, III, pp. 91, 105.
22 Letter of Augustus Toplady (1773), in Tyerman, *Life of Rev. John Wesley*, III, p. 159.
23 Cheshunt F1/545, John Forman to Selina Hastings, 5 September 1783.
24 Vincent Perronet to John Wesley, 22 November 1777, in *Arminian Magazine*, 20 (1797), 255.
25 Rylands, DD WES 1, Wesley Family Letters and Papers, Folio vol. 1, p. 120, Selina Hastings to Charles Wesley, 8 June 1771.
26 Rylands, Black Folio 24, Selina Hastings to Charles Wesley, 7 October 1752.
27 Cheshunt E4/1/19, Walter Shirley to Selina Hastings, 12 June 1773.
28 Cheshunt G2/1/8, Selina Hastings to John Hawksworth, 15 June 1773.
29 John Fletcher to Walter Shirley, 11 September 1771, in Tyerman, *Wesley's Designated Successor*, p. 195.
30 Cheshunt F1/140, Henry Mead to Selina Hastings, 16 November 1771.
31 NLW Trevecka Letter 2710, J. Thomas to Thomas Jones, 25 June 1772.
32 Ward and Heitzenrater (eds), *The Works of John Wesley*, XXII, p. 299 (4 December 1771), p. 354 (7 December 1772).
33 Cheshunt F1/134, John Cosson to Selina Hastings, 14 September 1771.

[34] John Wesley to Mrs Woodhouse, 22 October 1773, in Telford (ed.), *The Letters of the Rev. John Wesley*, VI, p. 51.

[35] Cheshunt E4/3/2, John Wesley to Selina Hastings, 15 September 1776.

[36] Ward and Heitzenrater (eds), *The Works of John Wesley*, XXII, pp. 103–4 (28 August 1778).

[37] Ibid., p. 138 (3 July 1779).

[38] Cheshunt F1/604, Committee of Norwich Chapel to Selina Hastings, 27 February 1784.

[39] Cheshunt F1/731, John Child and Thomas Skinner to Selina Hastings, 3 June 1788.

[40] Cheshunt A1/13/4, Robert Keen to Selina Hastings, 3 August 1775.

[41] John Wesley to Mary Bishop, 18 August 1784, in Telford (ed.), *The Letters of the Rev. John Wesley*, VII, pp. 227–8.

[42] *An Elegy on the Reverend Mr. G. Whitefield . . . Presented to Her Ladyship* (Carmarthen: J. Ross, 1771), p. 11.

[43] Rylands, Tyerman/Evertt transcripts, Thomas Rankin's Journal, 15 October 1775.

[44] John Fletcher to Joseph Benson, 12 February 1773, in Telford (ed.), *The Letters of the Rev. John Wesley*, VI, p. 20.

[45] For the story of the Bethesda mission, see Boyd Stanley Schlenther, '"To convert the poor people in America": the Bethesda Orphanage and the thwarted zeal of the countess of Huntingdon,' *Georgia Historical Quarterly*, 77 (1994), 225–56.

[46] George Whitefield to Mrs C__, 26 August 1757, in Gillies (ed.), *The Works of Rev. George Whitefield*, III, p. 211.

[47] Selina Hastings to Josiah Tatnall, John Glen and Nathaniel Hall, n.d., in [Aaron C. H. Seymour], *The Life and Times of Selina, Countess of Huntingdon* (2 vols, London: William Edward Painter, 1839), II, p. 266.

[48] Cheshunt A3/1/33 and A4/7/9, Anthony Benezet to Selina Hastings, 25 May 1774, 10 March 1775. (In this latter letter Benezet quotes from her letter to him.) Wesley's tract *Thoughts Upon Slavery* was published in 1774: the reference to slavery as a 'villainy' is quoted from p. 35.

[49] Recollections of John Eyre, *The Order Observed at the Countess of Huntingdon's College, at Cheshunt* (London: Edward Nodson, 1792), p. 79.

[50] Cheshunt E3/2/2, Frederick Cornwallis to Selina Hastings, 3 September 1777.

51 Boyd Stanley Schlenther, *Queen of the Methodists: The Countess of Huntingdon and the Eighteenth-Century Crisis of Faith and Society* (Durham: Durham Academic Press, 1997), pp. 69, 80 n. 8.

52 Cheshunt F1/1823, Thomas Wills to Selina Hastings, 10 March 1778.

53 Guildhall Library, Dissenting Deputies Minutes (1778) MS 3083/2, pp. 278, 280.

54 Dr Williams's Library, Congregational Library II.c.7/3, Selina Hastings to Thomas and Selina Wills, April 1778. As early as 1773 she had been searching for ground in Wapping to build a large chapel, but this 'plan was evidently shelved: a further temporary structure was put up in 1774 and the opening of a permanent chapel in the Gardens did not take place until 1778'. Alan Harding, *The Countess of Huntingdon's Connexion: A Sect in Action* (Oxford: Oxford University Press, 2003), p. 308.

55 Rylands, English MSS 338, Letters of Selina Countess of Huntingdon, 1774–1784, Selina Hastings to John Hawksworth, 16 February 1779.

56 Cheshunt E3/2/4, 8, Selina Hastings to Robert Lowth, 25 February, 19 March 1779.

57 Cheshunt E3/2/7, Robert Lowth to Selina Hastings, 11 March 1779.

58 Rylands, English MSS 338, Letters of Selina Countess of Huntingdon, 1774–1784, Selina Hastings to Selina Wills, 3 September 1779. As early as 1776 she had expressed the fear that she might be turned out of the Church of England. SMU 113a, Selina Hastings to anon. [1776].

59 Cheshunt E4/10/19, Selina Hastings to Mr Evans, 10 June 1782.

60 SMU 102, Selina Hastings to [Thomas Haweis], 17 September 1779.

61 Cheshunt F1/1856, Peter Williams to Selina Hastings, 18 August 1780.

62 Cheshunt F1/1855, William Taylor to Selina Hastings, 16 August 1780.

63 *An Authentic Narrative of the Primary Ordination* (London: Hughes and Walsh, 1784), p. 11.

64 Kenneth Morey, 'The theological position of the Countess of Huntingdon's Connexion', (unpublished BA thesis, Council for National Academic Awards, 1990), 31. 'On original sin, predestination, free will, justification, and good works before and after justification, the Connexion articles used passages verbatim from the Anglican Articles.' Harding, *The Countess of Huntingdon's Connexion*, p. 255.

65 The Anglican Articles 2, 7, 8, 14, 16, 18, 20–26, 30–39 were omitted, some of them 'because they were not sufficiently Calvinist'. Edwin

Welch, *Spiritual Pilgrim: A Reassessment of the Life of the Countess of Huntingdon* (Cardiff: University of Wales Press, 1995), p. 204. The connexion's fifteen articles are printed in *An Authentic Narrative of the Primary Ordination*, pp. 16–25 and are reprinted in Edwin Welch (ed.), *Two Calvinistic Methodist Chapels, 1743–1811: The London Tabernacle and Spa Fields Chapel* (London: London Record Society, 1975), pp. 88–92.

66 The connexion 'maintained, and continued to maintain, that it was not just another sect of dissenters, but a distinct group between them and the Church [of England]'. Alan Harding, 'The countess of Huntingdon and her connexion in the eighteenth century' (unpublished D.Phil. thesis, University of Oxford, 1992), 344.

67 Quoted in J. P. de Castro, *The Gordon Riots* (Oxford: Oxford University Press, 1926), p. 17.

68 Quoted in Christopher Hibbert, *King Mob: The Story of Lord George Gordon and the Riots of 1780* (London: Readers Union, 1959), p. 90.

69 See, for example, Duke, Frank A. Baker Collection, Selina Hastings to Mrs H. Leighton, 19 December 1768.

70 SMU 100, Selina Hastings to [Thomas Haweis], September 1778; Cheshunt F1/889, T. Watkins to Selina Hastings, 25 February 1790.

71 *Gospel Magazine*, 7 (1780), 266–70.

72 Cheshunt E3/3/2, Selina Hastings to Mr Way, 26 July 1780.

73 Cheshunt E4/10/15, Selina Hastings to Spa Fields Committee, 11 September 1781.

74 Cheshunt G2/2, Selina Hastings to [Thomas] Beale, 20 August 1779.

75 Rylands, Black Folio 79, Selina Hastings to Charles Wesley, 28 November 1770.

76 See Harding, *The Countess of Huntingdon's Connexion*, p. 289.

77 Rylands, Black Folio 133, Selina Hastings to Mr Carpenter, [2 November 1785].

78 Rylands, English Manuscripts 338, No. [12], Original Letters of Selina Countess of Huntingdon, 1774–1784, Selina Hastings to Mr Langston, 18 February 1784.

79 Cheshunt, F1/740, Abraham Gadd et al. to Selina Hastings, 7 July 1788.

80 Geoffrey F. Nuttall, 'Rowland Hill and the Rodborough Connexion, 1771–1833', *Transactions of the Congregational Historical Society*, 21, 3 (1972), 70.

81 Christopher Stell, *An Inventory of Nonconformist Chapels and Meeting-Houses in South-West England* (London: Stationary Office Books, 1991), p. 217.

82 Nuttall, 'Rowland Hill and the Rodborough Connexion', 69–71; R. Tudur Jones, *Congregationalism in England* (London: Independent Press, 1962), pp. 149–50.

83 D. Myrddin Lloyd, 'Nathaniel Rowland and the Tabernacle, Haverford-west', *JHSPCW*, 36 (1951), 33.

84 'A proposal for agreement between the Welsh Association and the Gloucestershire Connection, 1781', *JHSPCW*, 52 (1967), 40–1.

85 Cheshunt F1/1734, William Shirley to Selina Hastings, 14 November 1776.

86 James Phillips, 'The Tabernacle Church, Haverfordwest', *JHSPCW*, 7 (1922), 47.

87 Gloucestershire Record Office, Ebley D2538 8/1(8), Nathaniel Rowland to Selina Hastings, 11 August 1789.

88 Cheshunt F1/863, Nathaniel Rowland to Selina Hastings, 3 October 1789.

89 Harding, 'The countess of Huntingdon and her connexion', 145–6, 154.

90 NLW Howel Harris's Diary, 30 March 1769; Cheshunt F1/1347, Isaac Billing et al. to John Wesley, n.d; Dorothy E. S. Brown, 'Evangelicals and education in eighteenth-century Britain: a study of Trevecca College, 1768–1792' (unpublished Ph.D. thesis, University of Wisconsin-Madison, 1992), 243–4.

91 Matthew Wilks to Trevecca students, 6 May 1774, in *Evangelical Register* (1828–9), 205.

92 For example, Cheshunt F1/73, Richard De Courcy to Selina Hastings, 8 July 1769.

93 East Sussex Record Office NB 1/1/1A, pp. 2, 10, 29.

94 Cheshunt F1/2090, John Child to Selina Hastings, 23 July 1789; Cheshunt F1/848, Edward Irish to Selina Hastings, 11 August 1789.

95 National Archives, Kew, RG 4/3132, 4165.

96 Cheshunt F1/815, 'Mortgage for Birmingham Chapel', 23 February 1789; Cheshunt F1/533, Selina Hastings' power of attorney for Bath Chapel, 12 July 1783.

97 Cheshunt F1/209, Lady M. Manners to Selina Hastings, 7 January 1773.

98 Frank Baker, *John Wesley and the Church of England* (Peterborough: Epworth Press, 1970), p. 78; John Penrose to Peggy Penrose, 20 April 1766, *Letters from Bath 1766–1767 by the Rev. John Penrose* (Gloucester: Alan Sutton, 1983), p. 44; Duke, R. E. Hendrix MSS, ticket for Jane Cave, 3 February 1771.

99 Cheshunt F1/27, John Lloyd to Selina Hastings, 2 April 1768; Spa Fields Chapel minutes, 25 May 1781, in Welch (ed.), *Two Calvinistic*

Methodist Chapels, item 156; Spa Fields Committee to Selina Hastings, 9 August 1781, in Welch (ed.), *Two Calvinistic Methodist Chapels*, item 159.

[100] Cheshunt E4/1/18, Walter Shirley to Selina Hastings, 22 May 1773.

[101] Cheshunt G2/2, Selina Hastings to [Thomas] Beale, 20 August 1779.

[102] Hannah More to Bishop of Bath and Wells, 1801, in George W. E. Russell, *A Short History of the Evangelical Movement* (London: Mowbray, 1915), p. 45.

[103] Cheshunt F1.554, John Thornton to Selina Hastings, 7 October 1783; Birmingham University Library, Church Missionary Society Manuscripts: Venn MSS, C68, John Thornton to John Venn, 6 February 1790.

[104] Dr Williams's Library, Congregational Library II c. 7/22, Selina Hastings to Thomas Wills, 29 April 1785.

[105] George Waring, *The End of Time. A Sermon, preached at the Countess of Huntingdon's Chapel, Spa Fields, Clerkenwell, London, on Sunday Evening, August 22, 1790; by George Waring, one of Her Ladyship's Ministers* (2nd edn, n.p., n.d.), pp. 28–9, 33, 41.

[106] John Wesley to John Fletcher, 20 March 1768, in Patrick Streiff, *Jean Guillaume de la Fléchère* (Frankfurt: Lang, 1984), p. 277n.

[107] John Knyveton, 4 November 1763, in Ernest Gray (ed.), *Man Midwife* (London: Robert Hale, 1946), p. 158.

[108] NLW CMA 3154, Diaries of Thomas Roberts, 6 July 1774.

[109] NLW CMA 7021–30, Diary of Edmund Jones (1778).

[110] David Hempton, 'Methodism and the law, 1740–1820', *Bulletin of the John Rylands University Library of Manchester*, 70 (1988), 98.

[111] Cheshunt F1/2060, John Williams to Selina Hastings, 5 February 1789.

[112] Cheshunt F1/927, Thomas Jones to Selina Hastings, 5 July 1790.

[113] NLW CMA 7021–30, Diary of Edmund Jones (1780).

[114] Cheshunt F1/773, J. Sheppard and G. Ford to SH, 10 October 1788; Cheshunt F1/774, anon. to William Taylor (via Selina Hastings), 10 October 1788.

[115] Cheshunt F1/2175, Thomas Young to Selina Hastings, 11 April 1791.

[116] Spa Fields Chapel Minutes, 10 and 13 August 1782, in Welch (ed.), *Two Calvinistic Methodist Chapels*, items 177, 178.

[117] Rylands, Wesley Family Letters and Papers, Folio Vol. 4, Charles Wesley to Sally Wesley, 27 May [c.1780].

[118] Cheshunt E4/4/6, Walter Sellon to Selina Hastings, 20 November 1771.

[119] William Francis Platt, *The Waiting Christian* (Bristol: John Rose, 1791), p. 13.

[120] NLW Trevecka Letter 1643, anon. to SH, 20 April 1747.

[121] Mark Wilks, *Nonconformity: A Sermon, Delivered . . . Nov. 6, 1817, at the Monthly Association, of Congregational Ministers* (London: T. Hamilton, 1818), p. 116.

[122] NLW CMA 7021–30, Diary of Edmund Jones (1780).

[123] John Berridge to Selina Hastings (n.d.), *Evangelical Register*, 1 (1824–5), 236–7.

[124] Cheshunt F1/562, Samuel Phillips to Selina Hastings, 31 October 1783.

[125] Cheshunt F1/782, S. Seager to George Best, 12 November 1788; Cheshunt F1/572, A. Dixon to Selina Hastings, November 1783.

[126] Countess of Huntingdon Connexion Archives, Rayleigh, Selina Hastings to Thomas Pentycross, [1781].

[127] Dr Williams's Library, Congregational Library II.c.7/20, Selina Hastings to Selina Wills, 1 June 1784.

[128] Cheshunt F1/609, Samuel Phillips to SH, 19 March 1784.

[129] Cheshunt F1/480, Thomas Pentycross to Selina Hastings, 28 August 1782; Cheshunt F1/1918, Thomas Wills to Selina Hastings, 7 December 1783; Cheshunt C18/1, p. 1: 'Plan of Apostolic Society', 17 October 1787.

[130] SMU 122, Selina Hastings to [Thomas Haweis], 13 April 1790.

[131] For example, Gloucestershire Record Office, Ebley MSS D 2538/8/1, John Williams to George Best, 9 June 1788.

[132] Cheshunt E4/8/6, J. Meldrum to Selina Hastings, 12 February 1774.

[133] Cheshunt F1/882, David Jones to Selina Hastings, 8 February 1790.

[134] Cheshunt F1/888, David Griffiths, 24 February 1790.

[135] NLW T. C. Edwards Collection 228, Selina Hastings to Thomas Charles, 30 June 1781.

[136] See, for example, letters of Thomas Charles and Sarah Charles to Selina Hastings, 1789–91, printed in *JHSPCW*, 57 (1972), 42, 45–7, and new series, 1 (1977), 20–9. Indeed, he still came to London during the summer for a period following the countess's death, to preach at Spa Fields. Cheshunt F1/2189, 2222, 2229, Thomas Charles to Lady Anne Erskine, 13 July 1791, 31 May 1792, 25 September 1792.

[137] Cheshunt A1/13/14, Nathaniel Rowland to Selina Hastings, 6 April 1782.

[138] Dr Williams's Library, Congregational Library II.a.17/20, Selina Hastings to Thomas Charles, 12 March 1790.

[139] Dr Williams's Library, Congregational Library II.c.7/25, Selina Hastings to Selina Wills, n.d.

[140] Cheshunt F1/918, David Jones to Selina Hastings, 5 June 1790.

[141] Quoted in Harding, 'The countess of Huntingdon and her connexion', 335.

9

'The Lord's gift to the north': the spread of the movement throughout Wales, 1780–1791

Those clergy who found favour with the countess of Huntingdon were among the most prominent of the second generation of leaders of Welsh Methodism. David Jones, for instance, had been awarded the living of Llan-gan by Lady Charlotte Edwin through the countess's influence. It was evangelical Anglican clergy who remained at the forefront of the movement in Wales, although with staunch backing from a number of dedicated laymen, such as Dafydd Morris of Twr-gwyn, Cardiganshire, and Thomas Jones, originally from Flintshire but usually associated with his later base at Denbigh. Daniel Rowland, William Williams and Peter Williams were the longest-serving ordained members of the association by the 1780s, but they had recruited others, including not only Nathaniel Rowland, but also David Jones, William Davies curate of Neath, David Griffiths vicar of Nevern and Thomas Charles of Bala. Rowland and William Williams continued to take a lead in ensuring that secession from the Church was not seriously considered, despite the fact that, in many ways, Welsh Methodism was adopting some of the features and trappings of a denomination in its own right. Indeed, during this period, it succeeded in transforming itself into a more truly Wales-wide phenomenon, by establishing a far stronger footing in the new industrial areas and in the previously largely hostile north of the country. So whilst the Calvinistic Methodists in England may have been in some disarray, in Wales they were forging ahead with increasing confidence.

By the 1780s, the long-term effects of the evangelical revival had led to the Independents and Baptists also making substantial gains in Wales.[1] They shared a common purpose with the Methodists over the need to defend Calvinism and trinitarianism against threats from within and without. The emergence of Unitarianism in Wales was a particular irritant to the Methodists, especially given the location of the Unitarian stronghold, the so-called 'Black Spot', on the Cardiganshire–Carmarthenshire border, in close proximity to Daniel Rowland's parish of Llangeitho.[2] Not even his influence was sufficient to dislodge them, and they proved to be a remarkably tenacious minority. The Calvinist groups among the Dissenters tended to be the ones most affected by revival, and, if anything, this served to distance them even further from Arminian and Arian congregations who regarded themselves as more rational in their approach.[3]

From the 1780s onwards the influence of Thomas Charles in north Wales certainly helped bring greater success in that region, leading Daniel Rowland to proclaim that Charles was 'the Lord's gift to the north'.[4] The eighteen-year-old Charles had been converted in 1773 as a result of his response to a sermon by Daniel Rowland.[5] Educated at Carmarthen Dissenting Academy and Jesus College, Oxford, he was ordained in the Anglican Church in 1778.[6] It was perhaps ironic that this gift to the north came from south-west Wales and settled in Merionethshire only as a result of his marriage to Sally Jones of Bala in 1783, after a long and determined courtship. Sally Charles was an eminently capable businesswoman, who did much to sustain her husband financially in the years to come through her successful management of the family shop.[7] He himself was without a salary as, having yielded his curacy in South Barrow, Somerset, his Methodist associations meant that he struggled in vain to find a position in the Church in north Wales. Since his wife was loath to leave her native town and family connections, he resigned himself to being without a benefice. His decision to join the Bala Calvinistic Methodist society on 2 July 1784 was a sign that he had little expectation of finding a suitable appointment in the Church and that he had thrown in his lot completely with the Methodists.[8] He was thus free to embark on a programme of preaching tours in addition to serving the local evangelical community. Charles was the first ordained cleric in the north to commit himself to such an extent, and his presence was a vital factor in the growth of the cause in the region. Sporadic visits from prominent southern Methodists could not possibly have the same effect as the constant influence that Charles exerted for the rest of his life. As a result of his presence, Bala soon evolved as a major evangelical centre, setting a tradition which was to continue into the nineteenth century with the establishment there of a college to train candidates for the ministry. Prior to her conversion in 1796, Ann Griffiths sarcastically compared the sight of Methodists trudging along the road to Bala with Muslim pilgrims on the way to Mecca, as the town came increasingly to assume the role which Llangeitho in the south had played during Daniel Rowland's lifetime.[9] Llangeitho and Bala were not substantial centres of population, yet they attracted some of the largest gatherings in the country in the eighteenth century; only public executions, it seems, could rival the great Methodist preachers when it came to drawing a crowd.[10]

Bala under Thomas Charles also developed a strong association with publishing and education. It was around 1785 that Charles began to establish day schools, following the model of Griffith Jones's circulating schools.[11] As a native of Llanfihangel Abercywyn, only a few miles from Jones's parish of Llanddowror in south Carmarthenshire, Charles must surely have heard of the great man from an early age. The decline of the circulating schools following the death in 1779 of Bridget Bevan, their remaining organiser, was a general cause for concern for the Methodists, who had long urged their members to attend in order to learn to read the Bible and appreciate its message for themselves. The early leaders had strong personal links to Griffith Jones and a sincere admiration for his successor, Mrs Bevan. After their first meeting, Howel Harris enthused that she was 'the finest Lady I ever saw in all Respects, twas a taste of Heaven to be with her'.[12] Bridget Bevan had sought to ensure the survival of the scheme by setting up a trust fund of £10,000 through the terms of her will. Unfortunately, two of the four trustees she appointed, her relatives, Elizabeth Stepney and William Lloyd, chose to doubt the validity of this legacy, leading the remaining two trustees, George Bowen of Llwyngwair, Pembrokeshire, and Zachary Bevan of Laugharne, to seek redress in the Court of Chancery in 1784. Bowen was a member of a family with strong Methodist connections, and Methodist sympathies characterised fifteen of the forty-seven witnesses summoned to give evidence to the commissioners appointed in 1786 to investigate the legacy.[13]

But Chancery moved at the snail's pace satirised by Charles Dickens, ensuring that financial provision was hardly likely to be provided speedily, whatever the outcome, whilst the schools languished in uncertainty. It was the resulting decline in educational provision which is likely to have galvanised Thomas Charles into action, given that his first efforts to improve the situation concentrated on a revival of the circulating schools. Beginning with one teacher whom he had trained himself, by 1794 the system had expanded to include twenty teachers who had established an estimated forty schools in north Wales.[14] Like Griffith Jones, Charles was motivated by concerns about the underlying ignorance of the scriptures which preaching alone could not remedy. He was also similarly alert to the difficulty in persuading poorer families to send their children to school during daylight hours when they might be profitably engaged. Unlike Jones, however, his solution was increasingly to focus his attention on the role of Sunday schools as a means of providing effective education. He began to set up such schools from 1789, using teachers who had received instruction in the day schools.[15] Although Charles's name has become ineradicably associated with the Sunday school movement in Wales, he was by no means the pioneer of the idea and acknowledged that he had heard of the work of Robert Raikes in Gloucester before setting up his own schools. Moreover, it may well be the case that it was the Baptist Morgan John Rhys or possibly the Independent Edward Williams of Oswestry who was actually responsible for introducing the first Sunday school to Wales; but it was Charles's initiative which was to be the most enduring and influential.[16] The Calvinistic Methodists in Wales were, therefore, fortunate to be able to reap the early benefits of Charles's Sunday school system.

The growing importance of Thomas Charles was another sign of the emergence of a second generation of leaders to take the place of the old. With the start of a new decade in the early 1790s came a number of significant changes in personnel, as many of the more prominent Methodist figures passed away. The most notable of these passings was the death of Daniel Rowland on 16 October 1790. With the Methodist cause having grown so considerably since the death of Howel Harris, it is not surprising that Rowland's loss was possibly felt more widely. The seventeen-year-old John Elias was devastated by the news, with the realisation it brought that he would never now have the opportunity to hear the great evangelist speak.[17] Thomas Charles, who had been so deeply affected by Rowland's preaching and had developed a close relationship with him, was similarly grief stricken. Even the diarist William Thomas, no great lover of Methodism, spoke respectfully of Rowland as 'an extraordinary preacher' and as 'a chearfull man and clear of understanding, without Bigotry'.[18]

William Williams managed to rouse himself, despite his precarious state of health, to write an elegy to his old friend, which was, fittingly enough, to be his last work. At this stage Williams, acutely conscious that he was the last of the leaders who had steered the course of Methodism from its early years, seemed increasingly preoccupied with safeguarding the future of the movement after he too would pass away. He was determined that the leadership, at least in the south of the country, should pass to Nathaniel Rowland, whether from a sense of loyalty, from some notion that this was the most fitting form of succession, or from a genuine conviction that Rowland was best suited to carry the work forward. Deeply frustrated at the frailty which beset him in his final months, Williams devoted much of his remaining energy to attempting through the written word to press his last wishes regarding the future of Methodism. In his elegy to Daniel Rowland, Williams appeared to take for granted that Nathaniel would inherit his mantle, urging him to be 'a father' to the association and to guard the principles of Calvin.[19] He suggested that 'honest' David Jones of Llan-gan would be a source of guidance and support in this endeavour, although Rowland himself showed few signs of feeling himself in need of such advice.

A further reflection of Williams's concern with the future is evident in his final letters to Thomas Charles charging him to take care to guard the faithful from all potential heresy, a threat which also seemed to be preying on his mind. In both elegy and correspondence he emphasised the Thirty-Nine Articles of the Church of England, the classic Christian creeds and the creedal statements drafted by the seventeenth-century Puritan Westminster Assembly as the bedrock of Welsh Calvinistic Methodist faith:

the Articles of the Church of England, the Nicean, and Athanasian Creeds, the lesser & larger Catechisms of the assembly with their confession of faith are some of the grandest and most Illustrious beauties of the reformation. I think our young Exorters should study such orthodox tracts over & over . . . the Antitrinitarian, the socinian, & Arian Doctrine get ground dayly; our unwary new born Methodist preachers know nothing of these things, therefore pray much that no drop of this pernicious and poisonous Liquor may be mingled or privately thrown into the good delicious divine fountain of which the honest Methodists drink.[20]

The emergence of Unitarianism was a valid concern for those committed to the Calvinist cause, and the possibility that the Methodists might at some future point be tempted to desert their fundamental principles seemed to weigh heavily on Williams during his last days. He died less than three months after Daniel Rowland, on 11 January 1791, probably before his final letter to Thomas Charles, written on New Year's Day, was delivered.

Williams's concerns about heretical tendencies were far from unfounded, since doctrinal disputes had by no means been quelled after the reconciliation with Howel Harris in the early 1760s. The leaders in the association had frequently felt the need to defend the orthodoxy of their position against the dangers of Sandemanianism, Sabellianism and antinomianism and to expel some adherents as a result. The most notorious of these expulsions was that of Peter Williams in 1791. At this point, after the deaths of Rowland and William Williams, Peter Williams had some claim to being regarded as the last of the early Methodist fathers, since he had risen to prominence in the movement by the late 1740s, partly as a result of his inspired preaching and partly through the respect afforded by the Methodists to a man in holy orders. His position might indeed have been considered unassailable: as an ordained clergyman with an established publishing career and as an elder statesman of the association. Yet, as Harris had learnt previously, it could prove difficult to defend against accusations of heresy, particularly those which centred on the divine nature of the three persons of the Trinity. Although the Welsh Methodists tended to have fewer internal disputes than their English counterparts, when they did occur they seem to have been particularly bitter and personal.

Peter Williams hailed from the same area of south Carmarthenshire as Thomas Charles and as a boy had been taken by his mother to hear Griffith Jones in his parish church at nearby Llanddowror. During the three years he attended the reputable grammar school at Carmarthen he heard George Whitefield preach in the town, in April 1743, an experience which confirmed in Williams the desire he already cherished to be ordained in the Church of England. After ordination, he was dismissed from three curacies in turn, largely as a result of his Methodist tendencies, so that by 1747 he relinquished his career in the Church to concentrate on his Methodist activities. In this capacity, he gained a reputation as an effective preacher and also as one who suffered considerable persecution for his beliefs. His encounter with the arch-enemy of Methodism in north Wales, Sir Watkin Williams Wynn, led to his being fined for preaching, with the money being taken from his pockets forcibly by the constable of Ruabon parish.[21] The outrage concerning this ill-treatment had led Howel Harris to investigate the possibility of instituting a prosecution against those involved, as a result of which Sir Watkin was found to have acted illegally and was obliged to refund the confiscated fine.[22] Such enmity from the civil authorities in north Wales abated somewhat after the death of Sir Watkin in 1749, following a fall from his horse, a misfortune which many Methodists must have regarded as the work of providence. Indeed, to Howel Harris it was 'the miserable end of that great oppressor'.[23]

Peter Williams thus became something of a hero of the evangelical cause, but he was to attain a far wider reputation in Wales as an author and editor. His varied publications included *Blodau i Blant* ('Flowers for Children'), an anthology of scriptural verses for children to memorise, and volumes of hymns in both Welsh and English. The English volume, *Hymns on Various Subjects*, included his translation from Welsh of one of the most famous hymns by William Williams, Pantycelyn, 'Guide me O Thou great Jehovah', the first verse of which was preserved intact by Pantycelyn when he later produced his own version in English, no small compliment from the famous hymn writer. Perhaps Peter Williams's greatest achievement, however, was to be responsible for the first edition of the Bible to be published in Wales itself. This was issued in parts, each costing a shilling, from 1767 onwards, with the completed work published in its entirety in 1770, printed at

Carmarthen by John Ross and on sale for a guinea. Until 1695 the licensing laws had limited the founding of printing presses to London and the two university towns of Oxford and Cambridge, so it was only in the eighteenth century that the publishing industry began to thrive in Wales. As the publication of the scriptures was a substantial undertaking, it is not surprising that most of the relatively small printing houses within Wales were content to leave such work in the hands of the Society for Promoting Christian Knowledge (SPCK), which had been responsible for all of the Welsh Bibles produced in the first half of the eighteenth century. As the population grew and the literate proportion of society expanded with the influence of the circulating schools, demand for copies of the Bible increased. Printing Welsh Bibles in England had inevitably led to increased costs, difficulties with distribution and errors that might have been avoided by printers familiar with the Welsh alphabet. With the publication of the 1770 edition, Peter Williams opened a new chapter in the history of the scriptures in Welsh. This would prove to be the first of many editions of the publishing phenomenon fondly known as '*Beibl Peter Williams*' ('Peter Williams's Bible') which became the family Bible of choice in countless Welsh homes during the nineteenth century.[24]

Despite the long-term success of this version of the Bible, its publication caused some unease among Peter Williams's colleagues in the Methodist movement.[25] The 1770 edition had included the first commentary on the contents in Welsh, for which Williams noted that he was indebted to the guidance of a number of previous commentators. Yet some of the notes were undoubtedly derived from his own views of religious doctrine, particularly on the question of the Trinity. The section which gave rise to the greatest concern related to the first chapter of John's gospel, where Williams's gloss explained that 'the man Jesus is the everlasting Father', which seemed to suggest that he was not distinguishing sufficiently between the separate persons of the Trinity. The biblical commentary led to suspicions that he was, indeed, guilty of Sabellianism and had departed from the principles enshrined in the Athanasian creed.[26] Although these concerns were voiced in the association, no denunciation or chastisement followed. It seems clear that Daniel Rowland sought to avoid open confrontation by warning Williams privately about his viewpoint, and in Williams's elegy to Rowland he recalled the many rebukes he had received from his colleague. The storm broke again in 1781, when the second edition of Williams's Bible appeared with the contentious comments remaining unaltered. On both occasions, Nathaniel Rowland seems to have acted as one of the most vitriolic accusers of Williams, and it is most likely in 1781 that his father was moved to rebuke him, 'Nat, Nat, ti a gondemniaist dy well' ('Nat, Nat, you have condemned your better').[27]

There is no doubt that the memory of Howel Harris's expulsion cast a long shadow over the debates regarding Peter Williams. These were the two most prominent Welsh Methodists to be suspected of unorthodoxy, and the heresies of which they were accused bore a relation to each other, as both turned on the vexed question of the appropriate distinction between the separate persons of the Trinity. The fact that Harris had previously been found guilty helped Williams avoid reprisal for twenty years. Scarcely seven years had passed since the reconciliation with Harris when the questions regarding Williams's doctrine were raised, so the wounds of the division were still fresh. It was understandable that Daniel Rowland was keen to avoid any further rift which might lead to similar scandal and decline. He emerged as Peter Williams's chief protector and, with William Williams prepared to follow Rowland's lead, it is hardly surprising that the association adopted a lenient attitude. Even so, it would appear that Nathaniel Rowland was by no means appeased and may well have smarted under the suggestion that Peter Williams, a man who lacked his university education, might be deemed his 'better'.

Matters came to a head again in 1790 when Peter Williams, in collaboration with the Baptist David Jones, published a pocket version of the Bible, also with notes, based on the annotated English edition by John Canne.[28] This time it was not just the commentary which proved controversial but the text itself, to which Williams had made a few minor alterations. The Welsh translation of the Bible by William Morgan, as revised in 1620 by John Davies and Richard Parry, was considered virtually sacrosanct, and Williams's temerity in amending it caused some consternation. Worse than that, however, was the suspicion that he had done so in order to bolster his arguments regarding the nature of Christ's divinity. The ensuing discussion turned on subtleties of doctrine and language, with Williams insisting that the changes were utterly innocuous.[29] He had actually discussed the

amendments to the translation with the printers at Trefeca while
the text was being prepared for publication, urging them to examine
them impartially and to ignore anything they felt was mistaken. It
was his suggestion also that they consult John Williams, master at
Lady Huntingdon's 'college', to seek his approval of the amendments,
which hardly suggests any covert intent behind them.[30] The concern
was over the possible impact the Bible might have in leading its readers
into false doctrine, and this was considered a serious enough possibility
to merit discussion by the association. Without Daniel Rowland to
plead his cause, Peter Williams felt vulnerable and rightly anticipated
the result.[31] The Llandeilo Association of May 1791 decided to expel
him and to forbid the purchase and use of his Bible amongst the
membership.[32]

It has been suggested that Peter Williams's greatest fault was a lack
of clarity in thought and expression.[33] However, his writings certainly
indicate Sabellian tendencies which may have justified concern. At a
time when William Williams could express acute fears about the threat
of anti-trinitarian beliefs, it is easy to understand why alarm should
be raised at the notion that such heresies might taint the very text of
the Welsh Bible. It was not the seriousness of the offence which was
soon afterwards called into question, but the method of dispensing
so unceremoniously with one who had given years of dedicated service.
This did cause something of the backlash Daniel Rowland had feared,
with a general sense emerging that the Methodists had acted in an
unbecoming fashion, as Robert Jones acknowledged in 1820:

> mewn gormod o fyrbwylltra, yn lle gwneud pob ymgais tuag at ei at-
> gyweirio, bwriwyd ef allan o'r Synagog. Mae lle i amau i rai oedd yn
> blaenori yn y gwaith ruthro, ar ŵr cyfiawnach na hwy eu hunain.

> [. . . in too much rashness, instead of making every effort to correct
> him, he was cast out of the Synagogue. There is reason to suspect that
> some who took the lead in the work rushed on a man more righteous
> than themselves.][34]

This statement set the tone for nineteenth- and twentieth-century
historians whose tendency was to attribute much of the responsibility
for the expulsion of Peter Williams to Nathaniel Rowland alone. As

most of the early accounts of the controversy were written by members of the connexion, this approach may have been a convenient way of forestalling any criticism of the movement for acting too precipitately or harshly in the matter. Since Rowland had himself subsequently been ejected, ascribing any misdoing in this affair to his vindictiveness largely absolved the Methodists from blame in the matter. Rowland did appear to be the most eager to act against Williams, and many possible motivations can be suggested for his persistence. Williams himself believed that he had roused Rowland's animosity by befriending Torial Joss and Rowland Hill, who had opposed Rowland over the matter of the Tabernacle Chapel in Haverfordwest.[35] It was Hill who insisted that Nathaniel Rowland was the 'proudest devil he ever saw'.[36] It is conceivable that Rowland harboured a grudge over this and, indeed, over the success of Peter Williams's previous edition of the Bible. The association had minuted the proposal that Rowland and David Jones, Llan-gan, should produce a pocket Bible, in the belief that such a reasonably priced edition would be of great benefit to the membership. Rowland may, therefore, have felt that Williams had stolen a march on him when it came to the publication of the Bible. He may also still have resented his father's previous rebuke over his attitude towards Williams.

In emphasising Rowland's determined enmity, some commentators glossed over the involvement of Thomas Charles who held substantial influence in the association in the north, which made the same decision to repudiate Williams, on 8 June 1791. Charles may have felt that he was keeping faith with William Williams's dying wish that he root out heresy and may have acted out of the best possible motives, although Peter Williams certainly viewed him as one of his chief persecutors.[37] This controversy, arising as it did so soon after the deaths of Daniel Rowland and William Williams, suggests that the two had managed to ensure over the previous thirty years that any simmering disagreements did not boil over to damaging effect. It may also indicate a somewhat uneasy transition of leadership to the second generation, with Nathaniel Rowland perhaps not equipped to act as 'father' of the association and other, more temperate characters, such as David Jones, slow to push themselves forward. Williams continually begged to be readmitted, insisting that it was only a difference of wording which separated him from his Methodist brethren, but he died in

1796 before any reconciliation could take place. Ironically perhaps, Thomas Charles was among those who paid tribute to the substantial contribution Williams made to Methodism and to Welsh culture more generally.[38] Editions of his larger Bible continued to be read, regardless of the banning of the 1790 edition, and his expulsion did not do as much harm to the cause as the separation in 1750 had done. Williams was never as influential a figure as Harris, and the delay in taking action against him meant that the movement had so developed into a far stronger position that it was unlikely to be as adversely affected by the loss of one individual.

A fresh outbreak of revival in 1791 provided confirmation that the movement was not greatly shaken by this doctrinal controversy. In his last letter to Thomas Charles, on 1 January 1791, William Williams, Pantycelyn, mentioned a revival that was affecting several parts of the south, and estimated that hundreds of new converts had been awakened. By the end of the year, Charles was talking of a 'glorious outpouring of the Spirit of God' in the north as well, centring particularly on the town of Bala.[39] This was a clear indication of the steadily growing popularity of Methodism in the north of the country. Representatives of the six counties of the north (Anglesey, Caernarfonshire, Merionethshire, Montgomeryshire, Denbighshire and Flintshire) had kept separate records of the meetings of the association held in the north since 1780, but in 1791 they noted that they formally constituted a separate body.[40] They had already drawn up a list of rules at the Bala Association the previous year, which demonstrate an orderly approach to their business, whilst also insisting that one quarterly meeting should be set aside to concentrate on considerations of doctrine and spiritual experiences. Any of the southern brethren who happened to attend were afforded the same right to speak and decide as the regular members, as an expression of the determination to maintain the principle of a single, united movement throughout the country.[41]

These rules suggest the guiding hand of Thomas Charles, who remained the only ordained clergyman in the north at this point, although there were a number of diligent lay helpers, such as John Evans, Bala, who had been accepted as an exhorter by the association in 1765. He had been the inspiration behind the introduction of the 'halfpenny collection', whereby all the members contributed to the building and upkeep of the chapels in the north.[42] This practice would seem to have been emulated in the south, where it was also decided in 1791 that a halfpenny a week should be collected from all society members.[43] These collections were richly suggestive of a denominational form of organisation, which was also implied by the construction of around sixty-three new Calvinistic Methodist chapels between 1783 and 1791.[44]

The fact that so many of these chapels were located in the north was a sure sign of the way the movement was becoming firmly established there, with the buildings giving tangible indications of the Methodist presence in the region. In the south, chapels were largely being constructed in the traditional strongholds, as long-standing societies chose to find more permanent homes for their meetings: but Methodism was also breaking new ground. In the latter years of the eighteenth century many factors were changing the face of Wales, including a rapid growth of population, a rise in literacy levels and the advent of industrialisation. Methodism and the Nonconformist groups were better placed than the Established Church to gain ground in the developing industrial communities. The Church was tied to its parish structure and slow to adapt by setting up new congregations or parishes for new concentrations of population. Traditional chapels of ease which had helped serve the needs of bigger parishes had largely fallen into disuse or were only utilised by the Methodist-inclined clergy rather than for official Church services. New chapels and churches were not being built quickly enough for many parishes which were expanding at an unprecedented rate. Their readiness to make use of unconsecrated buildings to hold their meetings allowed Methodists and Dissenters to establish themselves in growing urban centres.[45]

However, it was not just the greater adaptability in comparison to the Established Church which enabled Methodism to strike roots in industrial communities. In such areas societies were able to provide social opportunities and fellowship to migrants who frequently felt dislocated and adrift in their new surroundings. They were also able to offer an assurance that meetings would be held in the first language of the members. The Anglican Church was obliged to cater for all its parishioners in its services, and in a number of increasingly bilingual communities that frequently meant conducting services in a combination of English and Welsh. Some of the clergy would only decide on how the service would be divided by language when they had ascertained the linguistic abilities of those present on the day. That might seem like a pragmatic response to a complicated issue, but it meant that neither Welsh nor English speakers could know beforehand what proportion of the worship they would understand.[46] The dissatisfaction this caused undoubtedly enhanced the appeal of the Methodist societies, which were largely conducted in Welsh, the language of the vast majority of the population. The ability to meet the linguistic needs of its members was, therefore, a valuable asset. English-medium societies had also been established from the start of the revival, in areas where the language was commonly used, such as in south Pembrokeshire and along the border. Care had always been taken to ensure that both Welsh- and English-speaking societies were adequately supplied with exhorters who could communicate through their language of choice. The result was that Methodists and Non-conformists appeared to be catering more effectively to Welsh speakers. Indeed, the bishop of St David's had to admit in 1811 that 'the Welsh Language is with the Sectaries a powerful means of seduction from the church'.[47]

Eighteenth-century Wales had experienced an unprecedented growth in literacy through the medium of Welsh, largely through the influence of the circulating schools. It had also witnessed a marked increase in Welsh-medium publications as changes in licensing laws enabled printing houses to be established in Wales for the first time, facilitating both the accuracy of the works produced and the process of their distribution. That these two developments had coincided in the early eighteenth century had been of vital importance to the emergence of Methodism. The Calvinistic Methodists had identified the potential of the written word from the outset and had sought to cultivate its use, publishing the first printed sermon in 1739, the rulebook in 1742, volumes of hymns in 1744 and a guide to orthodox doctrine in 1750.[48] The work of Peter Williams and Thomas Charles continued this long-standing tradition – greatly enriched by the efforts of William Williams – of supplying a range of literature to provide instruction and inspiration for the societies. The drive to maintain the association between Methodism and literacy was also reflected in the founding of the Sunday schools, inspired by the achievements of the circulating schools and with a similar aim of ensuring a solid foundation of biblical knowledge. Methodism in Wales thus continued to contribute to a religious literature and culture which helped enforce the perception that it was more closely associated with the Welsh language than was the Anglican Church.[49]

By the early 1790s, therefore, it was apparent that the movement in Wales was continuing to mature and was better placed to overcome internal strife than in the past. The loss of the first generation of leaders was deeply felt, but there was also an obvious sense of continuity with the emergence of Thomas Charles and Nathaniel Rowland in the north and south, both of whom could draw on able and committed support from the associations in both regions. The establishment of a separate association in the north during this period, however, perhaps confirmed that the Methodist centre of gravity was shifting slightly northwards, away from its early base in the diocese of St David's and towards Thomas Charles's Bala.

Notes

[1] T. M. Bassett, *The Welsh Baptists* (Swansea: Ilston House, 1977), pp. 92–122; R. Tudur Jones, *Congregationalism in Wales*, ed. Robert Pope (Cardiff: University of Wales Press, 2004), pp. 110–31.

[2] Geraint H. Jenkins, 'The Established Church and Dissent in Eighteenth-Century Cardiganshire', in Geraint H. Jenkins and Ieuan Gwynedd Jones (eds), *Cardiganshire County History*, vol. 3, *Cardiganshire in Modern Times* (Cardiff: University of Wales Press, 1998), pp. 472–4. See also D. Elwyn Davies, *Y Smotiau Duon* (Llandysul: Gomer, 1981); idem., *They Thought for Themselves* (Llandysul: Gomer, 1982).

[3] R. Tudur Jones, 'Y Dwym Ias a'r Sentars Sychion: Methodistiaeth ac Ymneilltuaeth yn y Ddeunawfed Ganrif', in D. Densil Morgan (ed.), *Grym y Gair a Fflam y Ffydd: Ysgrifau ar Hanes Crefydd yng Nghymru*, (Swansea: Cyhoeddiadau'r Gair, 1998), pp. 153–69.

[4] Thomas Jones, *Cofiant neu Hanes Bywyd a Marwolaeth Thomas Charles* (Bala: Robert Saunderson, 1816), p. 161.

[5] Ibid., pp. 8–9.

[6] Ibid., pp. 7–8, 11–13.

[7] See Gwen Emyr, *Sally Jones: Rhodd Duw i Charles* (Bridgend: Evangelical Press of Wales, 1996).

[8] Jones, *Cofiant*, p. 161.

9 John Hughes, 'Cofiant a Llythyrau Ann Griffiths', *Y Traethodydd* (1846), 421.

10 Russell Davies, *Hope and Heartbreak: A Social History of Wales and the Welsh* (Cardiff: University of Wales Press, 2005), p. 27.

11 Jones, *Cofiant*, pp. 168–9; Beryl Thomas, 'Mudiadau Addysg Thomas Charles', in Gomer M. Roberts (ed.), *Hanes Methodistiaeth Galfinaidd Cymru II: Cynnydd y Corff* (Caernarfon: Llyfrfa'r Methodistiaid Calfinaidd, 1978), pp. 431–55.

12 NLW Trevecka Letter 76, Howel Harris to Joseph Harris, undated, 1736.

13 G. J. Thomas, 'Madam Bevan's Will: the Chancery action', *Transactions of the Carmarthenshire Antiquarian Society*, 29 (1939), 431–52.

14 M. G. Jones, *The Charity School Movement* (Cambridge: Cambridge University Press, 1938), p. 315.

15 Jones, *Cofiant*, p. 173; Derec Llwyd Morgan, '"Ysgolion Sabothol" Thomas Charles', in Morgan, *Pobl Pantycelyn*, pp. 86–110.

16 Eryn M. White, 'Popular schooling and the Welsh language, 1650–1800' in Geraint H. Jenkins (ed.), *The Welsh Language before the Industrial Revolution* (Cardiff: University of Wales Press, 1997), pp. 337–8.

17 Goronwy P. Owen (ed.), *Hunangofiant John Elias* (Bridgend: Evangelical Press of Wales, 1974), pp. 55–6.

18 R. T. W. Denning (ed.), *The Diary of William Thomas of Michaelston-super-Ely near St Fagans, Glamorgan, 1762–1795* (Cardiff: South Wales Record Society, 1995), pp. 235, 393.

19 William Williams, 'Marwnad y Parch. Daniel Rowland, Llangeitho', in N. Cynhafal Jones (ed.), *Gweithiau Williams Pant-y-celyn* (2 vols, Holywell: P. M. Evans, 1887), I, p. 588.

20 NLW CMA Trevecka 4797, William Williams to Thomas Charles, 25 May 1790; Gomer M. Roberts, *Y Pêr Ganiedydd (Pantycelyn)* cyfrol I, *Trem ar ei Fywyd* (Aberystwyth: Gwasg Aberystwyth, 1949), p. 168.

21 NLW CMA Trevecka 3190a, 3 January 1748.

22 NLW Trevecka Letter 1831, Howel Harris to anon., 29 November 1748.

23 NLW Trevecka Letter 1892, Howel Harris to George Whitefield, 15 October 1749.

24 Eryn M. White, *The Welsh Bible* (Stroud: Tempus, 2007), pp. 74–5.

25 Gomer M. Roberts, *Bywyd a Gwaith Peter Williams* (Cardiff: University of Wales Press, 1943), pp. 73–80; R. T. Jenkins, 'Diarddeliad Peter Williams', in *Yng Nghysgod Trefeca: Ysgrifau ar Hanes Crefydd a Chymdeithas yng Nghymru yn y Ddeunawfed Ganrif* (Caernarfon:

Llyfrfa'r Methodistiaid Calfinaidd, 1968), pp. 154–71; Derec Llwyd Morgan, 'Peter Williams yn 1791', in idem, *Pobl Pantycelyn*, pp. 37–52; Eryn M. White, 'Peter Williams a'r Beibl Cymraeg', *Transactions of the Honourable Society of Cymmrodorion* (2007), 58–72.

26 Sabelius was excommunicated in the third century for arguing that the Son and Holy Spirit were aspects of the Father and did not constitute separate persons within the Trinity.

27 R. H. Evans, 'Y Dadleuon Diwinyddol (1763–1814)', in Roberts (ed.), *Hanes Methodistiaeth Galfinaidd Cymru*, cyfrol II, p. 398.

28 *Y Bibl Sanctaidd: sef yr Hen Destament a'r Newydd, â nodau ysgrythurol ar ymyl y ddalen* (Trefeca, 1790).

29 Peter Williams, *Llythyr at Hen Gydymaith mewn perthynas i gywirdeb cyfieithiad Bibl John Cann, yn ymddiffyn Diwygiad, ac yn gwrthbrofi Camachwyniad* (Carmarthen: Ioan Daniel, 1791), pp. 3, 6–7.

30 NLW Trevecka Letter 2760, Peter Williams to Evan Roberts and Evan Moses, 22 August 1789; 2844a, ibid. to ibid., 26 April 1790.

31 NLW CMA, Bala 755, Peter Williams to Eliezer Williams, his son, 7 May 1791.

32 NLW CMA Trevecka 2999.

33 J. M. Jones and W. Morgan, *Y Tadau Methodistaid* (2 vols, Swansea: Lewis Evans, 1895), I, p. 449; R. Tudur Jones, 'Peter Williams (1723–1796)', *Oxford Dictionary of National Biography* (Oxford: Oxford University Press, 2004).

34 Robert Jones, *Drych yr Amseroedd*, ed. G. M. Ashton (Cardiff: University of Wales Press, 1958), pp. 89–90.

35 NLW, Cwrt Mawr 150; D. Myrddin Lloyd, 'Nathaniel Rowland and the Tabernacle, Haverfordwest', *JHSPCW*, 36 (1951).

36 Jones and Morgan, *Y Tadau Methodistaidd*, II, p. 227.

37 NLW CMA, Bala 755, Peter Williams to Eliezer Williams, his son, 7 May 1791; D. E. Jenkins, *The Life of the Rev. Thomas Charles B.A. of Bala*, vol. 2 *(1784–1805)* (3 vols, Denbigh: Llywelyn Jenkins, 1908), pp. 73–8.

38 See Thomas Charles, 'Peter Williams', *Trysorfa Ysprydol* (1813), 483–5.

39 Jenkins, *The Life of the Rev Thomas Charles*, II, pp. 88–91.

40 Roberts, *Hanes Methodistiaeth Galfinaidd Cymru*, II, pp. 157–62.

41 Ibid., pp. 137–9.

42 See Goronwy P. Owen (ed.), *Atgofion John Evans y Bala: Y Diwygiad Methodistaidd ym Meirionnydd a Môn* (Caernarfon: Gwasg Pantycelyn, 1997).

43 Roberts, *Hanes Methodistiaeth Galfinaidd Cymru*, II, p. 167.

[44] Ibid., pp. 535–6.
[45] Ieuan Gwynedd Jones, *Explorations and Explanations: Essays in the Social History of Victorian Wales* (Llandysul: Gwasg Gomer, 1981), pp. 217–35; Chris Evans, *Labyrinth of Flames: Work and Social Conditions in Early Industrial Merthyr Tydfil* (Cardiff: University of Wales Press, 1998), pp. 179–84.
[46] Eryn M. White, 'The Established Church, Dissent and the Welsh language', in Jenkins (ed.), *The Welsh Language before the Industrial Revolution*, pp. 261–3.
[47] NLW, Church in Wales Records, SD/MISC/1085.
[48] Daniel Rowland, *Y Llaeth Ysbrydol, neu bregeth yn dangos mawr hiraeth y ffyddloniaid am laeth y gair ynghyd a'r ffordd i mae cynyddy trwyddo* (Carmarthen: Nicholas Thomas, 1739); *Sail Dibenion, a Rheolau'r Societies neu'r Cyfarfodydd Neilltuol a Ddechreusant Ymgynull yn Ddiweddar yng Nghymru* (Bristol: Felix Farley, 1742); Daniel Rowland, *Hymnau duwiol. Yw canu, mewn cymdeithiasau crefyddol* (Bristol: Felix Farley, 1744); William Williams, *Aleluja, neu, casgljad o hymnau ar amryw ystyriaethau* (Carmarthen: Samuel Lewis, 1744); Daniel Rowland, *Ymddiddan rhwng Methodist uniawn-gred, ac un camsyniol* (Bristol: Felix Farley, 1750).
[49] See Brynley F. Roberts, 'The Connexion in Print', *JHSPCW*, 16–17 (1992–3), 9–31; R. Tudur Jones, 'Nonconformity and the Welsh language in the nineteenth century', in Geraint H. Jenkins (ed.), *The Welsh Language and its Social Domains, 1801–1911* (Cardiff: University of Wales Press, 2000), pp. 239–63.

10

'A smooth and satisfactory order': towards a new denomination for Wales and decline in England, 1791–1811

As her health began to fail, the countess of Huntingdon was persuaded by a number of laymen in several of her chapels, centred on Spa Fields, to produce a structured and orderly form for the connexion following her death. During her serious illness at the end of 1789 several men from her London chapels met to draft such a plan, which was in distinct contrast to the single-handed leadership that had guided her enterprises. A broadly conciliar form was proposed, providing for an 'association', with a significant majority of laymen in decision-making processes. This plan would mean that her connexion would be put 'into such a line of general usefulness that when the Lord calls for me my absence will not make more than an old shoe cast aside'.[1] Thus was produced and published a clearly set-out and balanced *Plan of an Association*, dividing her chapels throughout England (and Wales) into twenty-three districts, each with a committee composed of ministers and laymen. Each district was to send one minister and two laymen to an annual general association which would govern all connexional affairs, including those of the Trevecca 'college'. Provision was made for regular and systematic collections to maintain all the work. Thomas Charles, who was preaching for most of the summer at Spa Fields, approved of the plan.[2] However, her main clerical associate, Thomas Haweis, utterly refused to accept it, because 'I should not chuse to be in Bondage to Laymen, or committees'.[3] He issued an ultimatum: if the scheme went ahead, the countess would lose both him and her close personal companion of many years, Lady Anne Erskine. Lady

Huntingdon was forced to execute a total and publicly painful dismantling of the plan, and the following year she was dead. It may well have been, as one writer put it in Welsh verse, that Lady Huntingdon was welcomed to and escorted into heaven by George Whitefield and Howel Harris.[4] However, the connexion she left behind was bereft of any reasonable form of organisation that would have prepared it for advance into the new century. In the event, her leadership and the care of her chapels had involved her in 'almost continual sorrow'.[5]

The countess's connexion without the countess

At her death, the countess possessed only seven chapels: Bath, Brighton, Hereford, Tunbridge Wells, together with the London chapels: Spa Fields, Sion and Mulberry Gardens. All others within her connexion had been built or rented by others and either transferred to the connexion, or more usually were simply dependent upon its services.[6] In 1788, three years before her death, the countess drew up a list of 'the chapels and preaching places in the Connexion being 116'.[7] Unfortunately, this has long since disappeared, and the only listing of chapels by name during this period is two years later as part of the 1790 *Plan of Association*. That list, astonishingly, gives only sixty-four chapels. Thus roughly half the enterprises that can be identified from correspondence as having had some association with the connexion during the 1770s and 80s had ended that relationship by 1790. This included such places flung as far as Guernsey, Mevagissey and Dublin. Her zeal to expand the number of chapels led the countess to pledge far more funds than she could ever deliver, and this caused resentment and desertion. There was a remarkable fluidity in the connexion and, without even a list of ministers associated with the denomination, it is impossible to speak with any certainty regarding its size. Although no one has heretofore attempted to remedy the loss of the 1788 list, an attempt is now made at an approximation. Using all known sources, we have constructed a notional list of 112 chapels and societies which at some stage during the period 1760 until 1800 were considered part of the connexion.[8]

Ironically, the countess apparently was prepared to give up her arbitrary leadership with the establishment of a presbyterian form under the 1790 *Plan of Association*, yet the scuppering of that plan contributed directly to the haemorrhaging of her connexion. As long as she lived she continued to insist it be her own hand that moved the appointment and removal of ministers, while, with very rare exceptions, she demanded that local congregations bear the full financial brunt of all their activities. It would also be reasonable to suppose that, since she had taken the fateful road to secession and her chapels gradually began to be registered as Dissenting chapels during the 1780s, there was little advantage for many of her former followers to remain in the new denomination. As long as there had been the heady attraction of belonging to the 'countess' while still maintaining the pretence of not rejecting the Established Church, the advantages of such an arrangement outweighed the drawbacks; but now no longer. With the collapse of the *Plan of Association*, the countess left the supervision of her work to four self-perpetuating trustees: Haweis, Erskine, Haweis's wife and a long-serving layman, John Lloyd. In her will the countess bequeathed to them all of her possessions. These possessions included the handful of chapels she owned outright. Yet she also left overall debts of £3,000, with no funds to endow her 'college' or chapels.[9]

Lady Anne Erskine sought life as a replicated Lady Huntingdon, slipping into the role of exercising a similar maternalistic control of affairs from the Spa Fields chapel, where she continued to live. These ranged from dealing with applications from prospective Cheshunt students, to appeals from chapels for money, to choosing a chapel minister.[10] Indeed, until her death over a decade later in 1804, Lady Anne bore responsibility for the general movement of ministers within the connexion. For his part, Thomas Haweis, though a trustee, played a strikingly minor role in the operation of connexional affairs. After the death of Janetta Haweis in 1799, her husband married, at the age of 68, his 24-year-old secretary and spent his last years at Bath. Although for a time Haweis led services at the connexion's chapel there, his preaching was increasingly unwelcomed, to the extent that the congregation finally 'induced him to decline his ministry among them, and also his attendance'.[11]

Upon Haweis's death in 1820 the connexion attempted to put into place the plan of association he had forced the countess to jettison thirty years earlier. It was too late. The trustee form of church government had set a pattern for religious strife that would continue for several decades deep into the nineteenth century, with ecclesiastical disruption and highly acrimonious civil law suits draining the denomination of resources and spirit. Stemming from Haweis's and Lady Anne's refusal to accept the countess's proposed presbyterially-based plan of government, it was nothing other than 'the decay of our Connexion'; and the resulting 'chronic dispute . . . nearly terminated both the usefulness and the existence of the Connexion', according to one of its leading mid-nineteenth-century ministers. Following the original four, subsequent trustees professed to have derived their power from the countess, 'a despotic power'.[12]

It has been noted that in the last years of her life the countess effectively abandoned the 'college' at Trevecca, starving it of funds that she herself did not have and leaving the institution in a parlous condition. Less than a year after the countess's death, the connexion moved the 'college' from Trevecca to Cheshunt, Hertfordshire. During the first decade at Cheshunt there were precious few students, and their circumstances there were far from salubrious. Sheets had been brought from Trevecca and were in such tattered condition that they had to be replaced, although they were then to be cut up and used as towels.[13] A trust deed for the college was adopted in 1792, making it clear that the institution was to be considered an evangelical rather than a denominational establishment. Without this alteration it would have been impossible to secure staff, students or financial subscriptions. The arrangement guaranteed the college's continued existence, but it directly contributed to the increasing strife in the connexion during the early decades of the nineteenth century as Cheshunt produced those who did not serve the denomination. Into the nineteenth century it trained men who rarely went into the ministry of the connexion but who largely served as ministers in Independent Congregationalism.[14] Conversely, it was observed in 1884 that of the connexion's twenty-two ministers, only four had been educated at Cheshunt.[15]

Welsh Calvinistic Methodist piety and publishing

In Wales, by way of contrast, the turn of the century saw the further consolidation of the Calvinistic Methodist cause, with increased recruitment leading to yet more chapel building. Some sixty-seven chapels were built or rebuilt between 1791 and the end of the century.[16] It was a measure of the way in which Methodism was spreading that two of these were located within the Welsh-speaking communities of Manchester. Calvinistic Methodism was imported into urban centres like Manchester and Liverpool by Welsh migrants who moved in sufficient numbers to be able to afford to build their own places of worship. Nearly a hundred more chapels were constructed during the first decade of the nineteenth century, a clear demonstration of the growing membership and their willingness to contribute financially to such buildings.[17] As a result, for a religious group which was still not a denomination, Welsh Calvinistic Methodism had a remarkable network of congregations and properties.

The success of the movement still owed much to its characteristic evangelical preaching, and its most effective speakers were often accorded semi-heroic status. But they were backed up by a number of instructional publications and the development of a range of com-munal activities. The fact that so many of the societies had chapel buildings at their disposal made it far easier for them to arrange add-itional meetings, so that they were increasingly evolving into congre-gations with an attendant culture of spiritual and social activities for groups of all ages. The Sunday school in particular was emerging as a vital element in Methodist life. Thomas Charles did much to establish a solid foundation for the schools in the guidelines he provided for teachers, *Rheolau i ffurfiaw a threfnu yr Ysgolion Sabbothawl* ('Rules for the forming and organising of the Sunday schools') (1813). He also provided one of the most popular elements in their syllabus through his catechism, *Hyfforddwr i'r Grefydd Gristionogol* ('Instructor in the Christian religion') (1807) and a reading primer in his *Sillydd Cymraeg, neu, Arweiniad i'r Frutaniaeth* ('Welsh primer or guide to the British language') (1807). Generations of Sunday school scholars would learn Charles's *Hyfforddwr* by rote, and it ran to eighty editions during the nineteenth century. This activity gave rise to the Sunday School Assemblies – public oral examinations of the children's attainments – the first of which was held at Blaenannerch Chapel in Cardiganshire on Easter Monday 1808.[18] There was thus a structure in place to help nurture future Methodist generations by supplying suitable religious instruction from an early age. As was the case with the earliest eighteenth-century societies, the communal activities provided for the members helped to keep them within the fold by shoring up their spiritual commitment and ensuring a reassuring sense of fellowship.

This period also saw the emergence of two of the most prominent female figures in Welsh Methodist tradition: Mary Jones and Ann Griffiths, both of whose stories demonstrated the ways in which membership of the movement could affect women, and both of whom to a large extent owed their part in posterity to their connection with Thomas Charles. Amongst those who had learnt to read in the circulating schools set up by Charles was Mary Jones, a young girl from Llanfihangel-y-pennant, Merionethshire. She was the only daughter of a widowed mother who took her child along to the Methodist society meetings from an early age. With this early exposure, Mary became a member of the society in her own right at the age of eight. Although she had learnt to read the Bible, she had no copy of her own. Once a week she had the opportunity to walk to a farm over a mile from her mother's cottage, where she was permitted to read the Bible and to attempt to memorise as much of it as possible. By the age of sixteen, in 1800, she had managed to save enough money to afford her own copy and so walked the 25 miles to Bala to purchase one from Thomas Charles. As a member of the SPCK, Charles would have had copies of the 1799 edition for distribution, at a probable cost of 3s. 6d. According to one version of the story, all the Bibles had been sold by the time she arrived, but Charles was so moved by her distress at this news that he gave her his own copy. It is believed that it was Mary Jones's experience which prompted Charles's statement to Joseph Tarn, the assistant secretary of the newly formed British and Foreign Bible Society in 1804:

> I have seen some of them overcome with joy, and burst into tears of thankfulness, on their obtaining possession of a Bible as their own property and for their free use. Young females, in service, have walked over thirty miles to me with only the bare hope of obtaining a Bible each; and returned with more joy and thanksgiving than if they had obtained great spoils. We who have half a dozen Bibles by us, and are in circumstances to obtain as many more, know but little of the value those put upon *one*, who before were hardly permitted to look into a Bible once a week.[19]

Charles, however, spoke of 'young females', which may indicate that there were a number of similar cases. Whatever the truth of the matter, the tale of Mary Jones, the girl without a Bible, caught the public imagination, as she came to represent the need for religious instruction which was to motivate philanthropic concerns like the Bible Society.[20] She was also a product of the growth in literacy which aided the spread of the Methodist movement in Wales.

Ann Griffiths's social sphere was rather more elevated than that of Mary Jones, and she had every opportunity to become steeped in knowledge of the Bible from an early age.[21] Her conversion to Methodism came rather later in life, at the age of 20, when in 1796 she joined the Methodist society at Pontrobert, near her home in Dolanog, Montgomeryshire. Given her detailed acquaintance with the scriptures and her familiarity with local traditions of folk music, it is not surprising that she sought to express the intensity of her spiritual experience through verse. She remains one of Welsh Methodism's most acclaimed hymn writers, despite the fact that she died in 1805 at the age of 29, leaving only thirty-eight hymns to establish her reputation. Those hymns had not been recorded during her lifetime and were preserved only in her maidservant's memory. They appeared in print for the first time in 1806 in a collection edited by Thomas Charles, who had met and admired Ann during her lifetime.[22] Her hymns followed the Calvinistic viewpoint of her Methodist training, combined, as with William Williams, Pantycelyn, with an intense personal experience. Her work was a further demonstration of the way the growth of Methodism contributed to the development of a literature of spiritual experience through the medium of Welsh, which included not only hymns but also spiritual autobiography, devotional manuals, expositions of the scriptures and biography.

A significant milestone in the history of Welsh Methodism and publishing was reached in April 1799 when Thomas Charles and Thomas Jones, Denbigh, produced the first issue of the sixpenny quarterly *Trysorfa Ysprydol* ('Spiritual Treasury'). It was designed along the lines of the English *Evangelical Magazine*, with accounts of congregations and ministers, as well as theological discussion. The Independent minister, Edmund Jones of Pontypool, had bemoaned the fact that the *Evangelical Magazine* could not be sold widely in Wales because 'the people who are very zealous for the truth cannot read

English'.[23] Having sought the blessing of the association in 1798, Charles and Jones set out to attempt to address that problem with this periodical. It was evident that the editors hoped to use the publication to provide the membership with a sense of the movement's past. To that end, John Evans supplied a series of seven conversations between 'Scrutator' and 'Senex', giving a history of early Methodism in the Bala area in the dialogue form so popular amongst early Methodist writers.[24] Charles also urged Robert Jones to contribute historical accounts, since 'I have a desire to leave to the coming age, a mirror in which they may see the form and aspect of religion in our days, and a memorial of God's goodness towards the children of men in our age and country'.[25] Jones went on to write for the *Trysorfa Ysprydol* but fulfilled Charles's brief more fully when he published his account of Methodist history, *Drych yr Amseroedd* ('A mirror of the times') in 1820.

It proved difficult to produce the magazine regularly, largely because of the editors' poor health, but it appeared between 1799 and 1801 and with Thomas Charles as the sole editor between 1809 and 1813. Yet, as the first denominational periodical in Welsh, it contrived to set a high standard for its successors to emulate. It was later superseded by titles such as *Y Drysorfa* ('The Treasury') and *Y Goleuad* ('The Illuminator'), which proved to have greater longevity; but they were based on the blueprint established by the *Trysorfa Ysprydol*.[26] Its editors had grasped the importance of regular communication with the movement's members, in order to spread information and to build a united sense of identity across the country. They realised Howel Harris's dream of a Welsh counterpart to the English-language periodicals of the 1740s such as the *Weekly History*, which had struggled in a movement composed largely of monoglot Welsh speakers.

Thomas Charles's partner in this venture was his close friend Thomas Jones, who emerged as one of the foremost Welsh Methodist authors of the period. The two had first met in 1784, after which Jones had been influential in advising Charles to join the Bala Methodist society. The son of a well-to-do farmer, Jones had received a grammar school education and had been intended for the Church before his conversion to Methodism. Originally from Caerwys in Flintshire, he was based for some time in Ruthin, although his name is usually associated with his later home at Denbigh, where he was pastor of the local societies.

A considerable scholar, whose wide range of works included a dictionary and a number of hymns, he shared Thomas Charles's appreciation of the usefulness of the printed word and the pressing need to ensure a solid foundation of religious knowledge amongst the Methodist membership. His financial situation was such that he was able to afford to establish his own printing press at Ruthin in 1808 in order to facilitate the production of works for the benefit of the society members. One of Jones's lasting legacies was the appointment of Thomas Gee to oversee the press, which moved to Denbigh in 1809. Having published some of his major works, Jones sold the press to Gee in 1813, heralding the start of one of the most significant publishing firms in nineteenth-century Wales, Gee a'i Fab (Gee and Son).[27]

The late eighteenth century and early nineteenth century was a time when the Methodists felt a particular need to write in defence of their situation and beliefs. With the commencement of the war against France during the 1790s, suspicions of treachery and sedition were widespread. The Welsh Methodists frequently felt compelled to clarify their position as upholders of the political status quo in contrast with some more radical Dissenting views and thus emerged as a strong force in favour of loyalism. They were impelled to do so by attacks in *The Anti-Jacobin Review* and in the writings of two Anglican clergymen, Hugh Davies and Thomas Ellis Owen.[28] In *Hints to the Heads of Families*, published anonymously in 1801, Owen insinuated that the Methodists were plotting anarchy and treachery behind the closed doors of their society meetings. Had not the French Revolution, he suggested, been fuelled by the same anti-clerical feelings as the Methodists sought to awaken? It was in response to such accusations that Thomas Charles put pen to paper to produce his *Welsh Methodists Vindicated* in 1801. Thomas Jones had already in 1798 published his *Gair yn ei Amser at drigolion Cymru*, which also appeared in English as *A Word in Season*. These loyalist writings proved to be far more popular than the works of more radical authors in Welsh, with *Gair yn ei Amser* being reprinted within a year of its first appearance. Such publications confirmed the somewhat conservative attitude of the Methodists in the field of politics.

Thomas Jones thus emerged as one of the movement's chief apologists and one of those responsible for forming its character during the early years of the nineteenth century. One of his incentives to publish was the need to defend Calvinist doctrine against the emerging Arminian challenge. John Wesley's influence in Wales had always been limited during his lifetime. The Welsh Methodists had adopted Calvinism since the beginning, and so their natural associations were with George Whitefield and the countess of Huntingdon. Whitefield invariably had Welsh-speaking escorts on his preaching trips in Wales, whereas Wesley had fewer local connections and bemoaned the fact that linguistic differences prevented him from communicating effectively.[29] The difficulties persisted after Wesley's death, with the Wesleyan denomination largely confined to more anglicised areas of south Wales. However, from 1800, a more determined effort was made to establish Wesleyan Methodism in Wales. This came as a result of a proposal to the Methodist Conference from Thomas Coke, who had been born in Brecon and had become increasingly convinced of the need to employ the Welsh language to reach out to the Welsh people. Owen Davies and John Hughes were dispatched to north-east Wales to assist the efforts of Edward Jones of Bathafarn, who founded a Welsh-speaking Wesleyan cause at Ruthin in 1800.[30] The mission was not without success, and sixty chapels were established by 1810.

This incursion on Thomas Jones's own doorstep was naturally a cause for concern, especially as he feared that the Wesleyans were misrepresenting the beliefs of their Calvinist counterparts in order to augment their own recruitment. He stated that it was with the encouragement of some of his brethren in the movement that he set out to counter such misrepresentation in a series of publications defending Calvinist doctrine.[31] The first such work was *Drych Athrawiaethol* ('Doctrinal Mirror') in 1806, followed by *Ymddyddanion Crefyddol* ('Religious Conversations') in 1807. In these works Jones sought to construct a defence of doctrines such as election, by demonstrating the biblical authority on which they were founded. He also used historical precedent by arguing that the early Protestant reformers and martyrs had all shared the same beliefs as Calvin, well before Arminius had developed his ideas. Jones's contention was that it was in fact sixteenth-century Catholicism as expressed in the decisions of the Council of Trent that had shared the Arminian beliefs of contemporary Wesleyanism. This provocative argument provoked a response from Owen Davies, *Amddiffyniad i'r Methodistiaid Wesleyaidd* ('Defence of the

Wesleyan Methodists') (1806). The appendix of Jones's *Ymddyddanion Crefyddol* gave a reaction to Davies's work as well as an examination of the perceived inconsistencies of John Wesley's teachings. When *Ymddyddanion* was at the press, it seems that a compositor showed the page proofs to Owen Davies, enabling him to formulate a rapid response, much to Jones's chagrin, a factor which may have prompted the further volume, *Sylwadau ar Lyfr Mr. Owen Davies* (1808) ('Observations on Mr Owen Davies's book').[32] It may also have motivated Jones to set up his own printing press, so that he might have greater assurance in future that unpublished copies of his works would not be leaked to his rivals.

In these works, Jones showed some of the detailed knowledge of the writings and viewpoints of the early Protestants which would become apparent in his magnum opus, *Diwygwyr, merthyron a chyffeswyr Eglwys Loegr* ('Reformers, martyrs and confessors of the Church of England') (1813). Heavily influenced by John Foxe's *Book of Martyrs*, it was obviously also the product of considerable research and continues to be deemed his greatest work, although it served to heighten Nonconformist prejudice against Catholicism. Through his publications, Thomas Jones became the chief spokesperson for moderate Calvinism in the Welsh Methodist camp. In that respect, there would be some disagreement between him and the supporters of a stricter interpretation of Calvinism.[33] Jones's death in 1820 in effect gave the victory to the higher Calvinist group and also removed one of the bars against the adoption of a declaration of faith for the movement. Thomas Jones, and indeed Thomas Charles, had always opposed such a measure, insisting that the articles of the Church of England were sufficient; and it was only in 1823 that its Confession of Faith, *Cyffes Ffydd y Corph o Fethodistiaid Calfinaidd yng Nghymru* ('The Welsh Calvinistic Methodist Confession of Faith'), was finally published, twelve years after the founding of the denomination.

The shaping of a denomination

In many respects, the Welsh Methodists had long displayed the characteristics of a separate denomination, despite their great care not to do so too ostentatiously. Chapels had been built from the 1740s onwards, although they had initially been called 'society houses' to avoid suggestions that they were forming a sect outside the Church.[34] The first rule book had been published as early as 1742, superseded by *Rheolau a dybenion y Cymdeithasau Neillduol* ('Rules and aims of the private societies'), drawn up by Thomas Charles and Thomas Jones and ratified by the association in 1801.[35] Although it was emphatically stated in the introduction that the Methodists had no intention to create schism or division, the very publication of these rules was suggestive of a separate institution with its own particular identity. The content was, indeed, largely reproduced in the 1823 Confession of Faith, an indication that these guidelines provided a potential framework for an independent religious institution, although they were quite obviously heavily dependent on the Anglican Thirty-Nine Articles. There were further signs of the emergence of a definite separate identity, including the publication of the first collection of hymns for use in the private societies, *Grawn-syppiau Canaan* ('A cluster of Canaan's grapes'), edited by Robert Jones in 1795.[36] Despite competition from old and new Dissenters, Welsh Calvinistic Methodism at the start of the nineteenth century was, therefore, in a strong position owing to its combination of a substantial number of adherents and an organisational structure which had stood the test of time.

Throughout the eighteenth century, the Methodists had remained within the confines of the Established Church, despite the many tensions arising from that relationship.[37] Central to the dispute which arose over separation in the early years of the nineteenth century was the issue of the administration of the sacraments, especially communion. Almost from the first, the lay preachers had argued the case for separation so that they might administer communion within the societies, but the first generation of leaders had contrived to keep the movement within the Anglican fold, despite the secession of some individuals and whole societies in certain instances. Thomas Charles seemed to have inherited this determination to abide by the Church, along with the mantle of leadership from Rowland and Williams. Yet, in many ways, the Methodist position appeared to be increasingly untenable, particularly given the scarcity of ordained clergy to minister to the needs of expanding congregations. The considerable dedication demonstrated by the lay preachers and society elders in the absence of ordained ministers was thus fundamental to the maintenance of Methodist activities. The movement had already assumed several of the characteristics of a denomination, including the growing trend towards chapel building. Some lay exhorters had exercised an unofficial pastoral ministry for years, as Dafydd Morris had done over the society of Twr-gwyn, Cardiganshire, from 1774 until his death in 1791, when his role was passed on to his son, Ebenezer Morris.[38] For the congregations served by such lay pastors, it seemed strange that those who took such pains to watch over their spiritual welfare should not be able to provide them with communion, conduct their funeral services and baptise their children. This appears to have troubled a number of the societies, including that of Pensarn, Cardiganshire, one of whose elders raised the question more than once in the southern association in the first decade of the nineteenth century.[39] From around 1806 onwards, it was a subject which was raising its head more and more frequently, with the association invariably deciding to seek counsel in prayer rather than to conduct a lengthy discussion.

It was in this context that Nathaniel Rowland's conservative attitude to the ministration of communion gave rise to considerable tension. He would only hold communion services in three chapels in Pembrokeshire which had previously been used for that purpose by Howell Davies: Monkton, Woodstock and Capel Newydd. He also opposed David Charles's request in 1801 that communion should be administered in the Water Street chapel in Carmarthen to save the local members the ten-mile trip to Llanlluan chapel of ease in Llanarthney parish, to which Methodists had journeyed to receive the sacrament since the 1740s.[40] Rumours that Rowland was sometimes intoxicated when he preached left his fellow members of the association with something of a dilemma, as their respect for his father's memory made them hesitant to act against the son. An association meeting was called at Newcastle Emlyn in 1807 specifically to discuss the matter and, despite the extreme reluctance of David Jones in the chair, David Charles seconded Ebenezer Morris's proposal that all ties to Rowland be severed. The motion was carried, although Rowland of course remained an ordained priest in the Anglican Church and in that capacity continued to hold services at Bridge Street Chapel in Haverfordwest until the congregation dwindled to the point where he was compelled to retire.[41]

Rowland's exclusion meant a further decline in the number of ordained clergy who were members of the movement. The situation was in fact far more critical in the north of the country, where Thomas Charles had laboured as the only Methodist-inclined cleric for many years until he was joined by Simon Lloyd of Bala in 1803 and later in 1805 by William Lloyd in Caernarfon. There were limits to what those three could hope to achieve, in the light of the growing communities of Methodists in the north who constantly called on their services. The frustration of the lay preachers who were unable to offer the same level of provision as their clerical brethren led to growing demands that the movement should move to ordain its own ministers. Such demands placed many of the Methodist-oriented clergy in a difficult position. Many saw their activities with the Methodist movement as an extension of their duties in the Church, not as an alternative to them. Any ordination would inevitably entail the formation of a separate denomination, so that the clergymen would have to dissent from the Church in order to remain members of the Methodist movement. For most of them, that would mean the sacrifice of their livelihoods, and David Jones, Llan-gan, pointed out that he had already risked his daily bread by his adherence to the Methodists.[42] Yet, for Jones and others it was not the matter of earning their daily bread which was paramount, but the fact of their genuine commitment to the Anglican Church and their determination not to leave it. Jones swore that he would go no further along the path to separation and died in August 1810 before he was obliged to make the choice. Although much mourned, his death did, however, remove one of the chief voices in opposition to ordination.

It was, not surprisingly, the lay preachers who argued most vehemently in favour of ordination. For Thomas Jones, one of the crucial factors in the debates over separation was that the scriptures seemed quite clearly to establish the practice of the two sacraments of baptism and communion, and to urge a more frequent administration of the latter than was common or practicable among the Methodists.[43] He could not but conclude that it was contrary to God's word to encourage members to seek the sacraments outside their own movement. He feared that many of the members, through unwillingness to have their children baptised by 'unawakened' clergy of the Church, were being forced, albeit reluctantly, to turn to Dissenting ministers for this service. It was after considerable prayer and soul-searching that he consented to baptise a child, called Evan Simner, on the understanding that the congregation who regarded him as their pastor called him to do so. The baptism took place in the parents' home in March 1810, but Jones subsequently performed further baptismal services in the Methodist chapel at Denbigh. Shortly afterwards, Jones proceeded to administer communion in the chapel in a spirit of 'godly fear, joy and thanksgiving'.[44]

Thomas Jones was deeply troubled that this action might cause distress to his close friend, Thomas Charles, who had hitherto been opposed to any move towards separation from the Church. As a priest without a parish, Charles had no cause to fear reprisal in the form of ejection from benefices or the loss of a salary, so in fact had less to lose than other Methodist-inclined clergymen. Yet Charles had argued along with all the supporters of the status quo that Methodism had thrived in its present condition for many years, so that any attempt to alter matters might well jeopardise its success. Charles had worked closely with Daniel Rowland and William Williams and may well have felt an obligation to continue along the path they had laid out for the movement. It has also been argued that he may not have been particularly impressed with the ministers ordained in Lady Huntingdon's Connexion and that he may have been reluctant to sever ties with the Church because it might injure the support he had won for his efforts to spread knowledge of the Bible.[45] Thomas Jones's first biographer, Jonathan Jones, believed that it was primarily an uncertainty regarding the procedure for ordination which had caused Charles to hesitate.[46] This seems unlikely, however, since there was little difficulty in devising an appropriate form once the decision had been made. Despite his previous opposition, however, at the Quarterly Association in Bala in June 1810, Charles announced his willingness to move gradually towards administering ordination.[47]

It is not entirely clear precisely how or why this change of heart came about, although it has been suggested that Thomas Jones's *fait accompli* forced Charles's hand, since the only alternative to accepting what had been done was to face the tricky task of disciplining Jones for actions which many members of the association would doubtless commend.[48] It has also been argued that Jones's actions were not likely to have precipitated Charles's change of attitude, as they were not the first of their kind: John Evans, Llwynffortun, apparently baptised children in Water Street Chapel in Carmarthen prior to 1811.[49] He was, however, ordained into deacon's orders by Bishop Richard Watson of Llandaff in 1807, which may have made it seem that he was not contravening the rules of the Established Church to the extent that Jones had done. The need to protect lay exhorters, who, without the security of the Toleration Act, risked being pressed into military service, may also have been something of a factor.[50] Ultimately, it would seem that it was not so much Thomas Jones's actions which persuaded Charles to capitulate, but the arguments put forward by him and the other advocates of ordination. It was difficult to continue to ignore the sheer number of lay preachers, monthly meetings and societies who called for the change. Those like Ebenezer Morris who argued the case in the association were evidently reluctant to force an open confrontation with Charles and wished above all to persuade him to their way of thinking; so it was evidently with some relief that they heard his declaration in 1810, as Thomas Jones recorded:

> yr oedd yr Arglwydd wedi gogwyddo meddyliau ei was, yr hwn yr oedd gan y corph oll y parch mwyaf . . .a'r ofn mwyaf rhag ei ofidio; ac, er mawr lawenydd i'r brodyr oedd yno yn gynnulledig, efe ym-roddodd yn ewyllysgar a llawen i ddwyn yr amcan y'mlaen mewn modd araf a graddol, fel yr oedd pawb o'r brodyr yn cydfarnu ei fod yn fwyaf cymhwys.

> [the Lord inclined the thoughts of his servant, for whom the entire connection had the greatest respect . . . and the greatest fear of troubling him: and, to the great joy of the brethren there assembled, he committed himself willingly and joyfully to carry the intention forward in a slow and gradual manner, as all the brethren judged to be most fitting.][51]

It was Thomas Charles who was responsible for drawing up the proposals on how to proceed with the ordination, which were accepted by both associations, in the north and the south. The monthly meetings in the counties were to nominate candidates to assist the clergy in their work of administering the sacraments. In order to maintain the centralised structure of the movement it was emphasised that the ministers were to be ordained by the connexion in the summer meetings of the associations. They were then to serve within their localities at the direction of the monthly meetings rather than be called to minister to individual chapels. They received their authority from the connexion as a whole, therefore, rather than from a call to serve a particular congregation. The first ordination service took place as part of the meeting of the northern association at Bala on 19 and 20 June 1811. Thomas Jones and John Davies of Denbighshire; John Elias and Richard Lloyd of Anglesey; Evan Richardson of Caernarfonshire; John Roberts of Merionethshire; Evan Griffiths and William Jones of Montgomeryshire; and Robert Ellis of Flintshire were ordained with the approval of the three hundred members said to have assembled, with Thomas Charles presiding.[52] It was a simple occasion, with the candidates being asked to answer a series of questions regarding their opinions on important questions of faith, before the congregation were called upon to consent to their ordination by a show of hands. The candidates were then asked if they were willing to accept the call and offered some words of counsel by Robert Jones, Rhoslan, as one of the movement's most respected elder statesmen. The occasion was repeated three weeks later in the southern association at Llandeilo on 10 and 11 July, with Thomas Charles presiding once again. It seems that the original idea had been to hold such a significant event at Llangeitho, but the opposition to ordination among members of the society there made that impossible. John Evans, David Rees, Arthur Evans and David Charles from Carmarthenshire; James James, David Parry and Evan Evans from Breconshire; Ebenezer Morris, John Thomas and Ebenezer Richard from Cardiganshire; Evan Harris from Pembrokeshire; Hopkin Bevan from Glamorgan; and John Rees of Monmouthshire were ordained at this ceremony.[53] Although the procedure adopted was quite straightforward and unostentatious, those present were deeply sensible of the significance of the occasion and approached it with a sense of awe and trepidation. Several could barely speak for nervousness, as one eyewitness later recounted:

> y gymdeithasfa hono oedd yr un fwyaf ofnadwy y bum ynddi yn fy mywyd. Yr oedd pob cnawd yn crynu, ïe, yr oedd hyd yn nod llawer o'r gweinidogion mwyaf duwiol, hyawdl, a chadarn yn yr Ysgrythyrau, bron yn methu ateb gan fawredd Duw.
>
> [that assocation was the most dreadful I was ever at in my life. All flesh trembled, yes, even many of the ministers who were the most

godly, eloquent and firm in the Scriptures, were almost unable to answer on account of the greatness of God.][54]

A joyous development for those who had longed for the opportunity to serve the societies more fully, the separation was not without its casualties. Over half the Methodist-oriented clergy in the south were lost to the movement, as they could not reconcile themselves to the prospect of dissenting from the Church. Pembrokeshire, for instance, lost all four of the clergymen who were members of the movement: David Griffiths of Nevern, William Jones of St Dogmaels, David Davies of Llanfyrnach and David Pugh of Newport, who had been granted the living by John Thornton in 1770 after Daniel Rowland had refused it. The schism there may have been due to the influence of David Griffiths, who had been a powerful figure in the Methodist movement for forty years. Efforts were made to mend the breach with Griffiths, but he remained bitterly and unalterably opposed to the ordinations.[55] In Glamorgan, the brothers Daniel and Hezekiah Jones withdrew from the association, but as both held a number of curacies this may have been at least partly a matter of financial necessity, since Hezekiah certainly continued to assist the Methodist cause at a local level.[56] In the same county, two of the clergy attempted to continue to serve both causes, with contrasting results. Richard Bassett, curate of St Athan, managed to maintain his place in the Church whilst continuing to associate with the Methodists and was even promoted to a rectorial benefice. Howel Howells, curate of St Lythan's, attempted a similar dual loyalty, but eventually, when forced by Bishop Marsh of Llandaff in 1818 to make a choice, decided to throw in his lot with the Methodists.[57] Matters were rather more straightforward for the unbeneficed, which included the three Methodist-inclined clergymen in the north and John Williams, Pantycelyn, and John Williams, Lledrod, in the south. Their ties to Anglicanism were inevitably rather looser, and their situation changed little as a result of the separation. It was only the unbeneficed clergy who were present at the first ordination ceremonies, indicating that this was a step too far for those still actively serving the Church. For some observers, however, the clerical presence may have lent a greater measure of authority and acceptability to the proceedings.

These divisions left a legacy of evangelically-inclined clergy within the Anglican Church, some of whom continued to conduct society meetings in their parishes. Complications arose in the case of some chapels where the Methodist-inclined clergy had been named as trustees and where the wording of the original deeds had been sufficiently ambiguous to prevent the new Methodist Church from being able to take possession of the buildings. This proved to be the case in Nevern, Newport and St Dogmaels, where the Methodists were bereft of their chapels as well as their ordained clerics.[58] The departure of so many of the clergy also made essential further ordinations in order to fill the gaps. Seven candidates were ordained at a second ceremony held in the southern association at Llandeilo in 1813 and another seven in the northern association at Bala in 1814.[59] The move to ordination also confirmed an inevitable shift in the way the movement was governed. Traditionally, ordained Anglican clergy had automatically been held in great esteem in the movement and had almost been guaranteed a prominent role amongst the leadership. However, the number of clergy decreased as a result of episcopal reluctance to accept known Methodists and because many gifted individuals preferred to serve as Methodist preachers first and foremost. The traditional prominence of the Anglican clergy was already being eroded prior to 1811 and finally came to an end with the death of Thomas Charles in 1814. From then on, those at the forefront of the movement would be men like Thomas Jones, John Elias and Ebenezer Richard, ordained as Methodist ministers and not as Anglican clergymen.

Despite some difficulties, however, the formation of the new denomination was a fairly smooth process, largely because so little changed. Robert Jones took pride in the fact that the connexion had succeeded in establishing 'a smooth and satisfactory order to carry the work forward without hurting anyone'.[60] In essence, 1811 could be said to denote a coming of age rather than a birth. Welsh Methodism had matured into a movement with a strong organisational structure which needed scarcely any adaptation to accommodate the change in situation. Each county had been divided into regions served by a group of lay preachers, who as ordained ministers continued with their labours much as before, save with the added responsibility of being able to perform baptism and administer communion. Many of the members had spent their entire lives in the evangelical Methodist fold, with occasional recourse to their parish priest for the essential rites of passage of baptism, marriage and burial, so their primary allegiance was unaltered by this development. Since the separation was not caused by any great theological difference with the Established Church, many other members found no difficulty in continuing to attend both Church and chapel. In such cases, the denominational lines remained somewhat blurred during the early years of the nineteenth century, until a generation had matured for whom Methodism and Anglicanism had always been separate entities. Thomas Charles, despite his late conversion to the idea of secession, never regretted his role in fashioning the Calvinistic Methodist Church of Wales and was said to have remained 'quiet and comfortable' in his mind regarding the momentous decision.[61] Yet, despite the relatively tranquil establishment of the denomination, the repercussions were considerable. The Methodist dissent from the Established Church did much to consolidate the strength of the Nonconformist cause in Wales during the nineteenth century. By the time of the religious census of 1851, Calvinistic Methodists represented the largest of the Nonconformist denominations in Wales, comprising 25 per cent of the worshipping population.[62] This growth would colour the social, cultural and political identity of the Welsh people and fuel the emerging arguments in favour of the disestablishment of the Anglican Church, confirming that the religious character of Wales was very different to that of neighbouring England.

The fading of English Calvinistic Methodism

In stark contrast to Wales, English Calvinism in the nineteenth century was to slip its earlier Methodist moorings to be found overwhelmingly in the Evangelical branch of the Church of England and in the Dissenting denominations of Independents (Congregationalists) and Baptists. As they went out on their preaching rounds, Lady Huntingdon's students and young preachers were often asked to preach in Dissenting chapels: this accelerated the attraction of Dissent for many of her young men, as they would be invited to settle in these chapels and offered immediate Dissenting ordination. All this increased the drain of her connexion towards Dissent. Many were particularly drawn to a settled ministry. The minister of her Wigan chapel, William Roby, departed for Independency because he could not abide the itinerancy demanded. Moreover, he believed that it undercut the need for a minister to exert discipline over his flock. Moving to an Independent chapel in Manchester, Roby became the leading Congregationalist minister of his generation in Lancashire.[63]

Following the list of sixty-four chapels in 1790, the next full tally of countess of Huntingdon chapels appeared in 1884, when only thirty-five are recorded. It might be suggested that the Countess of Huntingdon's Connexion played its part by furnishing Independent Dissent with the scores of ministers and chapels that defected from the connexion's ranks, although the irony of this suggestion is the countess's personal rejection and detestation of Independency. Even with the best will possible it would be difficult to maintain that the denomination otherwise made any distinctive or enduring contribution to Nonconformity. The simultaneous deaths in 1791 of John Wesley and the countess of Huntingdon placed punctuation marks against English Methodism: his a comma, hers for all intents a full stop. In 1811, London had forty-six Wesleyan and two countess of Huntingdon chapels.[64] Wesleyan leaders, who took considerable pleasure in reporting the atrophy in her connexion, had geared the organisation of their church to a carefully wrought ecclesiastical system. Lady Huntingdon's enterprises now became occluded. Once the heady enthusiasm of its eighteenth-century formative period had waned, Calvinistic Methodism in England sought the stability of settled ministry.

This was true not only for the Countess of Huntingdon Connexion, but also for all the other fragments of English Calvinistic Methodism: from Whitefield's chapels in London and elsewhere, to the Gloucestershire chapels of the Rodborough Connexion, to the Tabernacle chapel in Haverfordwest – all these enterprises moved into the welcoming arms of Independent Dissent. Perhaps the process had begun in 1763 when Andrew Kinsman, a Whitefield convert, had been ordained by a group composed not only of Methodist but also of Independent ministers in Bristol to serve the Devonport Tabernacle. There he reshaped the Calvinistic Methodist society into an Independent congregation.[65]

Not long after George Whitefield's death the Rodborough Connexion came under the supervision of the noted preacher at Wotton under Edge, Gloucestershire: Rowland Hill. However, although zealous in attempting to maintain an effective oversight, after a decade Hill established himself as the minister of the Surrey Chapel, Blackfriars, London, and it was only the summer months that he spent in Gloucestershire. Thus any lasting oversight of the Rodborough Connexion would have been seriously truncated. Even at the Rodborough chapel itself, when a new minister was ordained in 1774 it proceeded to separate from the connexion as an Independent body. A decade later the same procedure occurred at the equally important Dursley chapel. Similarly, when Cornelius Winter, a close follower of George Whitefield, assumed leadership of the Rodborough Connexion's Wiltshire meeting houses at Chippenham, Castle Combe and Christian Malford, he proceeded to reconstitute them along Congregationalist lines and was himself ordained as an Independent minister.[66] One by one chapels invited such men to settle with them permanently. Since a hallmark of Methodism in the eighteenth century was an itinerant ministry this development meant that, while many Independent chapels remained Calvinist, 'Methodist' was fading from English Calvinism. In the Rodborough Connexion, as with nearly all manifestations of Calvinistic Methodism in England, organisational heart had been removed as Independent Congregationalism won the day.

Notes

[1] SMU 108, Selina Hastings to [Thomas Haweis], 25 February 1790.
[2] Cheshunt F1/908, Thomas Charles to Selina Hastings, 28 April 1790; on the other hand, Nathaniel Rowland thought the Welsh clergy were lukewarm at best. Cheshunt F1/939, Nathaniel Rowland to Selina Hastings, 25 September 1790.
[3] Cheshunt F1/2121, Thomas Haweis to Selina Hastings, 27 February 1790.
[4] John Thomas, *Marwnad, ar Farwolaeth yr Anrhydeddus Arglwyddes Waddolog, Huntingdon* (Trevecka, 1791), p. 4.
[5] Thomas Cannon, *No. 5. The Family Library, being the Substance of a Funeral Sermon . . . on the Death of the . . . Countess . . . of Huntingdon* (London, [1791?]), p. 126.
[6] Alan Harding, *The Countess of Huntingdon's Connexion: A Sect in Action* (Oxford: Oxford University Press, 2003), p. 369.
[7] Cheshunt C1/1, Apostolic Society Minutes, p. 17.

8 See appendix C of this present work.

9 Huntington Library, San Marino, California, Hastings Personal Papers 31(7).

10 For examples: Cheshunt F1/2194, [Thomas] Cannon to Lady Anne Erskine, 7 November 1791; F1/2188, Robert Bradley to idem, 4 July 1791; F1/2198, Isaac Creswell and John Wilkes to [idem], 22 November 1791.

11 George Redford and John A. James (eds), *Autobiography of William Jay* (London: Hamilton, Adams & Co., 1854), pp. 479–80.

12 James Bridgman, *An Address to the Ministers, Deacons, and Friends of the Countess of Huntingdon's Connexion and College* (London: Ward & Co., [1857]), pp. 3, 8. See also [F. W. Willcocks], *Spa Fields Chapel and its Associations* ([London: n.p., 1886]), pp. 22–31; *Evangelical Register*, 6 (1834), 105–8, 418–21; *Countess of Huntingdon New Magazine* (1850), 270–2, 279.

13 Edwin Welch (ed.), *Cheshunt College, the Early Years* (n.p: Hertfordshire Record Society, 1990), p. 68.

14 S. C. Orchard, *Cheshunt College* (n.p: n.p., [1968]), pp. 8–10.

15 Welch (ed.), *Cheshunt College*, p. xvii.

16 Gomer M. Roberts (ed.), *Hanes Methodistiaeth Galfinaidd Cymru*, cyfrol II: *Cynnydd y Corff* (Caernarfon: Llyfrfa'r Methodistiaid Calfinaidd, 1978), pp. 537–8.

17 Ibid., pp. 538–41.

18 John Hughes, *Methodistiaeth Cymru* (3 vols, Wrexham: R. Hughes a'i Fab, 1851–6), II, p. 25; G. Wynne Griffith, *Yr Ysgol Sul: Penodau ar Hanes yr ysgol Sul yn bennaf ymhlith y Methodistiaid Calfinaidd* (Caernarfon: Methodistiaid Calfinaidd, 1936), pp. 44–51.

19 D. E. Jenkins, *The Life of the Rev. Thomas Charles B.A. of Bala* (3 vols, Denbigh: Llywelyn Jenkins, 1908), II, p. 518.

20 R. Tudur Jones, *Thomas Charles o'r Bala: Gwas y Gair a Chyfaill Cenedl* (Cardiff: University of Wales Press, 1979), pp. 26–8; E. Wyn James, 'Ann Griffiths, Mary Jones a Mecca'r Methodistiaid', *Llên Cymru*, 21 (1998), 74–87.

21 For Ann Griffiths, see Siân Megan, *Gwaith Ann Griffiths* (Llandybïe: Christopher Davies, 1982); A. M. Allchin, *Ann Griffiths: The Furnace and the Fountain* (Cardiff: University of Wales Press, 1987); R. M. Jones, 'Ann Griffiths and the Norm', in Branwen Jarvis (ed.), *A Guide to Welsh literature c.1700–1800* (Cardiff: University of Wales Press, 2000).

22 *Casgliad o hymnau gan mwyaf heb erioed eu hargraffu o'r blaen* (Bala: R. Saunderson, 1806); E. Wyn James, 'Pererinion ar y ffordd: Thomas Charles ac Ann Griffiths', *JHSPCW*, 29–30 (2005–6), 90–1.

23 Geoffrey Nuttall, 'Cyflwr Crefydd yn Nhrefddyn, Sir Fynwy 1793: Gan Edmund Jones', *Y Cofiadur*, 46 (1981), 26.

24 Goronwy P. Owen (ed.), *Atgofion John Evans y Bala: Y Diwygiad Methodistaidd ym Meirionnydd a Môn* (Caernarfon: Gwasg Pantycelyn, 1997), pp. 95–131.

25 Jenkins, *Life of Thomas Charles*, II, pp. 202–3.

26 Derec Llwyd Morgan, 'Llenyddiaeth y Methodistiaid', in Roberts (ed.), *Hanes Methodistiaeth Galfinaidd Cymru*, II, pp. 481–4; Huw Walters, 'The Welsh language and the periodical press' in Geraint H. Jenkins (ed.), *The Welsh Language and its Social Domains 1801–1911* (Cardiff: University of Wales Press, 2000), pp. 350–1; Aled G. Jones, 'The Welsh newspaper press', in Hywel Teifi Edwards (ed.), *A Guide to Welsh literature c.1800–1900* (Cardiff: University of Wales Press, 2000), pp. 2–3.

27 Philip Henry Jones, 'Two Welsh publishers of the Golden Age: Gee a'i Fab and Hughes a'i Fab', in P. H. Jones and Eiluned Rees (eds), *A Nation and its Books: A History of the Book in Wales* (Aberystwyth: National Library of Wales, 1998), p. 173.

28 Roberts (ed.), *Hanes Methodistiaeth Galfinaidd Cymru*, II, pp. 234–44.

29 A. H. Williams (ed.), *John Wesley in Wales, 1738–1790* (Cardiff: University of Wales Press, 1971), p. 36.

30 Glyn Tegai Hughes, 'Welsh-speaking Methodism', in Lionel Madden (ed.), *Methodism in Wales: A Short History of the Welsh Tradition* (Llandudno: Methodist Conference, 2003), pp. 23–8.

31 Idwal Jones (ed.), *Hunangofiant Thomas Jones, Dinbych* (Aberystwyth: Gwasg Aberystwyth, 1937), pp. 48–50.

32 Thomas Jones, *Ymddyddanion crefyddol, (rhwng dau gymmydog) Ystyriol a Hyffordd* ... (Bala: R. Saunderson, 1807); Thomas Jones, *Sylwadau ar lyfr Mr. Owen Davies* (Bala: R. Saunderson, 1808); Jonathan Jones, *Cofiant y Parch. Thomas Jones* (Denbigh: Thomas Gee, 1897), pp. 181–2.

33 Owen Thomas, *Cofiant y Parchedig John Jones, Talysarn* (2 vols, Wrexham: Hughes and Son, 1874), I, pp. 362–537; Jonathan Jones, *Cofiant y Parch. Thomas Jones*, pp. 158–80; Frank Price Jones, *Thomas Jones o Ddinbych 1756–1820* (Denbigh: Gwasg Gee, 1956), pp. 30–9.

34 Eryn M. White, *Praidd Bach y Bugail Mawr: Seiadau Methodistaidd De-orllewin Cymru* (Llandysul: Gwasg Gomer, 1995), pp. 15–16.

35 *Rheolau a dybenion y Cymdeithasau Neillduol yn mhlith y bobl a elwir y Methodistiaid yn Nghymru; a gyttunwyd arnynt mewn Cymdeithasfa Chwarterol, yn y Bala* (Caerleon: W. C. Jones, 1801).

36 Robert Jones (ed.), *Grawn-syppiau Canaan, neu gasgliad o hymnau; gan mwyaf o waith ... William Williams* (Liverpool: J. Dore, 1795).

37 See Eryn M. White, 'A "poor, benighted church"?, in R. R. Davies and Geraint H. Jenkins (eds), *From Medieval to Modern Wales* (Cardiff: University of Wales Press, 2004), pp. 124–7.

38 Hughes, *Methodistiaeth Cymru*, II, p. 34; John Morgan Jones and William Morgan, *Y Tadau Methodistaidd* (2 vols, Swansea: Lewis Evans, 1895), I, pp. 483–90; Roberts, *Hanes Methodistiaeth Galfinaidd Cymru*, II, pp. 67–8.

39 Hughes, *Methodistiaeth Cymru*, I, pp. 451–2; John Evans, *Hanes Methodistiaeth Rhan Ddeheuol Sir Aberteifi* (Dolgellau: E. W. Evans, 1904), pp. 223–4.

40 White, *Praidd Bach y Bugail Mawr*, pp. 12–14.

41 Euros Wyn Jones, 'Nathaniel Rowland (1749–1831)', *JHSPCW*, 7 (1983), 35–42; J. E. Wynne Davies, 'David Charles (1762–1834), Caerfyrddin', *JHSPCW*, 60 (1975), 39–44.

42 Hughes, *Methodistiaeth Cymru*, I, p. 459; Roberts, *Hanes Methodistiaeth Galfinaidd Cymru*, II, pp. 303–4.

43 Jones (ed.), *Hunangofiant Thomas Jones*, pp. 59–60.

44 Ibid., p. 54.

45 Jenkins, *Life of Thomas Charles*, III, p. 253.

46 Jones, *Cofiant y Parch. Thomas Jones*, p. 229.

47 Thomas Jones, *Cofiant Thomas Charles* (Bala: Robert Saunderson, 1816), p. 211.

48 Jones, *Cofiant y Parch. Thomas Jones*, pp. 238–9; Frank Price Jones, *Thomas Jones o Ddinbych*, pp. 54–60.

49 Jenkins, *Life of Thomas Charles*, III, pp. 260–1; Davies, 'David Charles', 42.

50 John Roberts, *Methodistiaeth Galfinaidd Cymru* (London: Gwasg Gymraeg Foyle, 1931), pp. 67–70.

51 Jones (ed.), *Hunangofiant Thomas Jones*, p. 54.

52 Hughes, *Methodistiaeth Cymru*, I, p. 462; Roberts, *Hanes Methodistiaeth Galfinaidd Cymru*, II, pp. 314–15.

53 Ibid., p. 462.

54 E. W. and H. Richard, *Bywyd y Parch. Ebenezer Richard* (London: W. Clowes, 1839), p. 48.

55 Hughes, *Methodistiaeth Cymru*, I, pp. 463–9; Jenkins, *Life of Thomas Charles*, III, pp. 322–3; Roberts, *Hanes Methodistiaeth Galfinaidd Cymru*, II, pp. 326–7.

56 Brian C. Luxton, 'Hezekiah Jones (c.1751–1833), the Red Priest of Colcot', *JHSPCW*, 55 (1970), 14–23, 33–48.

57 Roberts, *Hanes Methodistiaeth Galfinaidd Cymru*, II, pp. 332–3.

58 Hughes, *Methodistiaeth Cymru*, I, pp. 463–8.

59 Roberts, *Hanes Methodistiaeth Galfinaidd Cymru*, II, pp. 338–42.

60 '. . .[t]refn esmwyth a boddhaol i ddwyn y gwaith ymlaen heb friwo neb. . .', Robert Jones (ed.), *Drych yr Amseroedd*, ed. G. M. Ashton (Cardiff: University of Wales Press, 1958), p. 99.

61 Jones, *Cofiant Thomas Charles*, p. 212.

62 John Williams, *Historical Digest of Welsh Statistics* (Cardiff: Welsh Office, 1985), p. 352.

63 Henry D. Rack, *Reasonable Enthusiast: John Wesley and the Rise of Methodism* (London: Epworth Press, 1989), p. 286.

64 R. J. Helmstadter, 'The Reverend Andrew Reed', in R. W. Davis and R. J. Helmstadter (eds), *Religion and Irreligion in Victorian Society: Essays in Honour of R. K. Webb* (London: Routledge, 1992), p. 13.

65 R. Tudur Jones, *Congregationalism in England* (London: Independent Press, 1962), p. 150.

66 David E. Evans, *As Mad as a Hatter! Puritans and Whitefieldites in the History of Dursley and Cam* (Gloucester: Alan Sutton, 1982), pp. 84–5.

Conclusion

Apart from all other considerations, Calvinistic Methodism in England was distinguished from that in Wales by the chaotic nature of its 'organisation'. Whether under George Whitefield, the countess of Huntingdon or lesser figures, the groupings in England were dependent for their ongoing order on powerful charismatic individuals rather than structured representative meetings in which power and authority was vested. Certainly, the countess's connexion could have done better if it had adopted its 1790 plan; but, even then, geography would have worked against its effectiveness. Calvinistic Methodists in England were just too widely spread – and too limited in number – to have made a presbyterian structure work effectively. By the early nineteenth century there were simply too many other options for those who wished to adopt Calvinist theology, options that were often free from the quirky temper of many of the networks that had grown directly out of the eighteenth-century English Calvinistic Methodist movement. A further crucial consideration was that Calvinistic Methodism in England was thwarted by the far larger forces of Weslyanism.

In contrast, in Wales Wesleyanism made little inroad, at least until the early nineteenth century.[1] Calvinistic Methodism, free from obvious and aggressive competition, was given space to deepen and unsurprisingly strengthened its position. It was able to develop a distinct spirituality in the Welsh language which gave it the feel of an indigenous religious community, and the structure that Howel Harris had fashioned in the early days of the revival put down firm foundations and proved itself flexible enough to facilitate the growth of Welsh Methodism, especially in the aftermath of the 1762 Llangeitho revival. When the Welsh Methodists finally accepted the inevitable and reluctantly severed their links with the Church of England in 1811, they already had the sinews of a denomination in place. While they did not adopt the name Presbyterian at this stage, such a system was what they had, in effect, created. It was, therefore, natural for Lewis Edwards, one of the denomination's genuine intellectuals in the middle decades of the nineteenth century, to turn what had been a fairly loose presbyterian structure into a more classically defined Presbyterian church which had links with sister denominations throughout the Reformed world.[2]

However, by the early nineteenth century the Welsh Calvinistic Methodists had also been responsible for, or had at least inspired, the reinvigoration of the wider Nonconformist community in Wales. Baptists, Independents and others had all adopted a more evangelical outlook; and, fuelled by frequent waves of religious revivalism, often throughout Wales, generation after generation were brought into enthusiastic membership in one or other of the Welsh Nonconformist denominations. For much of the nineteenth century Calvinistic Methodism and Welsh Nonconformity were to become inextricably bound up with Welsh identity. When the government's Anglican educational commissioners published their infamous 'Blue Books' in 1847, castigating the Welsh as idle, immoral and largely ignorant, many already had the resources at their disposal to reinvent themselves as a respectable, well-ordered and deeply pious people.[3] Where English Calvinistic Methodism, therefore, struggled to be anything other than a bit player on the English religious stage, Welsh Calvinistic Methodism embedded itself as an indispensible part of nineteenth-century Welsh identity.

Notes

[1] A. H. Williams, *Welsh Wesleyan Methodism, 1800–1858: Its origins, Growth and Secessions* (Bangor: Llyfrfa'r Methodistiaid, 1935).

[2] D. Densil Morgan, 'Lewis Edwards (1808–87) and Welsh theology', *The Welsh Journal of Religious History*, 3 (2008), 18–19.

Notes

3 David Hempton, *Religion and Political Culture in Britain and Ireland: from the Glorious Revolution to the Decline of Empire* (Cambridge: Cambridge University Press, 1996), pp. 56–7.

Appendix A

Societies 'in Connexion together under the care of the Reverend Mr Whitefield', 12 November 1747

London
Tabernacle
Deptford
Bird Street

Gloucestershire
Gloucester
Minchinhampton
The Roadway
Stancombe

Bristol

Kingswood

Bath

Devon and Cornwall
Exeter
Plymouth
Kingsbridge
[St] Marychurch
Bovey

Buckinghamshire
Olney

Oxfordshire
Chinnor
Oxford

Wiltshire
Coombe
Foxham
Studley
Stratton
Avebury

Birmingham

Staffordshire
Wednesbury
Brewood Forge

Shrewsbury

Hereford

Portsmouth

Gosport

Source: NLW CMA Trevecka 2946 (corrected).

Appendix B

'Names of places for preaching where societies are not settled', 12 November 1747

London
Ratcliff (Stepney)
Southward
Lambeth

Kent
Chatham
Maidstone

Essex
Braintree
Coggeshall
Wethersfield

Gloucestershire
Tewkesbury
Ronneck (?)
Stroud
The Mill, near Stroud
Bismoure (?)
Tockington and Aust (?)

Devon and Cornwall
Axminster

Tavistock
Polperro
Devonport

Wiltshire
Calne and Preston
Longley (?)
Stanton (Upper and Lower)
Sutton

Buckinghamshire
Cludesle-row (?)
Speen

Source: NLW CMA Trevecka 2946 (corrected).

Appendix C

Chapels and congregations that were part of the Countess of Huntingdon's Connexion, up to 1800: a notional list drawn from all available sources

*Ashbourne, Derbyshire
*Ashby-de-la Zouch, Leicestershire

*Banbury, Oxfordshire
 Barton-upon-Humber, Lincolnshire
*Basingstoke, Hampshire
*Bath
 Berkhamsted, Hertfordshire
*Bilston, West Midlands
*Birmingham
 Bootle, Cumbria
 Brecon, Breconshire
*Brighton, Sussex
*Bristol
*Broad Oak, Herefordshire

 Castle Donington, Leicestershire
 Chatham, Kent
*Chatteris, Cambridgeshire
 Chelmsford, Essex
 Cheltenham, Gloucestershire
 Cheshunt, Hertfordshire
*Chichester, Sussex

*Coleford, Gloucestershire
 Cradley, Worcestershire

 Dartford, Kent
 Derby, Derbyshire
 Dorchester, Dorset
*Dover, Kent
*Dudley, West Midlands
 Dublin

 Ebley, Gloucestershire
*Edgbaston, Birmingham
*Ely, Cambridgeshire
*Evesham, Worcestershire

*Faversham, Kent
*Fordham, Essex
*Frome, Somerset

*Gainsborough, Lincolnshire
*Gloucester
*Goring, Oxfordshire
 Grantham, Lincolnshire
 Gravesend, Kent
 Great Yarmouth, Norfolk
 Guernsey, Channel Islands

*Handsworth, Birmingham
 Harwich, Essex
*Haxey, Lincolnshire
*Helmsley, Yorkshire
*Hereford
*Hull (Kingston Upon), Yorkshire
 Huntingdon, Huntingdonshire

 Kendal, Cumbria
*Kidderminster, Worcestershire

*Lewes, Sussex
*Lincoln
*Llangattock Lingoed, Monmouthshire

London
  Ewer Street Chapel, Southwark
  *Holywell Mount Chapel, Shoreditch
  *Mulberry Gardens Chapel, Wapping
  Princess Street Chapel, Westminster
  Rotherhithe
  *Sion Chapel, Whitechapel
  *Spa Fields Chapel, Clerkenwell
  Woolwich

Lyme Regis, Dorset

Maidstone, Kent
Margate, Kent
Melbourne, Derbyshire
Melksham, Wiltshire
Mevagissey, Cornwall
*Milton, Essex
*Monmouth
*Morpeth, Northumberland
  Mortimer West End, Hampshire

*Newark, Nottinghamshire
*Norwich

*Ote (Oat) Hall, Sussex
  Oundle, Northamptonshire

*Partney, Lincolnshire
*Peterborough, Northamptonshire
*Pinchbeck, Lincolnshire
  Preston, Lancashire

*Ramsey, Huntingdonshire

*Reading, Berkshire
*Rickmansworth, Hertfordshire
 Rochdale, Lancashire

 St Agnes, Cornwall
*St Columbe, Cornwall
 St Ives, Cornwall
 Sheffield, Yorkshire
 Sleaford, Lincolnshire
 South Petherton, Somerset
 Stamford, Lincolnshire

*Starcross, Devon
*Sudbury, Suffolk
*Swansea

Taunton, Somerset
*Tunbridge Wells, Kent

*Ulverston, Cumbria

*Wallingford, Berkshire
 Walsall, West Midlands
 Warwick
 Watchet, Somerset
 Wednesbury, West Midlands
*West Bromwich, West Midlands
 Weymouth, Dorset
*Whitehaven, Cumbria
*Wigan, Lancashire
*Wincanton, Somerset
*Wolverhampton, West Midlands
*Woodbridge, Suffolk
*Worcester

*York

*Indicates a location included in the sixty-four chapels listed in abortive *Plan of an Association for Uniting and Perpetuating the Connection of the Right Honourable the Countess Dowager of Huntingdon* (n.p., 1790).

Bibliography

Manuscripts

Birmingham University Library
Church Missionary Society Manuscripts
    Venn Manuscripts

Bridwell Library, Southern Methodist University, Dallas, Texas
Countess of Huntingdon Letters

Carmarthenshire Record Office, Carmarthen
Quarter Session Records, QS I/1

Cheshunt Foundation, Westminster College, Cambridge
College Archives
Connexional Archives
Countess of Huntingdon Correspondence

Countess of Huntingdon Connexion Archives, Rayleigh
Letters of Countess of Huntingdon

Dr Williams's Library, London
Congregational Library: Letters of Countess of Huntingdon

Drew University Library, Madison, New Jersey
Letters of the Countess of Huntingdon

Duke University Library, Durham, North Carolina
Frank A. Baker Collection
R. E. Hendrix Manuscripts
Wesley Family Papers

East Sussex Record Office, Lewes
NB 1/1/1A

Gloucestershire Record Office, Gloucester
Ebley Manuscripts

Guildhall Library, London
Dissenting Deputies Minutes

Huntingdon Library, San Marino, California
Hastings Personal Papers

John Rylands University Library of Manchester
English Manuscripts
     Countess of Huntingdon Letters, 1774–1784
Methodist Archives
     Countess of Huntingdon Black Folio of Letters

Lambeth Palace Library, London
Registers of Peers Chaplains

National Archives, Kew, London
RG 4/3132

National Library of Wales, Aberystwyth
Calvinistic Methodist Archives
     Howel Harris's Manuscript Diaries
     Thomas Charles Manuscripts
     Trevecka Manuscripts: Trevecka Letters
NLW Manuscripts
     NLW MS 5453: Diary of Thomas Morgan
     NLW MS 20515-6: Diary of John Thomas, Tre-main
     NLW MS 4797, William Williams to Thomas Charles,
         25 May 1790
     NLW Llwyngwair MS 16986a

Church in Wales Records
  SD/MISC/1085

Printed primary sources

'A proposal for agreement between the Welsh Association and the Glouces-
  tershire Connection', *Journal of the Historical Society of the Presby-
  terian Church in Wales*, 52 (1967), 40–1.
An Authentic Narrative of the Primary Ordination (London: Hughes and
  Walsh, 1784).
An Elegy on the Reverend Mr G. Whitefield . . . Presented to Her Ladyship
  (Carmarthen: John Ross, 1771).
Aveling, Thomas W., *Memorials of the Clayton Family* (London: Hodder
  and Walford, 1867).
Baker, Frank (ed.), *The Works of John Wesley*, vol. 25, *Letters I, 1721–1739*
  (Oxford: Oxford University Press, 1980).
—— (ed.), *The Works of John Wesley*, vol. 26, *Letters II, 1740–55* (Oxford:
  Oxford University Press, 1982).
Beynon, Tom, 'Howell Harris's Visits to Kidwelly and District', *Journal
  of the Historical Society of the Church in Wales*, 24, 1 (September
  1939), 49–61.
—— (ed.), 'Extracts from the diaries of Howell Harris', *Bathafarn: The
  Journal of the Historical Society of the Methodist Church in Wales*, 4
  (1949), 54–68; 6 (1951), 50–9.
—— (ed.), *Howell Harris, Reformer and Soldier (1714–1773)* (Caernarvon:
  The Calvinistic Methodist Bookroom, 1958).
—— (ed.), *Howell Harris's Visits to London* (Aberystwyth: The Cambrian
  News Press, 1966).
—— (ed.), *Howell Harris's Visits to Pembrokeshire (1739–1752)* (Aber-
  ystwyth: The Cambrian News Press, 1966).
Bridgman, James, *An Address to the Ministers, Deacons, and Friends of the
  Countess of Huntingdon's Connexion and College* (London: Ward &
  Co., [1857]).
Cannon, Thomas, *No. 5. The Family Library, being the Substance of a
  Funeral Sermon . . . on the Death of the . . . Countess . . . of Huntingdon*
  (London, [1791?]).
Casgliad o Hymnau gan mwyaf heb erioed eu hargraffu o'r blaen (Bala: R.
  Saunderson, 1806).
Cennick, John, *The Life of Mr J. Cennick* (Bristol: John Lewis and James
  Hutton, 1745).

——, 'An account of the most remarkable occurrences in the awakenings at Bristol and Kingswood till the brethren's labours began there in 1746', ed. H. J. Foster, *Proceedings of the Wesley Historical Society*, 6, 6 (June 1908), 101–11.

Charles, Thomas, 'Peter Williams', *Trysorfa Ysprydol* (1813), 483–5.

Claghorn, George S. (ed.), *The Works of Jonathan Edwards*, vol. 16, *Letters and Personal Writings* (New Haven, CT: Yale University Press, 1988).

Clap, Thomas, *A Letter from the Reverend Mr Clap, Rector of Yale College in New Haven, to the Rev. Mr. Edwards of North-hampton* (Boston: T. Fleet, 1745).

Cyffes Ffydd y Corph o Fethodistiaid Calfinaidd yng Nghymru (Bala, 1823).

Denning, R. T. W. (ed.), *The Diary of William Thomas of Michaelston-super-Ely, near St Fagans, Glamorgan, 1762–1795* (Cardiff: South Wales Record Society, 1995).

Erskine, Ebenezer and Erskine, Ralph, *Crist ym Mreichiau'r Credadyn: Wedi Ei Osod Allan Mewn Pregeth ar Luc. ii, 28* (Carmarthen: John Ross, 1744).

Erskine, Ralph, *Traethawd am Farw i'r Ddeddf, a Byw i Dduw* (trans. John Morgan) (Bristol: Felix Farley, 1743).

Evans, Eifion (ed.), *Pursued by God: A selective translation with notes of the Welsh religious classic Theomemphus, by William Williams of Pantycelyn* (Bridgend: Evangelical Press of Wales, 1996).

Evans, George Eyre (ed.), *Lloyd Letters (1754–1791)* (Aberystwyth: William Jones, 1908).

Eyre, John, *The Order Observed at the Countess of Huntingdon's College, at Cheshunt* (London: Edward Nodson, 1792).

Forsaith, Peter S. (ed.), *Unexampled Labours: Letters of the Revd John Fletcher to Leaders in the Evangelical Revival* (Peterborough: Epworth Press, 2008).

Gillies, John (ed.), *The Works of the Reverend George Whitefield* (6 vols, London: Edward and Charles Dilly, 1771–2).

Harris, Howell, *A Brief Account of the life of Howell Harris, Esq.* (Trevecka, 1791).

Heitzenrater, Richard P. (ed.), *Diary of an Oxford Methodist: Benjamin Ingham, 1733–1734* (Durham, NC: University of North Carolina Press, 1985).

Hill, Richard, *Pietas Oxoniensis* (2nd edition, London: J. and W. Oliver, 1768).

Hughes, Garfield H. (ed.), *Gweithiau William Williams Pantycelyn*, cyfrol 2, *Rhyddiaith* (Cardiff: University of Wales Press, 1967).

Hughes, John, 'Cofiant a Llythyrau Ann Griffiths', *Y Traethodydd* (1846), 420–33.

Jones, Idwal (ed.), *Hunangofiant Thomas Jones, Dinbych* (Aberystwyth: Gwasg Aberystwyth, 1937).

Jones, M. H., *The Trevecka Letters* (Caernarvon: Calvinistic Methodist Bookroom, 1932).

Jones, N. Cynhafal (ed.), *Gweithiau Williams Pant-y-celyn* (2 vols, Holywell: P. M. Evans, 1887).

Jones, Robert (ed.), *Grawn-syppiau Canaan, neu gasgliad o hymnau; gan mwyaf o waith...William Williams* (Liverpool: J. Dore, 1795).

——, *Drych yr Amseroedd*, ed. G. M. Ashton (Cardiff: University of Wales Press, 1958).

Jones, Thomas, *Ymddyddanion crefyddol, (rhwng dau gymmydog) Ystyriol a Hyffordd...* (Bala: R. Saunderson, 1807).

——, *Sylwadau ar lyfr Mr. Owen Davies* (Bala: R. Saunderson, 1808).

——, *Cofiant Thomas Charles* (Bala: Robert Saunderson, 1816).

Letters from Bath 1766–1767 by the Rev. John Penrose (Gloucester: Alan Sutton, 1983).

Lewis, W. S. (ed.), *Horace Walpole's Correspondence* (New Haven and Oxford: Yale University Press, 1937–83).

Meyer, John Henry, *The Saint's Triumph* (London: n.p., [1791]).

Minutes of the Methodist Conferences, vol. 1 (London, 1862).

Nuttall, Geoffrey, 'Cyflwr Crefydd yn Nhrefddyn, Sir Fynwy 1793: Gan Edmund Jones', *Y Cofiadur*, 46 (1981), 23–8; 47 (1982), 20–30.

Owen, Goronwy P. (ed.), *Hunangofiant John Elias* (Bridgend: Evangelical Press of Wales, 1974).

Platt, William Francis, *The Waiting Christian* (Bristol: John Rose, 1791).

Redford, George and James, John A. (eds), *Autobiography of William Jay* (London: Hamilton, Adams & Co., 1854).

Rheolau a dybenion y Cymdeithasau Neillduol yn mhlith y bobl a elwir y Methodistiaid yn Nghymru; a gyttunwyd arnynt mewn Cymdeithasfa Chwarterol, yn y Bala (Caerleon: W. C. Jones, 1801).

Rowland, Daniel, *Y Llaeth Ysbrydol, neu bregeth yn dangos mawr hiraeth y ffyddloniaid am laeth y gair ynghyd a'r ffordd i mae cynyddy trwyddo* (Carmarthen: Nicholas Thomas, 1739).

——, *Hymnau duwiol. Yw canu, mewn cymdeithiasau crefyddol* (Bristol: Felix Farley, 1744).

——, *Ymddiddan rhwng Methodist uniawn-gred, ac un camsyniol* (Bristol: Felix Farley, 1750).

——, *Tair Pregeth a bregethwyd yn yr Eglwys Newydd, gerllaw Llangeitho* (Carmarthen, John Ross, 1775).

Sail, Dibenion, a Rheolau'r Societies neu'r Cyfarfodydd Neilltuol a Ddechreusant Ymgynull yn Ddiweddar yng Nghymru (Bristol: Felix Farley, 1742).

Shirley, Walter, *A Narrative of the Principal Circumstances relative to the Rev. Mr Wesley's Late Conference* (Bath: W. Gye, 1771).

Telford, John (ed.), *The Letters of the Rev. John Wesley* (8 vols, London: Epworth Press, 1931).

Thomas, Graham C. G., 'George Whitefield and friends: the correspondence of some early Methodists', *National Library of Wales Journal*, 26, 3 (summer 1990), 251–80; 26, 4 (winter 1990), 367–96; 27, 1 (summer 1991), 65–96; 27, 2 (winter 1991), 175–203; 27, 3 (summer 1992), 289–318; 27, 4 (winter 1992), 431–52.

Thomas, Ioan, *Rhad Ras*, ed. J. Dyfnallt Owen (Cardiff: University of Wales Press, 1949).

Thomas, John, *Marwnad, ar Farwolaeth yr Anrhydeddus Arglwyddes Waddolog, Huntingdon* (Trevecka, 1791).

Thomas, Joshua, *Hanes y Bedyddwyr* (Carmarthen: John Ross, 1778).

Tyson, John R. with Schlenther, Boyd S., *In the Midst of Early Methodism: Lady Huntingdon and her Correspondence*, (Lanham, MD: Scarecrow Press, 2006).

Ward, W. Reginald and Heitzenrater, Richard P. (eds), *The Works of John Wesley*, vol. 19, *Journal and Diaries II (1738–43)* (Nashville, TN: Abingdon Press, 1990).

—— (eds), *The Works of John Wesley*, vol. 20, *Journal and Diaries III (1743–54)* (Nashville, TN: Abingdon Press, 1991).

—— (eds), *The Works of John Wesley*, vol. 22, *Journals and Diaries V (1765–75)* (Nashville, TN: Abingdon Press, 1993).

Waring, George, *The End of Time. A Sermon, preached at the Countess of Huntingdon's Chapel, Spa Fields, Clerkenwell, London, on Sunday Evening, August 22, 1790; by George Waring, one of Her Ladyship's Ministers* (2nd edn, n.p, n.d.).

Welch, Edwin (ed.), *Two Calvinistic Methodist Chapels, 1743–1811: The London Tabernacle and Spa Fields Chapel* (London: London Record Society, 1975).

—— (ed.), *Cheshunt College, the Early Years* (n.p: Hertfordshire Record Society, 1990).

Wesley, John, *Free Grace: A Sermon Preach'd at Bristol* (Bristol: S. and F. Farley, 1739).

Whitefield, George, *The Nature and Necessity of our New Birth in Christ Jesus, in order to Salvation* (London: C. Rivington, 1737).

Whitefield, George, *A Journal of a Voyage from London to Savannah in Georgia. In two parts. Part I, From London to Gibraltar. Part II. From Gibraltar to Savannah* (London: James Hutton, 1738).

Whitefield, George, *A Continuation of the Reverend Mr Whitefield's Journal, during the time he was detained in England by the Embargo* (London: W. Strahan, 1739).

Whitefield, George, *A Continuation of the Reverend Mr Whitefield's Journal from his arrival at London to his departure from thence on his way to Georgia (December 1738–June 1739)* (London: James Hutton, 1739).

Whitefield, George, *A Continuation of the Reverend Mr. Whitefield's Journal, from his arrival at Savannah, to his return to London* (London: James Hutton, 1739).

Whitefield, George, *A letter from the Rev. Mr George Whitefield to the religious societies, lately set on foot in several parts of England and Wales* (London: W. Strahan, 1740).

Whitefield, George, *Three letters from the Reverend Mr G. Whitefield: viz to a friend in London, concerning Archbishop Tillotson* (Philadelphia: B. Franklin, 1740).

Whitefield, George, *A letter to the Reverend Mr John Wesley: in answer to his sermon, entitled, Free-Grace* (London: W. Strahan, 1741).

Whitefield, George, *A letter to the Reverend the President, and Professors, Tutor, and Hebrew Instructor of Harvard College in Cambridge* (Boston: T. Fleet, 1745).

Whitefield, George, *A farther account of God's dealings with the Reverend Mr George Whitefield from the time of his ordination to his embarking for Georgia (June 1736–December 1737)* (London: W. Strahan, 1747).

Whitefield, George, *An Expostulatory Letter, addressed to Nicholas Lewis, Count Zinzendorf, and Lord Advocate of the Unitus Fratrum* (London: G. Keith and J. Oswald, 1753).

Whitefield, George, *The two first parts of his life, with his journals, revised, corrected and abridged* (London: W. Strahan, 1756).

Wilks, Mark, *Nonconformity: A Sermon Delivered . . . Nov. 6, 1817, at the Monthly Association of Congregational Ministers* (London: T. Hamilton, 1818).

Williams, A. H., (ed.), 'The leaders of Welsh and English Methodism, 1738–1791', *Bathafarn: Historical Society of the Methodist Church in Wales*, 16 (1961), 23–40; 17 (1962), 5–26; 22(1967), 24–36; 23 (1968), 7–13; 24 (1969), 20–5.

—— (ed.), *John Wesley in Wales, 1738–1790* (Cardiff: University of Wales Press, 1971).

Williams, Peter, *Llythyr at hen Gydymaith mewn perthynas i gywirdeb cyfieithiad Bibl John Cann, yn ymddiffyn Diwygiad, ac yn gwrthbrofi Camachwyniad* (Carmarthen: John Ross, 1791).

Williams, William, *Aleluja, neu, casgljad o hymnau ar amryw ystyriaethau* (Carmarthen: Samuel Lewis, 1744).

———, *Hosanna i fab Dafydd, neu gasgliad o hymnau* (Bristol: Felix Farley, 1751).

———, *Rhai hymnau a chaniadau duwiol ar amryw ystyrjaethau* (Carmarthen: Evan Powel, 1757).

———, *Marwnad er coffadwriaeth am Mr. Howel Harries...1773* (Brecon: E. Evans, 1773).

———, *Templum Experientiae apertum; neu, Ddrws y Society Profiad Wedi ei agor o Led y Pen* (Brecon: E. Evans, 1777).

———, *The Experience Meeting – an introduction to the Welsh Societies of the Evangelical Awakening* (Bridgend: Evangelical Movement of Wales, 1973). Translated by M. Lloyd Jones.

Y Bibl Sanctaidd: sef yr Hen Destament a'r Newydd, â nodau ysgrythurol ar ymyl y ddalen (Trefeca, 1790).

Newspapers and Magazines

Arminian Magazine.

Countess of Huntingdon New Magazine.

Evangelical Register.

Gospel Magazine.

Lewis, John (ed.), *The Christian's Amusement: containing letters concerning the progress of the gospel both at home and abroad &c. Together with an account of the Waldenses and Albigenses: People that never fell into the Popish errors, but retained the truth of the gospel from the time of the Apostles, under all Popish persecution down to the Reformation*, 1–27, (September 1740–March 1741).

——— (ed.), *The Weekly History: An account of the most remarkable particulars relating to the present progress of the gospel, by the encouragement of the Rev. Mr Whitefield*, 1–84 (11 April 1741–13 November 1742).

——— (ed.), *An Account of the Most Remarkable Particulars of the Present Progress of the Gospel*, vol. 2, nos. 1, 2, 3; vol. 3, nos 1, 2, 3; vol. 4, nos 1, 2 and 3 (autumn 1742–autumn 1743).

——— (ed.), *The Christian History: or a general account of the progress of the gospel, in England, Wales, Scotland and America: so far as the Rev.*

Mr Whitefield, his fellow-labourers, and assistants are concern'd, vol. 5, nos 1, 2, 3, 4; vol. 6, nos 1, 2, 3, 4; vol. 7, nos 1, 2, 3, 4; vol. 8 (autumn 1743–June 1748).

Secondary sources

Abraham, William J. and Kirby, James E. (eds), *The Oxford Handbook of Methodist Studies* (Oxford: Oxford University Press, 2009).

Allchin, A. M., *Ann Griffiths: The Furnace and the Fountain* (Cardiff: University of Wales Press, 1987).

Baker, Frank, *John Wesley and the Church of England* (Peterborough: Epworth Press, 1970).

Baker-Jones, Leslie, *Princelings, Privilege and Power: The Tivyside Gentry in their Community* (Llandysul: Gwasg Gomer, 1999).

Barry, Jonathan and Morgan, Kenneth (eds), *Reformation and Revival in Eighteenth-Century Bristol* (Bristol: Bristol Record Society, 1994).

Bassett, T. M., *The Welsh Baptists* (Swansea: Ilston House, 1977).

Bebbington, David W., *Evangelicalism in Modern Britain* (London: Unwin Hyman, 1989).

——, 'Evangelical conversion, c.1740–1850', *Scottish Bulletin of Evangelical Theology*, 18, 2 (autumn, 2000), 102–27.

Bennett, Richard, *Methodistiaeth Trefaldwyn Uchaf*, cyfrol I: *Hanes Cyfnod Howel Harris, 1738–1752* (Bala: R. Evans a'i Fab, 1929).

——, *The Early Life of Howell Harris* (London: The Banner of Truth Trust, 1962).

Bogue, D. and Bennett, J., *History of Dissenters from the Revolution in 1688 to the Year 1808* (4 vols, London, 1808–12).

Brown, Raymond L., 'The expulsion of Daniel Rowland from his curacies: an oral tradition?', *JHSPCW*, 20 (1996), 31–5.

Brown, Roger Lee, 'The marriage of George Whitefield at Caerphilly', *JHSPCW*, 7 (1983), 24–30.

Brown-Lawson, A., *John Wesley and the Anglican Evangelicals of the Eighteenth Century* (Edinburgh: The Pentland Press, 1994).

Campbell, Ted A., *The Religion of the Heart: A Study of European Religious Life in the Seventeenth and Eighteenth Centuries* (Columbia, SC: University of South Carolina Press, 1991).

Clark, J. C. D., *English Society, 1660–1832: Religion, Ideology and Politics during the Ancien Régime* (2nd edn, Cambridge: Cambridge University Press, 2000).

Claydon, Tony, *Europe and the Making of England, 1660–1760* (Cambridge: Cambridge University Press, 2007).

Clement, Mary, *The S.P.C.K. and Wales, 1699–1740* (London: SPCK, 1954).

Clifford, Alan C., *Atonement and Justification: English Evangelical Theology, 1640–1790* (Oxford: Oxford University Press, 1990).

Collins, Kenneth J., *John Wesley: A Theological Journey* (Nashville, TN: Abingdon Press, 2003).

—— and Tyson, John H. (eds), *Conversion in the Wesleyan Tradition* (Nashville, TN: Abingdon Press, 2001).

Cooper, J. H. (ed.), *Extracts from the Journals of John Cennick: Moravian Evangelist* (Glengormley: The Moravian History Magazine, 1996).

Cragg, George G., *Grimshaw of Haworth: A study in Eighteenth Century Evangelicalism* (Norwich: Canterbury Press, 1947).

Crawford, Michael J., *Seasons of Grace: Colonial New England's Revival Tradition in its British Context* (New York: Oxford University Press, 1991).

Cross, F. L. and Livingstone, E. A. (eds), *The Oxford History of the Christian Church* (Oxford: Oxford University Press, 1983).

Dallimore, Arnold A., *George Whitefield: The Life and Times of the Great Evangelist of the 18th Century Revival* (2 vols, London and Edinburgh: The Banner of Truth Trust, 1970 and 1980).

Davies, D. Elwyn, *Y Smotiau Duon* (Llandysul: Gomer, 1981).

——, *They Thought for Themselves* (Llandysul: Gomer, 1982).

Davies, J. E. Wynne, 'David Charles (1762–1834), Caerfyrddin', *JHSPCW*, 60, 2 (1975), 31–44; 3 (1976), 61–72.

Davies, John, 'Howell Harris and the Trevecka Settlement', *Brycheiniog*, 60 (1963), 103–7.

Davies, R. R. and Jenkins, Geraint H. (eds), *From Medieval to Modern Wales* (Cardiff: University of Wales Press, 2004).

Davies, Russell, *Hope and Heartbreak: A Social History of Wales and the Welsh* (Cardiff: University of Wales Press, 2005).

Davis, Harold E., *The Fledgling Province: Social and Cultural Life in Colonial Georgia, 1733–1776* (Chapel Hill, NC: University of North Carolina Press, 1976).

De Castro, J. P., *The Gordon Riots* (Oxford: Oxford University Press, 1926).

Dickinson, H. T. (ed.), *A Companion to Eighteenth-Century Britain* (Oxford: Blackwell, 2002).

Drummond, Andrew L. and Bulloch, James, *The Scottish Church, 1688–1843: The Age of the Moderates* (Edinburgh: St Andrew Press, 1973).

Duffy, Eamon, 'Primitive Christianity revived: religious renewal in

Augustan England', in Derek Baker (ed.), *Renaissance and Renewal in Christian History, Studies in Church History*, 14 (Oxford: Oxford University Press, 1977), pp. 287–300.

Durden, Susan, 'A study of the first evangelical magazines, 1740–1748', *Journal of Ecclesiastical History*, 27, 3 (1976), 255–75.

Edwards, Hywel Teifi (ed.), *A Guide to Welsh Literature, c.1800–1900* (Cardiff: University of Wales Press, 2000).

Emyr, Gwen, *Sally Jones: Rhodd Duw i Charles* (Bridgend: Evangelical Press of Wales, 1996).

Evans, Chris, *Labyrinth of Flames: Work and Social Conditions in Early Industrial Merthyr* (Cardiff: University of Wales Press, 1998).

Evans, David E., *As Mad as a Hatter! A History of Nonconformism in Dursley and Cam* (Gloucester: Alan Sutton, 1982).

Evans, Eifion, 'Nathaniel Rowland's ordination and curacy at Stock, Essex', *JHSPCW*, 45 (1960), 67–70.

——, *Howel Harris, Evangelist 1714–1773* (Cardiff: University of Wales Press, 1974).

——, *Daniel Rowland and the Great Evangelical Awakening in Wales* (Edinburgh: The Banner of Truth Trust, 1985).

——, *Fire in the Thatch: the True Nature of Religious Revival* (Bridgend: Evangelical Press of Wales, 1996).

——, 'Howel Harris and the printed page', *JHSPCW*, 23 (1999), 33–62.

——, *Bread of Heaven: The Life and Work of William Williams, Pantycelyn* (Bridgend: Bryntirion Press, 2010).

Evans, John, *Hanes Methodistiaeth Rhan Ddeheuol Sir Aberteifi* (Dolgellau: E. W. Evans, 1904).

Fairs, Geoffrey L., 'Notes on the death of William Seward at Hay, 1740', *JHSPCW*, 58, 1 (March 1973), 12–17.

Fawcett, Arthur, *The Cambuslang Revival: The Scottish Evangelical Revival of the Eighteenth Century* (Edinburgh: The Banner of Truth Trust, 1971).

Field, C. D., 'The social composition of English Methodism to 1830: a membership analysis', *Bulletin of the John Rylands University of Manchester Library*, 76 (spring 1994), 153–69.

Field, David P., *Rigide Calvinisme in a Softer Dresse: The Moderate Presbyterianism of John Howe, 1630–1705* (Edinburgh: Rutherford House, 2004).

Gentry, Peter and Taylor, Paul, *Bold as a Lion: The Life of John Cennick (1718–1755), Moravian Evangelist* (Leicester: Life Publications, 2007).

Gillies, John, *Memoirs of the Life of the Reverend George Whitefield* (London: Edward and Charles Dilly, 1772).

Gray, Ernest (ed.), *Man Midwife* (London: Robert Hale, 1946).

Griffith, G. Wynne, *Yr Ysgol Sul: Penodau ar Hanes yr ysgol Sul yn bennaf ymhlith y Methodistiaid Calfinaidd* (Caernarfon: Llyfrfa Methodistiaid Calfinaidd, 1936).

Griffiths, Rhidian, 'Howel Davies: Apostol Sir Benfro', *JHSPCW*, 11 (1987), 2–14.

Gruffydd, R. Geraint, 'Diwygiad 1762 a William Williams o Bantycelyn', *JHSPCW*, 54, 3 (1969), 68–75; 55, 1 (1970), 4–13.

——, 'John Thomas, Tre-main: Pererin Methodistaidd', *JHSPCW*, 9–10 (1985–6), 46–68.

Halévy, Elie, *The Birth of Methodism in England*, trans. and ed. B. Semmel (Chicago: University of Chicago Press, 1971).

Harding, Alan, *The Countess of Huntingdon's Connexion: A Sect in Action* (Oxford: Oxford University Press, 2003).

Hayden, Roger, *Continuity and Change: Evangelical Calvinism among Eighteenth-Century Baptist Ministers Trained at Bristol Academy, 1690–1791* (Milton under Wychwood: Baptist Historical Society, 2006).

Haykin, Michael A. G. and Stewart, Kenneth J. (eds), *The Emergence of Evangelicalism: Exploring Historical Continuities* (Nottingham: Apollos, 2008).

Heitzenrater, Richard P., *Mirror and Memory: Reflections on early Methodism* (Nashville, TN: Abingdon Press, 1989).

——, *Wesley and the People called Methodists* (Nashville, TN: Abingdon Press, 1995).

——, 'Wesley in America', *Proceedings of the Wesley Historical Society*, 54, part 3 (October 2003), 85–114.

Helmstadter, R. J., 'The Reverend Andrew Reed', in R. W. Davis and R. J. Helmstadter (eds), *Religion and Irreligion in Victorian Society: Essays in Honour of R. K. Webb* (London: Routledge, 1992).

Hempton, David, *Methodism and Politics in British Society, 1750–1850* (London: Hutchinson, 1984).

——, 'Methodism and the law, 1740–1820', *Bulletin of the John Rylands University Library of Manchester*, 70 (1988), 93–107.

——, *Religion and Political Culture in Britain and Ireland: From the Glorious Revolution to the Decline of Empire* (Cambridge: Cambridge University Press, 1996).

——, 'Established churches and the growth of religious pluralism: a case study of Christianisation and secularisation in England since 1700', in Hugh McLeod and Werner Ustorf (eds), *The Decline of Christendom in Western Europe, 1750–2000* (Cambridge: Cambridge University Press, 2003), pp. 81–98.

——, *Methodism: Empire of the Spirit* (New Haven, CT: Yale University Press, 2005).

—— and Hill, Myrtle, *Evangelical Protestantism in Ulster Society, 1740–1890* (London: Routledge, 1992).

—— and Walsh, John, 'E. P. Thompson and Methodism', in Mark A. Noll (ed.), *God and Mammon: Protestants, Money and the Market, 1790–1860* (New York: Oxford University Press, 2002), pp. 99–122.

Hibbert, Christopher, *King Mob: The Story of Lord George Gordon and the Riots of 1780* (London: Readers Union, 1959).

Hindmarsh, D. Bruce, '"My chains fell off, my heart was free": early Methodist conversion narrative in England', *Church History*, 68, 4 (1999), 910–29.

——, *The Evangelical Conversion Narrative: Spiritual Autobiography in Early Modern England* (Oxford: Oxford University Press, 2005).

Hughes, Garfield H., 'Herbert Jenkins', *JHSPCW*, 32 (1947), 1–8.

Hughes, Glyn Tegai, *Williams Pantycelyn* (Cardiff: University of Wales Press, 1983).

Hughes, Hugh J., *Life of Howell Harris: The Welsh Reformer* (London: James Nisbet & Co., 1892).

Hughes, John, *Methodistiaeth Cymru* (3 vols, Wrexham: R. Hughes a'i Fab, 1851–6).

James, E. Wyn, 'Ann Griffiths, Mary Jones a Mecca'r Methodistiaid', *Llên Cymru*, 21 (1998), 74–87.

——, 'The Evolution of the Welsh Hymn', in Isabel Rivers and David Wykes (eds), *Dissenting Praise: Religious Dissent and the Hymn in England and Wales* (Oxford: Oxford University Press, 2011), pp. 229–68.

——, '"The new birth of a people": Welsh language and identity and the Welsh Methodists, c.1740–1820', in Robert Pope (ed.), *Religion and National Identity: Wales and Scotland, c.1700–2000* (Cardiff: University of Wales Press, 2001), pp. 14–42.

——, 'Pererinion ar y Ffordd: Thomas Charles ac Ann Griffiths', *JHSPCW*, 29–30 (2005–6), 73–96.

Jarvis, Branwen (ed.), *A Guide to Welsh Literature c.1700–1800* (Cardiff: University of Wales Press, 2000).

Jenkins, D. E., *The Life of the Rev. Thomas Charles B.A. of Bala* (3 vols, Denbigh: Llywelyn Jenkins, 1908).

Jenkins, Geraint H., *Literature, Religion and Society in Wales, 1660–1730* (Cardiff: University of Wales Press, 1978).

——, '"An old and much honoured soldier": Griffith Jones, Llanddowror', *Welsh History Review*, 11, 4 (1983), 449–68.

——, *The Foundations of Modern Wales, 1642–1780* (Oxford: Oxford University Press, 1987).

—— (ed.), *The Welsh Language Before the Industrial Revolution* (Cardiff: University of Wales Press, 1997).

—— (ed.), *The Welsh Language and its Social Domains, 1811–1911* (Cardiff: University of Wales Press, 2000).

—— and Jones, Ieuan Gwynedd (eds), *Cardiganshire County History*, vol. 3, *Cardiganshire in Modern Times* (Cardiff: University of Wales Press, 1998).

Jenkins, R. T., *The Moravian Brethren in North Wales* (London: Honourable Society of Cymmrodorion, 1938).

——, *Yng Nghysgod Trefeca: Ysgrifau ar Hanes Crefydd a Chymdeithas yng Nghymru yn y Ddeunawfed Ganrif* (Caernarfon: Llyfrfa'r Methodistiaid Calfinaidd, 1968).

Jones, David Ceri, '"The Lord did give me a particular honour to make [me] a peacemaker": Howel Harris, John Wesley and Methodist Infighting, 1739–1750', *Bulletin of the John Rylands University Library of Manchester*, 82, 2 and 3 (summer and autumn 2003), 73–98.

——, *'A Glorious Work in the World': Welsh Methodism and the International Evangelical Revival, 1735–1750* (Cardiff: University of Wales Press, 2004).

——, '"A glorious morn"? Methodism and the rise of Evangelicalism in Wales, 1735–62', in Mark Smith (ed.), *British Evangelical Identities, Past and Present*, vol. 1, *Aspects of the History and Sociology of Evangelicalism in Britain and Ireland* (Milton Keynes: Paternoster, 2008), pp. 97–113.

——, 'Narratives of conversion in English Calvinistic Methodism', in Kate Cooper and Jeremy Gregory (eds), *Revival and Resurgence in Christian History*, *Studies in Church History*, 44 (Woodbridge: Boydell, 2008), pp. 128–41.

——, 'John Lewis and the promotion of the international evangelical revival, 1735–1756', in Dyfed Wyn Roberts (ed.), *Revival, Renewal and the Holy Spirit* (Milton Keynes: Paternoster, 2009), pp. 13–26.

——, '"We are of Calvinistical principles": how Calvinist was early Calvinistic Methodism?', *The Welsh Journal of Religious History*, 4 (2009), 37–54.

——, '"Sure the time here now is like New England": what happened when the Welsh Calvinistic Methodists read Jonathan Edwards', in Kelly Van Andel, Kenneth Minkema and Adriaan Neele (eds), *Jonathan Edwards and Scotland* (Edinburgh: Dunedin Press, 2011), pp. 49–62.

——, '"Unlike our fathers of old": John Elias and the contest over Calvinism in early nineteenth-century Welsh Calvinistic Methodism', in Peter Nockles and Vivienne Westbrook (eds), *Reinventing the Reformation* (Manchester, forthcoming).

——, '"Like the time of the Apostles": the fundamentalist mentality in eighteenth-century Welsh evangelicalism', *Welsh History Review*, 25, 3 (June, 2011), 374–400.

Jones, D. J. Odwyn, *Daniel Rowland Llangeitho (1713–1790)* (Llandysul: Gomer, 1938).

Jones, Euros Wyn, 'Nathaniel Rowland (1749–1831)', *JHSPCW*, 7 (1983), 35–42.

Jones, Frank Price, *Thomas Jones o Ddinbych, 1756–1820* (Denbigh: Gwasg Gee, 1956).

Jones, Ieuan Gwynedd, *Explorations and Explanations: Essays in the Social history of Victorian Wales* (Llandysul: Gwasg Gomer, 1981).

Jones, John Morgan and Morgan, William, *Y Tadau Methodistaidd* (2 vols, Swansea: Lewis Evans, 1895).

Jones, Jonathan, *Cofiant y Parch. Thomas Jones* (Denbigh: Thomas Gee, 1897).

Jones, M. G., *The Charity School Movement* (Cambridge: Cambridge University Press, 1938).

Jones, Philip Henry and Rees, Eiluned (eds), *A Nation and its Books: A History of the Book in Wales* (Aberystwyth: National Library of Wales, 1998).

Jones, R. Tudur, *Congregationalism in England* (London: Independent Press, 1962).

——, *Thomas Charles o'r Bala: Gwas y Gair a Chyfaill Cenedl* (Cardiff: University of Wales Press, 1979).

——, *Congregationalism in Wales*, ed. Robert Pope (Cardiff: University of Wales Press, 2004).

——, 'Peter Williams (1723–1796)', in *Oxford Dictionary of National Biography* (Oxford: Oxford University Press, 2004).

Kidd, Thomas S., *The Great Awakening: The Roots of Evangelical Christianity in Colonial America* (New Haven, CT: Yale University Press, 2007).

Kling, David W. and Sweeney, Douglas A. (eds), *Jonathan Edwards at Home and Abroad: Historical Memories, Cultural Movements, Global Horizons* (Columbia, SC: University of South Carolina Press, 2003).

Knox, R. A., *Enthusiasm* (Oxford: Clarendon Press, 1950).

Lambert, Frank, 'Subscribing for profits and piety: the friendship of Benjamin Franklin and George Whitefield', *The William and Mary Quarterly*, 50, 3 (July 1993), 529–48.

——, *'Pedlar in Divinity': George Whitefield and the Transatlantic Revivals, 1737–1770* (Princeton, NJ: Princeton University Press, 1994).

——, *James Habersham: Loyalty, Politics, and Commerce in Colonial Georgia* (Athens, GA: Georgia University Press, 2005).

Langford, Paul, *A Polite and Commercial People: England, 1727–1783* (Oxford: Oxford University Press, 1989).

Lindberg, Carter (ed.), *The Pietist Theologians: An Introduction to Theology in the Seventeenth and Eighteenth Centuries* (Oxford: Blackwell, 2005).

Lloyd, D. Myrddin, 'Nathaniel Rowland and the Tabernacle, Haverford-west', *JHSPCW*, 36, 2 (July 1951), 33–41.

Lloyd, Gareth, *Charles Wesley and the Struggle for Methodist Identity* (Oxford: Oxford University Press, 2007).

Lloyd, J. Trefor, 'Nathaniel Rowland (1749–1831)', *JHSPCW*, 45 (1960), 60–6; 46 (1961), 10–16.

Lloyd, J. T. and Jenkins, R. T. (eds), *The Dictionary of Welsh Biography down to 1940* (London: Honourable Society of Cymmrodorion, 1959).

Lovegrove, Deryck W., *Established Church, Sectarian People: Itinerancy and the Transformation of English Dissent, 1780–1830* (Cambridge: Cambridge University Press, 1988).

Luxton, Brian C., 'Hezekiah Jones (c.1751–1833), the Red Priest of Colcot', *JHSPCW*, 55 (1970), 14–23; 33–48.

McGonigle, Herbert Boyd, *Sufficient Saving Grace: John Wesley's Evangelical Arminianism* (Carlisle: Paternoster, 2001).

McKendrick, Neil, Brewer, John and Plumb, J. H., *The Birth of a Consumer Society: The Commercialization of Eighteenth-Century England* (Bloomington, ID: Indiana University Press, 1982).

Mack, Phyllis, *Heart Religion in the British Enlightenment: Gender and Emotion in Early Methodism* (Cambridge: Cambridge University Press, 2008).

Madden, Lionel (ed.), *Methodism in Wales: A Short History of the Welsh Tradition* (Llandudno: Methodist Conference, 2003).

Maddox, Randy L. and Vickers, Jason E. (eds.), *The Cambridge Companion to John Wesley* (Cambridge: Cambridge University Press, 2010).

Mahaffey, Jerome Dean, *Preaching Politics: The Religious Rhetoric of George Whitefield and the Founding of a New Nation* (Waco, TX: Baylor University Press, 2007).

Marsden, George M., *Jonathan Edwards: A Life* (New Haven, CT: Yale University Press, 2003).

Mason, J. C. S., *The Moravian Church and the Missionary Awakening in England 1760–1800* (Woodbridge: The Boydell Press, 2001).

Megan, Siân, *Gwaith Ann Griffiths* (Llandybïe: Christopher Davies, 1982).

Moore, Jonathan D., *English Hypothetical Universalism: John Preston and the Softening of Reformed Theology* (Grand Rapids, MI: Eerdmans, 2007).

Morgan, D. Densil (ed.), *Grym y Gair a Fflam y Ffydd: Ysgrifau ar Hanes Crefydd yng Nghymru* (Swansea: Cyhoeddiadau'r Gair, 1998).

——, 'Lewis Edwards (1808–87) and Welsh theology', *The Welsh Journal of Religious History*, 3 (2008), 15–28.

——, *Wales and the Word: Historical Perspectives on Welsh Identity and Religion* (Cardiff: University of Wales Press, 2008).

Morgan, Derec Llwyd, *Y Diwygiad Mawr* (Llandysul: Gomer, 1981).

——, *William Williams Pantycelyn* (Caernarfon: Gwasg Pantycelyn, 1983).

——, *Pobl Pantycelyn* (Llandysul: Gwasg Gomer, 1986).

——, *The Great Awakening in Wales* (Peterborough: Epworth Press, 1988).

——, 'Daniel Rowland (?1711–1790): Pregethwr Diwygiadol', *Ceredigion*, 10 (1991), 217–37.

——, 'Howell Davies (?1717–1770)', *Oxford Dictionary of National Biography* (Oxford: Oxford University Press, 2004).

Morgan, Edward, *The Life and Times of Howell Harris* (Holywell: W. Morris, 1852).

Morgan, Kenneth, *John Wesley in Bristol* (Bristol: Historical Association, 1990).

Noll, Mark A., *The Rise of Evangelicalism: the Age of Edwards, Whitefield and the Wesleys* (Leicester: Inter-Varsity Press, 2004).

Nuttall, Geoffrey F., *Richard Baxter and Philip Doddridge: A Study in Tradition* (Oxford: Oxford University Press, 1951).

——, *Howel Harris, 1714–1773: The Last Enthusiast* (Cardiff: University of Wales Press, 1965).

——, 'Rowland Hill and the Rodborough Connexion, 1771–1833', *Transactions of the Congregational Historical Society*, 21, 3 (1972), 69–73.

——, 'George Whitefield's "curate": Gloucestershire dissent and the revival', *Journal of Ecclesiastical History*, 27, 4 (October 1976), 369–86.

——, 'Welsh students at Bristol Baptist College, 1720–1797', *Transactions of the Honourable Society of Cymmrodorion* (1978), 171–99.

——, 'Howel Harris and "The Grand Table": a note on religion and politics, 1744–50', *Journal of Ecclesiastical History*, 39, 4 (October 1988), 531–44.

O'Brien, Susan, 'A transatlantic community of saints: the Great Awakening and the First Evangelical Network, 1735–1755', *American Historical Review*, 91 (1986), 811–32.

O'Connell, Neil J., 'George Whitefield and Bethesda Orphan-House', *The Georgia Historical Quarterly*, 54 (1970), 41–62.

Olsen, Gerald Wayne (ed.), *Religion and Revolution in Early Industrial England: the Halévy Thesis and its Critics* (Lanham, MD: Scarecrow Press, 1990).

Orchard, S. C., *Cheshunt College* (n.p: n.p, [1968]).

Owen, Goronwy P. (ed.), *Atgofion John Evans y Bala: Y Diwygiad Methodistaidd ym Meirionnydd a Môn* (Caernarfon: Gwasg Pant-ycelyn, 1997).

Owen, John, *Coffhad am y Parch. Daniel Rowlands, gynt o Llangeitho, Ceredigion* (Caerlleon: Edward Parry, 1839).

Philip, Robert, *The Life and Times of George Whitefield* (London: George Virtue, 1837).

Phillips, James, 'The Tabernacle Church, Haverfordwest', *JHSPCW*, 7, 2 (August 1922), 37–50.

Podmore, Colin J., *The Moravian Church in England, 1728–1760* (Oxford: Oxford University Press, 1998).

Rack, Henry D., 'Religious societies and the origins of Methodism', *Journal of Ecclesiastical History*, 38, 4 (October 1987), 582–95.

——, *Reasonable Enthusiast: John Wesley and the Rise of Methodism* (London: Epworth Press, 1989).

——, 'Survival and revival: John Bennett, Methodism and the old dissent', in Keith Robbins (ed.), *Protestant Evangelicalism: Britain, Ireland, Germany and America, c.1750–c.1950* (Oxford: Basil Blackwell, 1990, pp. 1–23.

Richard, E. W. and H., *Bywyd y Parch. Ebenezer Richard* (London: W. Clowes, 1839).

Rivers, Isabel, *Reason, Grace and Sentiment: A Study in the Language of Religion and Ethics in England, 1660–1780*, vol. 1, *Whichcote to Wesley* (Cambridge: Cambridge University Press, 1991).

——, 'The First Evangelical Tract Society', *The Historical Society*, 50, 1 (March, 2007), 1–22.

—— and Wykes, David L. (eds), *Dissenting Praise: Religious Dissent and the Hymn* (Oxford: Oxford University Press, 2011).

Roberts, Brynley F., 'The Connexion in print', *JHSPCW*, 16–17 (1992–3), 9–31.

Roberts, Gomer M., *Bywyd a Gwaith Peter Williams* (Cardiff: University of Wales Press, 1943).

——, 'Henry Thomas, Gelli Dochlaethe', *Y Cofiadur*, 17 (1947), 72–7.

——, *Y Pêr Ganiedydd (Pantycelyn)*, cyfrol I, *Trem ar ei Fywyd* (Aberystwyth: Gwasg Aberystwyth, 1949).

——, 'The Moravians, John Relly and his people', *JHSPCW*, 38, 1 (March 1953), 2–6.

——, *Y Pêr Ganiedydd (Pantycelyn)*, cyfrol II, *Arweiniad i'w Waith* (Aberystwyth: Gwasg Aberystwyth, 1958).

——, 'Methodistiaeth Gynnar Gwaelod Sir Aberteifi', *Ceredigion*, 5 (1964), 1–13.

——, *Portread o Ddiwygiwr* (Caernarfon: Llyfrfa'r Methodistiaid Calfinaidd, 1969).

——, 'William Gambold a'i Deulu', *Y Genhinen*, 22 (1972), 194–6.

——, *Hanes Methodistiaeth Galfinaidd Cymru*, cyfrol I, *Y Deffroad Mawr* (Caernarfon: Llyfrfa'r Methodistiaid Calfinaidd, 1973).

——, 'Calvinistic Methodism in Glamorgan, 1737–1773', in Glanmor Williams (ed.), *Glamorgan County History*, vol. 4, *Early Modern Glamorgan: From the Acts of Union to the Industrial Revolution* (Cardiff: Glamorgan County History Trust, 1974), 499–533.

——, *Hanes Methodistiaeth Galfinaidd Cymru*, cyfrol II, *Cynnydd y Corff* (Caernarfon: Llyfrfa'r Methodistiaid Calfinaidd, 1978).

Roberts, Griffith T., *Howell Harris* (London: Epworth Press, 1951).

Roberts, John, *Methodistiaeth Galfinaidd Cymru* (London: Gwasg Gymraeg Foyle, 1931).

Russell, George W. E., *A Short History of the Evangelical Movement* (London: Mowbray, 1915).

Schlenther, Boyd Stanley, '"To convert the poor people in America": the Bethesda Orphanage and the thwarted zeal of the countess of Huntingdon', *Georgia Historical Quarterly*, 77 (1994), 225–56.

——, *Queen of the Methodists: The Countess of Huntingdon and the Eighteenth-Century Crisis of Faith and Society* (Durham: Durham Academic Press, 1997).

——, 'Religious faith and commercial empire', in P. J. Marshall (ed.), *The Oxford History of the British Empire*, vol. 2, *The Eighteenth Century* (Oxford: Oxford University Press, 1998), pp. 128–50.

——, 'George Whitefield (1714–1770)', in *Oxford Dictionary of National Biography* (Oxford: Oxford University Press, 2004).

—— and White, Eryn Mant, *Calendar of the Trevecka Letters* (Aberystwyth: National Library of Wales, 2003).

Schwenk, James L., *Catholic Spirit: Wesley, Whitefield, and the Quest for Evangelical unity in Eighteenth-Century British Methodism* (Lanham, MD: Scarecrow Press, 2008).

[Seymour, Aaron C. H.], *The Life and Times of Selina, Countess of Huntingdon* (2 vols, London: William Edward Painter, 1839).

Snead, Jennifer, 'Print, predestination, and the public sphere: transatlantic evangelical periodicals, 1740–1745', *Early American Literature*, 45, 1 (2010), 93–118.

Stead, Geoffrey and Margaret, *The Exotic Plant: A History of the Moravian Church in Great Britain, 1742–2000* (Peterborough: Epworth Press, 2003).

Stein, Stephen J., 'George Whitefield and slavery: some new evidence', *Church History*, 42, 2 (June 1973), 243–56.

—— (ed.), *The Cambridge Companion to Jonathan Edwards* (Cambridge: Cambridge University Press, 2007).

Stell, Christopher, *An Inventory of Nonconformist Chapels and Meeting-Houses in South-West England* (London: Stationery Office Books, 1991).

Stout, Harry S., *The Divine Dramatist: George Whitefield and the Rise of Modern Evangelicalism* (Grand Rapids, MI: Eerdmans, 1991).

Streiff, Patrick, *Jean Guillaume de l Fléchère* (Frankfurt: Lang, 1984) (in German).

——, *Reluctant Saint: A Theological Biography of Fletcher of Madeley* (Peterborough: Epworth Press, 2001) (an English translation of the preceding item).

Thickens, John, *Howel Harris yn Llundain* (Caernarfon: Argraffdy'r Methodistiaid Calfinaidd, 1938).

Thomas, G. J., 'Madam Bevan's Will: the Chancery action', *Transactions of the Carmarthenshire Antiquarian Society*, 29 (1939), 431–52.

Thomas, Owen, *Cofiant y Parchedig John Jones, Talsarn* (2 vols, Wrexham: Hughes and Son, 1874).

——, *The Atonement Controversy in Welsh Theological Controversy and Debate, 1707–1841*, translated by John Aaron (Edinburgh: The Banner of Truth Trust, 2002).

Thuesen, Peter, *Predestination: The American Career of a Contentious Doctrine* (New York: Oxford University Press, 2009).

Toon, Peter, *The Emergence of Hyper-Calvinism in English Nonconformity, 1689–1765* (London: Olive Tree, 1967).

Tudur, Geraint, 'The king's daughter: a reassessement of Anne Harris of Trefeca', *Journal of Welsh Religious History,* 7 (1999), 55–76.

——, *Howell Harris: From Conversion to Separation, 1735–1750* (Cardiff: University of Wales Press, 2000).

——, '"Thou bold champion, where art thou": Howell Harris and the issue of Welsh Identity', in Robert Pope (ed.), *Religion and National Identity: Wales and Scotland, c.1700–2000* (Cardiff: University of Wales Press, 2001), pp. 43–60.

——, '"Like a right arm and a pillar": the story of James Beaumont', in Robert Pope (ed.), *Honouring the Past and Shaping the Future: Religious and Biblical Studies in Wales: Essays in Honour of Gareth Elwyn Jones* (Leominster: Gracewing, 2003), pp. 133–58.

Tyacke, Nicholas (ed.), *England's Long Reformation, 1500–1800* (London: Routledge, 1998).

Tyerman, Luke, *The Oxford Methodists: Memoirs of the Rev. Messrs. Clayton, Ingham, Gambold, Hervey, and Broughton, with biographical notices of others* (London: Hodder and Stoughton, 1873).

——, *The Life of the Rev. George Whitefield* (2 vols, London: Hodder and Stoughton, 1876).

——, *The Life of the Rev. John Wesley* (3 vols, 4th edn, London: Hodder and Stoughton, 1878).

——, *Wesley's Designated Successor: The Life, Letters and Literary Labours of the Rev. John William Fletcher* (London: Hodder and Stoughton, 1882).

van Wetering, J. E., 'The Christian history of the Great Awakening', *Journal of Presbyterian History*, 44 (1966), 122–9.

Vickers, John (ed.), *Dictionary of Methodism in Britain and Ireland* (Peterborough: Epworth Press, 2000).

Wallace, Peter G., *The Long European Reformation* (Basingstoke: Palgrave Macmillan, 2004).

Walsh, John, 'Origins of the evangelical revival', in G. V. Bennett and J. D. (eds), *Essays in Modern Church History: in Memory of Norman Sykes* (London: Black, 1966), pp. 141–61.

——, 'Methodism and the mob in the eighteenth century', in G. J. Cuming and Derek Baker (eds), *Popular Belief and Practice, Studies in Church History*, 8 (Cambridge: Cambridge University Press, 1972).

——, 'The Cambridge Methodists', in Peter Brooks (ed.), *Christian Spirituality: Essays in Honour of Gordon Rupp* (London: Epworth Press, 1973), pp. 249–83.

——, 'Methodism and the origins of English-speaking Evangelicalism', in Mark A. Noll, David W. Bebbington and George A. Rawlyk (eds), *Evangelicalism: Comparative Studies of Popular Protestantism in North America, the British Isles, and Beyond* (New York: Oxford University Press, 1994), pp. 19–37.

Ward, W. R., 'The renewed unity of the brethren: ancient church, new sect or inter-confessional movement?', *Bulletin of the John Rylands University Library of Manchester*, 70, 3 (autumn 1988), 77–92.

——, *The Protestant Evangelical Awakening* (Cambridge: Cambridge University Press, 1992).

——, *Christianity under the Ancien Régime, 1648–1789* (Cambridge: Cambridge University Press, 1999).

——, *Early Evangelicalism: A Global Intellectual History, 1670–1789* (Cambridge: Cambridge University Press, 2006).

Watson, C. E., 'Whitefield and Congregationalism', *Transactions of the Congregational Historical Society*, 8, 4 (1922), 172–80, 5 (1922), 227–45.

——, 'Rodborough Tabernacle: an account by John Knight, written in 1844', *Congregational Historical Society Transactions*, 10, 6 (September 1929), 172–80.

Watts, Michael, *The Dissenters: From the Reformation to the French Revolution* (Oxford: Clarendon Press, 1978).

Welch, C. E., 'Andrew Kinsman's churches at Plymouth', *Report and Transactions of the Devonshire Association for the Advancement of Science, Literature and Art*, 97 (1965), 212–36.

Welch, Edwin, *Spiritual Pilgrim: A Reassessment of the Life of the Countess of Huntingdon* (Cardiff: University of Wales Press, 1995).

——, 'Willielma Campbell, Viscountess Glenorchy (1741–1786)', in *Oxford Dictionary of National Biography* (Oxford: Oxford University Press, 2004).

White, Eryn M., *Praidd Bach y Bugail Mawr: Seiadau Methodistaidd De-orllewin Cymru* (Llandysul: Gwasg Gomer, 1995).

——, '"The world, the flesh and the devil" and the early Methodist societies of south-west Wales', *Transactions of the Honourable Society of Cymmrodorion*, 3 (1996), 45–61.

——, '"Myrdd o Wragedd": Merched a'r Diwygiad Methodistaidd', *Llên Cymru*, 20 (1997), 62–74.

——, 'Popular schooling and the Welsh language, 1650–1800', in Geraint H. Jenkins (ed.), *The Welsh Language Before the Industrial Revolution* (Cardiff: University of Wales Press, 1997), pp. 317–42.

——, 'Women in the early Methodist societies in Wales', *Journal of Welsh Religious History*, 7 (1999), 95–108.

——, 'Daniel Rowland (1711?-1790)', *Oxford Dictionary of National Biography* (Oxford: Oxford University Press, 2004).

——, '"A breach in God's house": the division in Welsh Calvinistic Methodism, 1750–63', in Nigel Yates (ed.), *Bishop Burgess and his World: Culture, Religion and Society in Britain, Europe and North America in the Eighteenth and Nineteenth Centuries* (Cardiff: University of Wales Press, 2007), pp. 85–102.

——, 'Peter Williams a'r Beibl Cymraeg', *Transactions of the Honourable Society of Cymmrodorion* (2007), 58–72.

——, *The Welsh Bible* (Stroud: Tempus, 2007).

——, '"I will once more shake the heavens": the 1762 Revival in Wales', in Kate Cooper and Jeremy Gregory (eds), *Revival and Resurgence in Christian History, Studies in Church History*, 44 (Woodbridge: Boydell, 2008), pp. 154–63.

——, 'The eighteenth-century evangelical revival and Welsh identity', in Mark Smith (ed.), *British Evangelical Identities, Past and Present*, vol. 1, *Aspects of the History and Sociology of Evangelicalism in Britain and Ireland* (Milton Keynes: Paternoster, 2009), pp. 85–96.

——, '"Gwnaeth ei farwnad yn ei fywyd": cofio Daniel Rowland, Llangeitho (1711?–1790)', *Y Traethodydd*, 166 (October 2011), 250–67.

——, 'Women, work and worship in the Trefeca family, 1752–1773', in Peter Forsaith and Geordan Hammond (eds), *Religion, Gender and Industry* (Eugene, OR: Wipf and Stock, 2011), pp. 109–22.

Whitebrook, J. C., 'Wesley and William Cudworth', *Proceedings of the Wesley Historical Society*, 12 (1919), 34–6.

Wicks, George Hasking, *Whitefield's Legacy to Bristol and the Cotswolds* (Bristol: Taylor Bros, 1914).

[Willcocks, F. W.], *Spa Fields Chapel and its Associations* ([London]; n.p, 1886).

Williams, A. H., *Welsh Wesleyan Methodism, 1800–1858: Its Origins, Growth and Secessions* (Bangor: Llyfrau'r Methodistiaid, 1935).

Williams, D. Emrys, 'The Popkin Family', *The Carmarthenshire Antiquary*, 7 (1971), 120–34.

Williams, Glanmor, *Welsh Reformation Essays* (Cardiff: University of Wales Press, 1967).

——, Jacob, William, Yates, Nigel and Knight, Frances, *The Welsh Church from Reformation to Disestablishment, 1603–1920* (Cardiff: University of Wales Press, 2007).

Williams, John, *Historical Digest of Welsh Statistics* (Cardiff: Welsh Office, 1985).

Yrigoyen Jr, Charles (ed.), *The T&T Clark Companion to Methodism* (London: T&T Clark, 2010).

Unpublished theses

Brown, Dorothy E. S., 'Evangelicals and education in eighteenth-century Britain: a study of Trevecca College, 1768–1792', (unpublished Ph.D. thesis, University of Wisconsin-Madison, 1992).

Durden, Diane Susan, 'Transatlantic communications and literature in the religious revivals, 1735–1745', (unpublished Ph.D. thesis, University of Hull, 1978).

Evans, R. W., 'The eighteenth century Welsh awakening, with its relationship to the contemporary English evangelical revival', (unpublished Ph.D. thesis, University of Edinburgh, 1956).

Harding, Alan, 'The countess of Huntingdon and her connexion in the eighteenth century' (unpublished D.Phil. thesis, University of Oxford, 1992).

Hughes-Edwards, W. G., 'The development and organisation of the Methodist society in Wales, 1735–1750', (unpublished MA thesis, University of Wales, 1966).

Hull, James E., 'The controversy between John Wesley and the countess of Huntingdon' (unpublished Ph.D. thesis, University of Edinburgh, 1959).

Morey, Kenneth, 'The theological position of the Countess of Huntingdon's Connexion' (unpublished BA thesis, Council for National Academic Awards, 1990).

Owen, Alun W., 'A study of Howell Harris and the Trevecka "family" (1752–1760), based upon the Trevecka letters and diaries and other Methodist archives at the National Library of Wales' (unpublished MA thesis, University of Wales, 1957).

Sangster, P. 'The life of the Rev. Rowland Hill (1744–1833) and his position in the evangelical revival', (unpublished D.Phil. thesis, University of Oxford, 1964).

Walsh, J. D., 'The Yorkshire evangelicals in the eighteenth century with special reference to Methodism' (unpublished Ph.D. thesis, University of Cambridge, 1956).

Index

T. Haweis and Lady Anne Erskine, 213–14, 239; chapels listed in (marked *), Appendix C

Plymouth: Calvinistic Methodism in, 146; chapel at, 71; clash with Wesleyans, 75–6; and Kinsman, 76, 149

Podmore, Colin, 72

Pontrobert, Montgomeryshire, 219

Popkin, John, 108; and testy opposition to H. Harris, 129, 131–2

Potter, John, Archbishop of Canterbury, 113

Powell, John, 60

Predestination, 115; defined, xiii–xiv, 154; and Calvin, xiii–xiv; effects on evangelism, 2, 24; and Whitefield, 24–5, 157, 158; and H. Harris, 24–5, 33–4, 57, 75, 157; and Watts, 24; J. Wesley's detestation of, and conflict with Whitefield over, 32, 33–6, 42, 44, 57, 74–5, 112, 142, 154–5; and C. Wesley, 33–4, 57, 112; and Cennick, 146; and countess of Huntingdon, 111–13, 154, 157–9; English Calvinistic Methodists affirm belief in but reject double predestination, 147, 158; and St Edmund Hall, Oxford, expulsion, 142, 155, 159; continuing Calvinist conflict with Wesleys over, 112, 114, 154–63, 182, 185. *See also* Double Predestination; Toplady

Prince, Thomas, 30

Princess Street, London: Countess of Huntingdon chapel at, 165

Printing and the Calvinistic Methodist movement in England: Whitefield's sermons and journals, 7–8; *The Christian's Amusement and The Weekly History*, 29–30, 45; *An Account of the Most Remarkable Particulars*, 78–9, 80; *Gospel Magazine*, 158, 170; *Arminian Magazine*, 158; countess of Huntingdon's hymn book, 160

Printing and the Calvinistic Methodist movement in Wales, 79; and education, 197, 208; and William Williams, 79, 123, 124–6, 127, 128, 201, 208, 219; and Peter Williams, 201–2; and Thomas Charles, 217, 219–20; and Thomas Jones, 219–23; and *Trysorfa Ysprydol*, 219–20; and hymns, 125, 201; and Welsh Bible, 201–4, 218–19

Pritchard, James, 105

The Protestant Association, 169–70

Pugh, David, 230

Pugh, Philip, 13

Puritans: efforts in Wales during mid-17th century, 11; H. Harris admires, 2, and reads works of, 24; Whitefield reads works of, 24; piety of, 12; and the Westminster Assembly's creedal formulas, 169, 199

Radnorshire: Calvinistic Methodism in, 103

Raikes, Robert, 198

Reading, Berkshire, 9

Rees, Dafydd Thomas, 108